Managing Talent for Success

Talent Development in Law Firms

Consulting Editor **Rebecca Normand-Hochman**
on behalf of the International Bar Association

Consulting editor
Rebecca Normand-Hochman on behalf of the International Bar Association

Publisher
Sian O'Neill

Editor
Carolyn Boyle

Production
Paul Stoneham

Publishing directors
Guy Davis, Tony Harriss, Mark Lamb

Managing Talent for Success: Talent Development in Law Firms
is published by
Globe Law and Business
Globe Business Publishing Ltd
New Hibernia House
Winchester Walk
London SE1 9AG
United Kingdom
Tel +44 20 7234 0606
Fax +44 20 7234 0808
Web www.globelawandbusiness.com

Printed and bound by CPI Group (UK) Ltd, Croydon, CR0 4YY

ISBN 9781909416031

Managing Talent for Success: Talent Development in Law Firms
© 2013 Globe Business Publishing Ltd

All rights reserved. No part of this publication may be reproduced in any material form (including photocopying, storing in any medium by electronic means or transmitting) without the written permission of the copyright owner, except in accordance with the provisions of the Copyright, Designs and Patents Act 1988 or under terms of a licence issued by the Copyright Licensing Agency Ltd, 6-10 Kirby Street, London EC1N 8TS, United Kingdom (www.cla.co.uk, email: licence@cla.co.uk). Applications for the copyright owner's written permission to reproduce any part of this publication should be addressed to the publisher.

DISCLAIMER
This publication is intended as a general guide only. The information and opinions which it contains are not intended to be a comprehensive study, nor to provide legal advice, and should not be treated as a substitute for legal advice concerning particular situations. Legal advice should always be sought before taking any action based on the information provided. The publishers bear no responsibility for any errors or omissions contained herein.

Table of contents

Time for a new approach _____ 5
to talent management in
law firms
    Rebecca Normand-Hochman
    Mentoring Collegium Limited,
    Institute of Mentoring

Driving business results _____ 19
through talent
    Marc Bartel
    Caroline Vanovermeire
    Heidrick & Struggles

Talent development in _____ 27
law firms
    Tony King
    Clifford Chance LLP

Coaching _____ 41
    Jonathan Middleburgh
    Simon Pizzey
    Huron Legal

Leading lawyers through _____ 53
change
    Amber Sharpe
    Psychologist
    Robert Sharpe
    Psychologist

Facilitating fast and _____ 69
smooth transitions from
law school
    Sarah Hutchinson
    The University of Law

'Generation Y' – key talent _____ 83
management drivers
    Sally Woodward
    Sherwood PSF Consulting

Into partnership: building _____ 103
sustainable client relationships
    Kevin Doolan
    Eversheds LLP
    Moray McLaren
    KermaPartners

Managing talent in _____ 113
global law firms
    Jay Connolly
    Dentons US LLP

Women lawyers and _____ 127
how to improve gender balance
    Rachel Brushfield
    EnergiseLegal

Effective teamwork and _____ 145
collaboration
    Heidi K Gardner
    Harvard Business School

Creating effective _____ 161
relationships
    Sarah Martin
    Coombs Martin

Cultural intelligence _____ 173
– an indispensable talent
    Peter Alfandary
    PRA CrossCultural

The future of legal talent management: adopting an innovative mindset for future challenges —— 185
    Shelley Dunstone
    Legal Circles

About the authors —— 199

Time for a new approach to talent management in law firms

Rebecca Normand-Hochman
Founder and director, Mentoring Collegium Limited, Institute of Mentoring

1. Introduction

A few years ago, at the end of a meeting, a managing partner looked at me with despair and said: "You can't imagine how difficult it is to motivate lawyers!"

Those words struck me at the time as symptomatic of the issue that many law firms were facing: they were reaching a dead end in the way that they managed talent.

Lawyers are naturally driven and motivated individuals. The principal challenge of law firms is thus not to motivate their lawyers, but to create the conditions for them to maintain this natural drive and motivation, sense of direction and achievement over the years.

Research in this area confirms that law firms not only should, but most importantly could do better at supporting the development of their lawyers. However, this is not an easy task.

The current changes that are reshaping the legal industry are now leading the most advanced firms to consider talent management as a strategic driver of competitiveness; this is unlikely to be a short-term trend.

This chapter proposes a new approach to law firm talent management, which has been developed over the course of three years of research into best practices in the corporate world and professional services firms (with a particular focus on international law firms). It incorporates interview feedback from managing partners and partners – capturing their experiences, challenges and aspirations – as well as input from the invaluable discussions and debates that I have had with talent management experts and professional colleagues over the years.

2. What is 'talent'?

'Talent' is a former weight and unit of currency, used especially by the ancient Romans and Greeks. The origin of the word as a description of monetary value is interesting to note, given the growing importance of talent as a business performance driver across all industries.

Today, there are many ways in which 'talent' can be defined. *The Oxford English Dictionary* defines it as "natural aptitude or skill".

In its most general sense, as defined by Ed Michaels, Helen Handfield-Jones and Beth Axelrod in their book *The War for Talent*[1]:"talent is the sum of a person's abilities

---

1   E. Michaels, H Handfield-Jones and B Axelrod, *The War for Talent*, Harvard Business School Press (2001).

– his or her intrinsic gifts, skills, knowledge, experience, intelligence, judgment, attitude, character and drive. It also includes his or her ability to learn and grow."

This broad definition is inspiring and illustrates the concept's many aspects. For the purposes of this book, the word 'talent' is deemed to have this meaning.

This definition includes not only abilities and skills, but also the notion of 'learning agility' – that is, the ability to adapt, learn and perform quickly under new and challenging conditions.

This reveals a paradox of our profession: lawyers are intellectuals who thrive on learning, and yet tend to be uncomfortable with change and find it difficult to embrace new paradigms. This chapter explains some of the reasons for this paradox.

Whatever the chosen definition, having a clear and well-communicated definition of 'talent' across the firm is a foundation to any sound talent management strategy.

2.1 Talent management

Is 'talent management' just another way to describe human resources/human capital functions or does it describe something fundamentally different?

As with talent, there are many possible definitions of 'talent management', but there tends to be an even greater lack of clarity about what this covers in practice.

In some organisations, talent management is still the sole responsibility of the human resources department; it involves recruiting, developing and retaining the right people with the right skills to meet the organisation's business needs.

What distinguishes the most advanced and talent-centred firms from others is their focus on the partners' role in managing talent, as opposed to reliance on human resources to drive the lifecycle of a lawyer.

In this sense, 'talent management' is the ability for senior management and partners to create the conditions for their lawyers to develop, perform and grow, and contribute to the firm's success. Talent management as referred to in this book is deemed to have this meaning.

Beyond human resources, leading talent management practices are shifting the responsibility for development onto the partners, for them to develop and engage the talent needed to succeed, individually and collectively.

3. Why does talent management matter?

Law firms have traditionally prioritised client development and service – everyone understands the reason for this. However, as important as client service is managing the main asset of the firm: talent.

Most law firms are good at competing for client service, but not at managing the talent of their lawyers. David Maister observes in his book *Managing the Professional Service Firm*: "Most professional service firm strategic thinking has focused overwhelmingly on the client market place alone. This is however about to change. In the next decade and beyond, the ability to attract develop, retain and deploy staff will be the single biggest determinant of a professional service firm's competitive success."[2]

---

2   D Maister, *Managing the Professional Service Firm*, Free Press – Simon and Schuster (1993).

Managing talent has become a business issue of prime importance and law firms lack the vision, experience and tools to address it.

In 1997, a large international study by McKinsey[3] examined how companies manage leadership talent and identified talent management as a business challenge and critical driver of corporate performance. Since then, research on the subject has shown the significant value that better talent creates.

The study contrasts the old approach to development with the modern approach. The most relevant aspects for law firms are as follows:

Old approach	New approach
• Development just happens • 'Development' means 'training' • Only poor performers have development needs • A few lucky people find mentors	• Development is woven into the fabric of the firm • 'Development' means challenging experiences, coaching, feedback and mentoring • Everyone has development needs and receives coaching • Mentors are assigned to every high-potential person

Talent management needs differ depending on the size and culture of individual firms, but the principles of creating the conditions for lawyers to develop remain the same. What vary across the industry are the ways in which these conditions can be created and applied.

3.1 Managing talent in a changing world

The legal industry is going through a number of unprecedented changes that are reshaping the traditional law firm model.[4] These include:
- globalisation;
- technological advances;
- economic downturn;
- commoditisation;
- alternative business structures;
- diversity; and
- 'Generation Y'.

The tendency for most businesses is to cut down on talent management investment during economic downturns. But the most progressive companies and firms are continually building their edge and competitiveness through better talent to improve their position.

---

3   Described in *The War For Talent*, see note 1 above.
4   R Susskind, *Tomorrow's Lawyers*, Oxford University Press (2013).

Some law firms will discover that being talent centred does not necessarily mean buying more external training programmes and leadership courses for partners and associates to attend. Instead, investing in talent is about creating a culture of feedback, coaching and mentoring, which is more cost effective and produces incomparable results in terms of lawyers' engagement, performance and retention.

3.2 Are lawyers different?

The legal industry has many points in common with the consulting and accounting industries in terms of tasks, organisational structures and people.

Legal and medical professionals also share many characteristics, in particular in their approaches to leadership and teamwork.

Lawyers are difficult to manage because they tend to:
- need constant challenge;
- require continuous intellectual progression;
- have high expectations of their careers;
- be reluctant to follow procedures; and
- need to be highly motivated to perform well.

It is a well-known concept in the profession that managing talent for professionals is like 'herding cats'.

In the last 15 years, all of the big consulting and accounting firms, such as Boston Consulting Group, PwC and Deloitte, have put in place talent management initiatives and career models that are highly structured, as well as innovative.

So why have law firms been unable to follow this trend?

To answer this question in context, let us first of all review what it takes for lawyers to be motivated and, most importantly, what makes them keep their natural drive.

(a) Motivation and performance

'Motivation' derives from the Latin word *'movere'*, meaning 'to move'. It can be defined as the forces that cause people to engage in one behaviour, rather than some alternative behaviour.

Abraham Maslow developed the 'Hierarchy of Needs' model in the 1940s and 1950s, and the theory remains valid today for understanding human motivation, management training and personal development. Maslow's ideas concerning the responsibility of organisations to provide an environment that encourages and enables people to fulfil their own unique potential (self-actualisation) are today more relevant than ever.

(b) What drives lawyers?

Lawyers have a strong need for achievement and are motivated by many drivers, but at their core they are motivated to perform as well as possible.[5]

Lawyers' internal motivational drivers include:

---

5   T J Delong, J J Gabarro and R J Lees, "When Professionals Have to Lead", *Harvard Business Review* (2007).

- challenging work;
- clear, timely and actionable feedback;
- the ability to measure their performance against clear objectives;
- autonomy;
- control over task parameters; and
- desire to take calculated risks.

In his book *Drive*,[6] Daniel Pink describes how old-fashioned ideas of management are slowly but inexorably giving way to a new emphasis on self-direction. He describes the three elements of drive as autonomy, mastery and purpose.

In my personal experience as a lawyer, these words resonate particularly well in the context of our profession.

(c) **What do lawyers need to stay motivated?**
This is a key question for law firm leaders like the managing partner referred to in the introduction of this chapter, who seemed so desperate to find ways to motivate his lawyers. Based on the internal motivational drivers described above, the authors of "When Professionals Have to Lead"[7] concluded that to stay motivated, lawyers need:
- ongoing tactical feedback;
- periodical developmental feedback;
- coaching and mentoring;
- challenging work; and
- recognition.

What it takes for lawyers to maintain their motivation and commitment is clear and known to most experts and law firm leaders by now. So why do most firms still fail to build the appropriate systems and cultures to achieve these?

Senior professionals who have a high need for achievement are rarely disposed to coach, mentor and give feedback to their juniors because they are impatient with anything that distracts them from the real work of serving clients and enhancing the book of business.[8]

For many partners, on-the-spot corrective feedback, coaching and mentoring are still not considered as central to their responsibility of finalising deals and so are ignored. Until now, they have failed to recognise or acknowledge the link between great talent development and business performance.

There are, however, clear indications that this is about to change.

4. **Adopting a new approach**
Sophisticated talent management initiatives have been introduced in law firms over the past decade. From performance management systems to leadership development,

---

6   Daniel H Pink, *Drive*, Penguin Group (2009).
7   See note 5 above.
8   See note 5 above.

Time for a new approach to talent management in law firms

coaching and mentoring programmes, the range and scope of talent management activities are now considerably more diverse and innovative than ever before.

The question is whether these initiatives produce the expected results on the levels of lawyers' engagement, performance and retention.

In all firms, unless talent management activities are directly linked and aligned – horizontally to HR management and vertically to the firm's strategy – they have a low impact.

4.1 What does a talent-centred firm look like?
The new approach proposed here is based on three aspects.

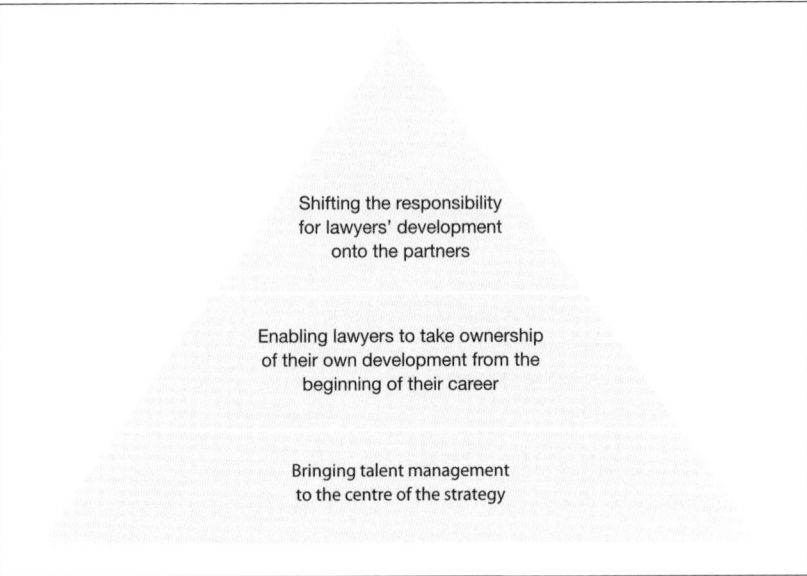

(a)   Shifting responsibility for lawyers' development onto the partners
Development does not happen through training, however sophisticated this may be; it happens through a combination of challenging work, feedback, coaching and mentoring.[9]

Developing a culture in which senior lawyers and partners have the tools to support the development of others is a cost-effective and powerful way to invest in talent.

For lawyers, performance is directly linked to motivation, and motivation is to a large extent dependent on the ability to measure progress against clearly defined goals.

Giving feedback and carrying out performance reviews are not easy, and partners need to be coached appropriately. Effective feedback and performance reviews require competence, not more time.

---

9   See note 1 above.

The shift of responsibility for lawyers' development onto the partners starts with the day-to-day interactions that partners and associates have in the course of client work.

Effective feedback: In order for feedback to be directly linked to performance, it is fundamental that a well-designed system (tailored to the specificities of how lawyers work) be established, so that supervising associates and partners can nurture associates and give them the feedback that they need.

To become part of the firm's culture, the ability to provide good feedback needs to be measured, rewarded and embedded into the performance review process.

Skills and tools must be provided to supervising associates and partners to ensure that they give feedback effectively.

Ideally, partners should be coached individually or in small groups to enable them to deliver effective feedback as part of their ongoing management and leadership responsibilities.

Performance reviews: Some law firms understand the importance and impact that delivering high-quality performance reviews has on lawyers' levels of engagement, performance and retention. But in the vast majority of firms, performance reviews are managed by the human resources department and partners simply follow the procedures, often reluctantly.

Performance reviews enable performance to be discussed in greater detail and development goals to be set.

Most of the time, performance reviews are seen as an administrative task or burden by partners and associates. To avoid this feeling, partners need to rely on a good performance review system, as well as being briefed and coached on how to achieve satisfying results when carrying out reviews.

Tips for an effective, light and motivating performance review system include the following:
- The forms need to be drafted to enable an open, constructive and creative exchange between associates and partners.
- The forms must be designed specifically for each level of seniority.
- The emphasis should be on development.
- There should be no surprises when performance is discussed, as every lawyer will have received constant feedback about his work.
- A less formal review twice a year is better practice than lengthy annual reviews.

Understanding the firm as a business: Among other aspects, the business of law involves management and business development, skills that all lawyers must acquire as part of their professional development. Clients expect all lawyers to understand their business. It is just as important that associates understand how the firm works, how business is generated and how they can contribute to developing the firm.

Requiring associates to carry out marketing activities is only a start.

Ultimately, if associates understand the business of the firm, they will also understand clients' businesses.

(b) **Enabling lawyers to take ownership of their own development from the beginning of their career**

As well as receiving quality feedback and constructive performance reviews, encouraging lawyers to work with mentors and be coached is the most effective way to support them in taking ownership of their development.

Mentoring – a modern approach: In order for partners to be able to support the development of their associates, it is important for them to have a clear understanding of the distinction between mentoring and coaching.

The distinction is clearly explained by Anne Scouler, founder of Meyler Campbell and one of the most experienced and respected business coaches in Europe, in her book on business coaching.[10]

In essence, traditional mentoring in the legal profession is mainly directive (mentors provide specific advice and guidance based on their experience), while coaching is mainly non-directive (coaches enable people to identify and explore their own options and solutions).

In practice, there is a significant overlap between the two and both are effective when they raise self-awareness. In the modern approach to mentoring, mentors are required to apply coaching skills as much as possible, to guide the mentees towards identifying their own solutions to the challenges.

As David Clutterbuck, one of Europe's thought leaders on mentoring, says: "No other developmental intervention has such a significant impact as mentoring does on retention, career success and talent management. It's hard to find a truly successful person who didn't have the benefit of one or more mentors in their career."

In the past, mentoring always existed informally in law firms. Senior lawyers had *protégés* whom they mentored, trained and promoted. This tradition no longer exists, but young lawyers expect to be guided and supported in their professional development.

Recent development in mentoring has favoured a new approach that is becoming the norm. Unlike traditional mentoring, the modern approach is for mentees to take responsibility for the mentoring relationship. Mentees now have a number of mentors, are the initiators and drive the mentoring relationships to achieve their learning objectives.

The modern approach to mentoring has also encouraged the development of new forms of mentoring, such as peer mentoring, reverse mentoring and group mentoring, which are interesting to explore in the context of large international firms.

An illustration of this modern approach to mentoring in the context of a professional service firm is described in the *Harvard Business Review* article "Why Mentoring Matters in a Hypercompetitive World".[11]

---

10 A Scouler, *Financial Times Guide to Business Coaching*, Financial Times Prentice Hall (2011).
11 T J Delong, J J Gabarro and R J Lees, "Why Mentoring Matters in a Hypercompetitive World", *Harvard Business Review*, January 2008.

McKinsey encourages associates to "build their own McKinsey" by seeking out subordinates, peers and partners with whom they share mutual chemistry, interests and goals. These individuals eventually form a "personal advisory board" – a core group of people invested in the associates' development.

Successful mentoring in law firms is based upon:
- having a clear programme goal and purpose;
- making mentoring voluntary;
- having senior management commitment;
- including mentoring skills in the performance system;
- training mentors and mentees;
- having a dedicated, trained programme coordinator; and
- monitoring and evaluating on a continuous basis for constant improvement.

Lawyers as mentors: It is the quality of attention that a mentor pays to the mentee that facilitates better mental engagement so that clearer ideas, greater vision and better solutions can emerge.[12]

Lawyers find it easier to explain and tell than to listen and guide. Because of their training and their inclination to put greater importance on intellectual and technical knowledge, it is hard for them to step back and not jump to conclusions about what seems right or wrong.

However, this does not mean that lawyers cannot be good mentors. In fact, when briefed on the required skills, the vast majority make good mentors.

Mentoring fails to work when:

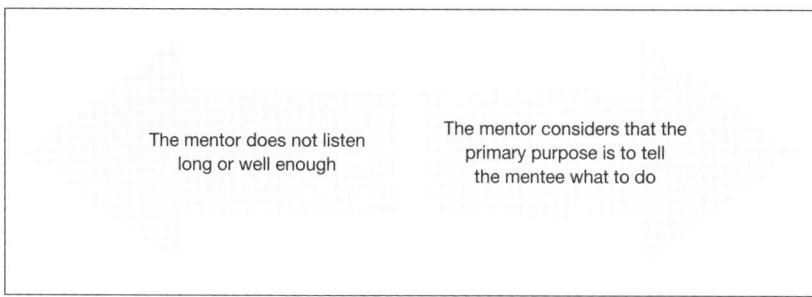

The modern approach to mentoring therefore requires mentors to use coaching techniques so that they can listen and guide, rather than explain and tell.

What mentors gain: While the benefits to the mentee are reasonably well understood and enable lawyers to take control of their own career, partners in law firms are often unaware of the benefits that good mentoring can bring to them. Partners can:
- enhance their own skills;

---

12   Nancy Kline, *Time to Think*, Ward Lock (1999).

- gain insight into their relationships with their own teams;
- have the satisfaction of seeing someone else grow;
- renew their focus on their own career and business development;
- rediscover business principles and practices;
- gain an opportunity to take time out and reflect;
- gain a broader understanding of employees' needs; and
- extend their professional and personal networks.[13]

The impact of good mentoring, both on lawyers and on law firms, is often underestimated because it is not measured.

Effective mentoring in law firms:

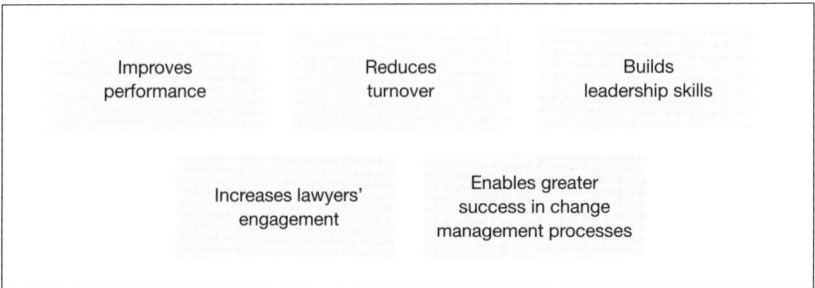

To achieve these outcomes, law firms need to design and run modern, flexible mentoring programmes that are tailored to the specificities of how lawyers work.

This means assimilating the best of informal mentoring into structured, formal programmes, which incorporate best practice.

A case study of an international mentoring programme that embodies the modern approach to mentoring in the context of the legal profession can be found in the appendix to this chapter.

Coaching skills for partners: The chapter in this book on coaching for lawyers deals with coaching from external providers. Here, 'coaching' refers to partners' abilities to use coaching skills to effectively support talent development in their teams.

Coaching is a real challenge for most partners, more so than mentoring.

It is nevertheless essential that partners learn the appropriate coaching skills (through focused, tailored individual or small group workshops, such as the type that Meyler Campbell delivers with its 'Elements' programme) so that, through the day-to-day interactions of client work, they can enable and encourage associates to take ownership of their development.

(c) *Bringing talent management to the centre of the strategy*
The direct link between great talent and a firm's ability to compete for and win work

---

13   Clutterbuck Associates, *Mentoring Programme Manager's Workshop* (2011).

means that it is imperative to align talent management with the firm's strategy.

The degree of alignment can be measured by the maturity of talent management in a firm.

The five stages of maturity for talent management are as follows:
- No talent management strategy exists; where talent is developed, it is incidental.
- Talent management activities occur in isolated, tactical pockets; there is no overall plan for talent management.
- Talent management activities are integrated and coordinated for a particular segment of the firm – for example, senior lawyers on partnership track.
- A talent management strategy designed to deliver the firm's overall strategy is in place.
- Talent management informs and is informed by the firm's strategy.

Alignment of talent management with the strategy of the firm[14]

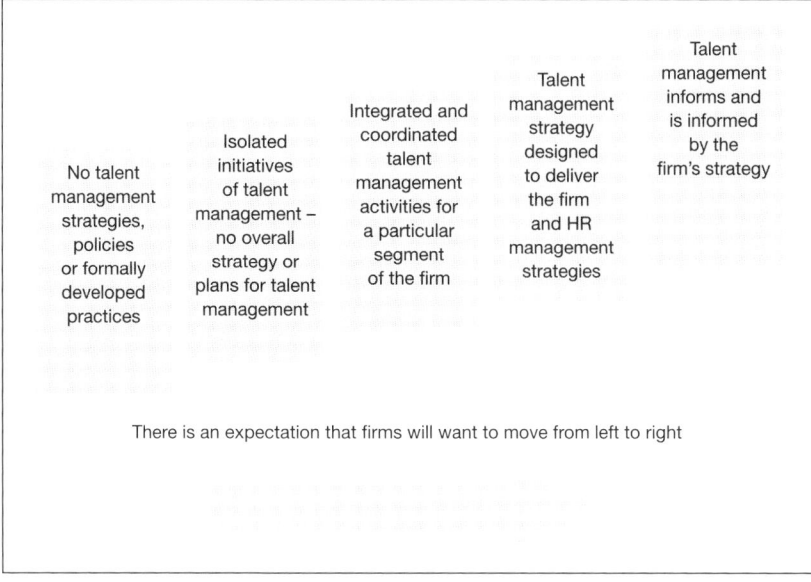

Moving to the next level of maturity: Moving talent management to the next level of maturity is a strategic process that starts by identifying the current level of maturity and ends by implementing integrated talent management measures that have been carefully designed and adapted to the structure, culture and specific challenges of the firm.

The level of maturity of talent management depends not only, but to a large extent, on the size of a firm. Experience shows that few firms manage to reach stage five (where talent management is put at the heart of the firm's strategy). This is the

---

14   CIPD, *Talent Management: Understanding the Dimensions*, p6 (2006).

stage which provides the best results on the firm's overall performance and should be the goal for law firms to aim for over the coming years, in order to remain capable of attracting, developing and retaining the best lawyers.

To measure the impact of talent management in law firms, success criteria must be defined at the outset of each initiative, while continuous monitoring will enable constant alignment and improvement.

5. Conclusion

I have occasionally heard partners say that developing others in the firm was getting in the way of client work. Luckily, this view is now rarely expressed (even if it is understandingly sometimes felt), and partners are becoming more aware of the link between great talent and business performance.

The unsurpassed levels of complexity and pressure with which lawyers practise law today require firms to have more skilled and self-aware partners than in the past.

The good news is that the profession is slowly but surely moving towards new talent management practices – it is just a matter of time before law firms fully embrace practices that shape the next generation law firms.

Appendix
Launching the International Bar Association Law Firm Mentoring Programme

A case study

The International Bar Association (IBA), established in 1947, is the world's leading organisation of international legal practitioners, bar associations and law societies. The IBA influences the development of international law reform and shapes the future of the legal profession throughout the world. It has a membership of more than 50,000 individual lawyers and over 200 bar associations and law societies spanning all continents. The Law Firm Management Committee, with over 3,000 members, is the biggest committee of the IBA.

In 2009, the Law Firm Management Committee decided to launch a law firm mentoring programme. The initiative links law firm partners with lawyers from around the world to help them start or grow their practice. Initially, the programme was aimed primarily at providing guidance and advice to IBA lawyers in emerging markets or developing economies who had no access to law firm management expertise.

With very little promotion, the programme rapidly attracted an impressive number of mentors who were respected members of the profession, from various parts of the world. The challenge that the programme encountered was to reach out to the mentees who either did not know of the IBA mentoring opportunities or did not know how to get involved.

In 2012, the programme was redesigned to enable proper promotion, coordination and monitoring on a bigger scale. The initiative was made available to mentees regardless of IBA membership and location.

The IBA is now partnering with local bar associations so that they can promote and coordinate the programme directly to their members. The first example of this is a partnership with the Costa Rican Bar, which is launching the initiative in six central American countries.

Since the formal relaunch of the Law Firm Mentoring Programme at the IBA annual conference in Dublin in October 2012, mentors and mentees are joining the programme on an ongoing basis and from a growing number of jurisdictions (100 participants from 35 jurisdictions are currently involved).

At the beginning of the initiative, some senior partners were questioning whether distance mentoring could build meaningful mentoring relationships. Fortunately, and due to the attention and support that the programme has attracted, most of them are now convinced that this can be achieved.

The challenge ahead relates to providing sufficient mentoring skills for participants so that once they have joined the programme, the mentoring pairs quickly engage in strong mentoring relationships.

Driving business results through talent

Marc Bartel
Caroline Vanovermeire
Heidrick & Struggles

The term 'strategy' has strong corporate connotations and hence is often perceived as something which is less relevant to smaller law firms. However, it remains essential in today's highly competitive legal market to know where one is going and why one has decided to become an independent adviser.

When a couple of lawyers decide to set up a new firm, establishing a strategy is not usually an initial concern. Yet their efforts to launch their new enterprise are nonetheless the first step towards establishing a strategy. They must ask themselves how they wish to differentiate their offering and what kind of clientele they are targeting.

1. A focused strategy

Historically, factors such as bar regulations that restrict business development and high demand for quality advisers in certain sectors fuelled an assumption that clients would come knocking on firms' doors to seek their help. Indeed, this might still be the case in a few limited situations. However, this reactive attitude can no longer be considered a viable way to develop a sustainable client base in today's challenging market. In the not so distant past, some even suggested that lawyers should not respond to clients too quickly, for fear that such quick turnaround times would come to be expected as a matter of course. At a session at the International Bar Association's 2012 annual conference in Dublin, by contrast, a US partner revealed that his firm now has a 20-minute return phone call policy.

A coherent strategy is crucial to ensure success in this demanding new environment. The most common flaw when considering a strategy is to overlook the fact that its success is entirely dependent on the talent available to implement it. In a professional service organisation, whose sole assets are its people, this omission is critical and often damaging. A second common flaw is a lack of focus, where the strategy is continually adapted to fit whatever talent might be available. Another common mistake is the partners' failure to communicate their strategy clearly and consistently to all other staff members. Finally, while the partners may agree on what their strategy should be, they may be less clear on how to go about implementing it.

Considering the first problem, then, a flawed evaluation of the available talent pool too often results in a compromise on the quality of the staff leading implementation of the strategy. For example, a strategy aimed at becoming a key player in a specific sector or developing niche expertise will not materialise as hoped if it is led by lawyers without the necessary talent to implement it successfully. If plans to attract a star lawyer from another firm or to groom up-and-coming internal talent to this end fall through, less experienced people may be hired or asked to lead, resulting in at best much slower implementation, at worst failure of the strategy. The financial expectation to return profits over the short term may thus result in a loss-making operation, putting pressure on profitability. Management will often argue that the market turned out to be more challenging than expected, when in fact it was poor talent planning which caused the losses. This resembles a situation where a company hopes to tap a potentially lucrative market and seeks the necessary equipment to profitably build and sell a product, but on discovering that such equipment is unavailable or unaffordable, still persists in its plan by investing in old technology which will not deliver the expected profits – or any profits, for that matter.

Those in smaller firms may think that a focused talent plan is unrealistic at this stage of their evolution. However, even a single-partner firm should consider how it intends to grow and whether or how available talent could help achieve its goals. In smaller firms especially, it is crucial that all lawyers share a common vision and purpose. Building synergies around skills and clients will deliver results and unify the partners. It is also much easier to develop work from existing clients than to win new ones. Once again, a simple plan or common objective should be determined, based on the specific talent which the firm can afford, access or attract.

An unfocused approach of accepting any talent that happens to come along is common, but is frequently problematic. The temptation to hire talent with a solid book of business or revenues is understandable, but not optimal. Depending on the size of the firm, this may be regarded as a way to boost overall revenues or counterbalance a risky or challenging revenue stream. There is often a false sense that the new hire will mean success for all, as he will make an immediate contribution to the bottom line. But if this were so simple, all or most such lateral hires – and even promotions – would end in success. By contrast, history has shown that, like all other professionals, lawyers who move firm rarely deliver the anticipated contribution in the short term. A study published by Heidrick & Struggles in collaboration with Winmark revealed that it "takes lawyers longer to bring their so-called following along, which normally ends up being about a third of that they say they would bring".[1] Too often, great expectations become disappointments on both sides and the bottom line may be endangered as a result.

Such hires can also undermine synergy in the firm, as partners focus on individual revenues instead of working together towards a common purpose. The most commonly overlooked issue, despite what firms may claim, is the importance of cultural fit. Too often in the rush to consider a potential lateral hire, or even an internal promotion, billing ends up being the decisive factor. In many jurisdictions, this is driven by an aggressive recruitment market or the fear of losing out on future talent. No one could disagree with the statement that the success of any business depends on quality. The impact of quality – or lack thereof – is quickly felt in the legal sector, where you are only as good as your last advice. Furthermore, a firm or

---

1 Heidrick & Struggles, *Bridging the Gap: Talent Strategies to align law firms with client needs*, 2011.

individual's career will span several decades, and a short-term view on quality thus has the potential to seriously damage the firm's brand, clientele and very survival. Despite this, however, for many firms internal promotions and lateral recruitment are still driven by existing or potential revenue. I have rarely heard management say that someone is a brilliant lawyer who delivers outstanding quality and hence will be promoted or hired despite a lack of revenues or clientele. I would not venture to say that the reverse is true, but billing or billing potential is too often the decisive criterion.

As mentioned, another common mistake is the partners' failure to communicate strategy clearly and consistently to all other staff members. Inevitably, a firm's primary focus tends to be on its lawyers, and thus strategy may be discussed at length within the partners' forum. However, firms tend to underestimate the importance of support functions in ensuring that lawyers can thrive and perform effectively. It is therefore crucial to familiarise all staff members with the strategy and how they can contribute towards achieving it.

Even once a strategy has been clearly articulated and consistently understood, the partners may not be aligned as to how it should be implemented. There may be disagreements about pace and timing, as well as 'softer' elements such as values which are reflected in daily client and colleague interactions, as well as in decisions made on behalf of or within the partnership.

2. **Building a brand**

There are numerous definitions of the term 'brand'. In some ways it can be equated to the culture of a firm, which can be hard to describe. It may be easy to intuit, but difficult to describe beyond basic adjectives such 'collegiate' or 'client-centric'. Essentially, the brand reflects the culture of the people working within the firm, and hence is a blend of their values, styles, personalities and aspirations.

From this perspective, then, a firm's strategy should include the objective of building or preserving a coherent brand. This could mean reinforcing the existing culture, ensuring that people can articulate the culture and identify with it, or reshaping the culture to facilitate implementation of the new strategy. A famous quote from Peter Drucker sums it up: "Culture eats strategy for breakfast." If the culture is not aligned with the strategy, implementation will be difficult and may ultimately come to naught.

One of the main principles highlighted by culture consultant firm Senn Delaney is that the firm is a mirror of its own leadership. In other words, a successful firm that is making great progress in line with its strategy will have partners who behave in line with the brand and culture. All too often, where this is not the case, firms try to solve the issue of culture by reviewing their structure. A leading law firm once approached us with the aim of increasing cross-selling activities as part of its growth strategy. However, we quickly established that we first had to tackle a lack of trust among partners and the absence of a common set of values. In other words, the partners needed to decide whether they wanted to operate as a real team or as franchisees. Both options work; however, they each require a different strategy and reflect a different culture and brand position on the market.

It is difficult to dissociate a firm's brand from that of each individual member. When developing or acquiring talent, this issue should not be overlooked. No partner would be happy to hear that a colleague delivers poor quality, lacks ethics or is not pleasant to work with when pitching to a client. Word of mouth about a bad experience with one partner may mean that the others are suddenly ignored by existing or potential clients. Sadly, such experiences generally arise post-promotion or recruitment, and are hard to predict. However, while we all tend to question, check and run simulations on portable revenue streams, we rarely invest the same energy on assessing the reputation or values of individual partners; and if there is any doubt, strategic needs and billing will inevitably take priority. The misperception is that the firm's culture and procedures will improve and correct some of the individual's perceived flaws.

3. **Differentiating the firm on the market**

Clients instruct a firm due to the perceived quality of its service, which makes it stand out from the crowd. Consolidation on the legal services market is continuing and more work is now being undertaken in-house – factors which have served to make this environment more competitive. Market positioning, brand building and differentiation are thus becoming increasingly important for law firms of all sizes. Admittedly, the 'friendship factor' does still apply at some level and can carry significant weight in certain cultures and countries. However, if the competition can offer a better service at the same price – or even at a higher price – even hitherto loyal clients may eventually move on.

A sole practitioner defines his brand by his actions. As soon as two lawyers begin to work together, their individual actions will reflect on one another. Even if the firm's name is just a basic combination of their surname, that name will develop a brand of its own on the market. Clients' perceptions will also be informed by the type of work and advice provided. There is nothing worse – except a reputation for poor quality, which may eventually prove fatal – than confused market perceptions about the types of services on offer. If clients do not understand what services the firm is offering and how good it is at providing them, they will not consider even asking it for more information about what it does. It is therefore essential to identify the clientele that the firm will target and what is required to serve and please that clientele. Clients and the market should have a clear understanding of what they can expect from the firm. In deciding on how the firm will differentiate itself, the partners must consider what kind of service they wish to offer and therefore what kind of talent they need. In a smaller firm, one person may be so well known that he effectively 'is' the brand – the magnet that attracts more work. This situation may create unrest among other more entrepreneurially aspirational lawyers or those seeking a greater say in the firm's day-to-day or future plans.

4. **Developing a dynamic talent strategy**

4.1 An evolving partnership

The economic landscape is changing increasingly rapidly. Client demand for services and advice is mirroring this trend, as new markets, products and issues emerge. In an ailing economy such as Europe, for example, there is heightened need for restructuring skills and hence talent who can offer these skills. In some emerging markets, on the other hand, new legislative regimes may develop quickly and clients will need up-to-date advice to support and protect them in entering those markets.

A static partnership – that is, a group of partners with few synergies or little desire to cooperate, or with rigid or siloed views of clients' needs – risks misreading or simply missing these economic changes altogether, or failing to adapt its offering accordingly.

It is thus essential that lawyers, like all other professionals, accept that the era of a single job or skill for life is over. We will all have to change jobs, position or function several times during our working careers. Lawyers cannot expect to be the exception to this rule and must commit to continual learning in order to stay agile, flexible and adaptable. Equally, firms must support the continued development of their lawyers, to ensure that they are well equipped to deal with the increased complexities and ambiguities of the sector and to promote their employability. At times, internal talent will need to be complemented by the acquisition of new talent, and offices or practices may need to be opened or closed. It is imperative to keep a finger on the pulse of the market and to anticipate trends in a proactive manner. Those who truly care about their clients' business challenges must pick up on early signs of change. However, inertia may make it difficult to adapt the talent and skills within the partnership sufficiently quickly to keep pace with market changes. Successful firms and partners will know how to break out of siloed thinking and develop talent with a wider skill set. Indeed, for smaller firms or in some jurisdictions, it is already a basic requirement to be more versatile.

4.2 **Identifying the necessary talent to achieve the strategy**
The law firm's strategy must be clear, realistic and focused. It must further be dynamic and reviewed regularly – although not excessively, as this will mean it is neither focused nor realistic, and will further blur the brand and confuse clients. The strategy must rely on existing or easily accessible talent. As market opportunities are identified and regularly reviewed and refined, it is thus critical to conduct in-depth analysis of the firm's talent and ensure that this talent is capable of adapting to market and demand changes. Lawyers tend to be resistant to the notion of developing new skills, which requires that billable time be set aside as an investment towards the future. But each professional should commit to keep learning – and not just by attending interesting presentations. Learning also involves humility and a willingness to accept new challenges. Lawyers often have abundant potential to learn, but less motivation to do so. A positive attitude towards learning is even more important in smaller firms, where a sudden drop in work and hence revenues will have a quicker, more dramatic impact on the firm as a whole, rapidly creating tension between the partners and possibly isolating the weakest link.

4.3 **Support professionals are a vital asset**
As previously observed, there is a common misconception that a firm's sole talent is its lawyers. They generate billable hours (many of which, in fact, are unbillable or of

poor quality), and hence revenues. But whatever the size of the firm, one cannot deny the added value of support professionals. Some still feel that it is easier to find a good secretary than a good lawyer, and thus show little interest in the recruitment and development of this talent. Lawyers for the most part sell their time, packaged up in a quality service; so ensuring that they can optimise this time will help to ensure success. A great professional support team will assist in implementing the strategy, as it can facilitate the delivery of a quality service. On the business development front, professionals can also help lawyers to identify new opportunities. Some firms have understood this strategic advantage and have invested in their support professionals well beyond the salary element.

5. **Integration**

One word which is always used following the hiring of new talent is 'integration'. Many firms have thought at length about the issues and challenges facing new recruits, and have designed integration programmes in response. In most cases, however, such programmes suffer from three major flaws. First, they are condensed: the vast majority of the information is usually shared in the first week that the new hire joins. Second, they cover only objective rules and procedures, neglecting unwritten rules or key aspects of the firm's culture. Third, where the programme is extended over several months, it is rarely fully implemented as originally intended, because all parties are too busy, do not prioritise it or forget about it all together.

Any new recruit who does not quickly grasp the culture or who thinks he can impose his own culture on the firm will face a rude awakening. Resistance is futile, as ultimately the prevailing culture will win out. Anecdotal data shows that one of the mains reasons why external hires do not work out is cultural misalignment.

The standard approach to integration seems to involve touring the office, reading the firm's rules and procedures, possibly signing an elaborate code of conduct and attending a couple of lunches with various members of the office. The IT manager will stop by to explain briefly how to use the computer system and other devices, and will provide the helpdesk phone number. It also seems that the more senior the new recruit, the quicker the process. The attitude is that the new recruit has joined to sell his time, and enough billable hours have already been invested in the recruitment process, so the priority is to get down to work and start making a return on that investment. What is forgotten is that the recruitment process is effectively a kind of courtship, in which both parties tend to oversell their qualities and potential, and fail to assess objective and/or subjective criteria with rigour. To complicate things further, many head hunters enthusiastically exaggerate the candidate's abilities and the firm, charmed by the promised revenues on offer, feels obliged to promise more than it can deliver.

By structuring the integration process over several months, and past the classic 90 or 100 days, unspoken rules can be clearly iterated over time and answers given to any unfulfilled expectations. The process can be compared to a training session for a newly acquired software program. A lot of information is thrown at the user, of which only a fraction is understood and assimilated. Those functionalities which are not used within a few days are easily forgotten, and suddenly the helpdesk telephone number provided earlier becomes so much more useful. Slowly, over time, one comes to learn the basic applications. Refresher courses are essential.

6. **Selling and cross-selling**

   As outlined elsewhere in this book, successful cross-selling requires a culture that supports cross-practice collaboration and talent which has the necessary skillsets to do so.

   Adding new talent to the firm without a common interest or potential synergies is unlikely to deliver the benefits of collaborative working. The end result may be a group of talented attorneys who share nothing more than costs and a coffee in the morning. The ultimate goal in creating a firm should be to help each other and chase, share and advise common clients, thus cross-pollinating both skillsets and potential and existing client bases. Cross-selling skills should always be considered when creating or growing a law firm. This might be more challenging for someone who is just starting out on a legal career or who has always worked by himself. However, it is nonetheless an essential skill. Aside from the obvious additional value it creates by increasing the flow of work from clients and hence strengthening the firm's client base, it further ties the client more closely to the firm and reduces the risk of defection to the competition. The client will also take comfort from the fact that two partners are clearly involved in protecting each other's clients and trust in each other's abilities to provide a quality service.

7. **Transition management**

   A partnership is a living structure in many ways: over the years, new partners are hired or appointed, while others are asked to leave or retire.

   Significant investments in terms of effort and money are made in order to attract the best possible talent, and to promote business development activities aimed at protecting or developing a profitable client base. In today's challenging economic climate and increasingly competitive legal market, some firms are further investing in chasing down alumni in the hope that they may send on work to their old firm, or at least say a few good words about it. A much easier way to secure future revenues or the firm's brand is to help partners transition out of the firm and prepare them for the next stage of their journey in life. Some partners who have retired may wish to utilise their knowledge or experience for the benefit of charities; others may still need to work to support their family; other may wish to continue working in a different position; and still others may wish to become non-executive directors. Firms should start investing time in understanding what their partners may wish to do later in their careers and offer advice or external help to prepare them for life after leaving the firm. These partners will only be thankful for the help they have received and will speak highly of the human qualities of their former firm – valuable word-of-mouth praise for the firm.

8. **Conclusion**

   Talent is vital for the successful implementation of any strategy. However, this issue is normally considered only after a strategy has been determined, which can lead to the acquisition of sub-optimal talent and to failures or tensions between partners. Other industries have realised that their main competitive advantage is their talent, its adaptability and its ability to help realise a strategy – law firms need to do likewise.

Talent development in law firms

Tony King
Clifford Chance LLP

1. Introduction

Law firms are knowledge businesses: the product they sell is the knowledge and expertise of their lawyers.

While law firms make significant investments in the infrastructure that enables them to deliver services to their clients (eg, premises, technology), the most important investment they can make is in their people.

To achieve success, a law firm must ensure that it has the right people working together to help achieve its strategic goals. The link between a law firm's overarching vision (and the strategy it has adopted to achieve that vision) and the recruitment, development and management of its people is covered elsewhere in this book.

The lawyers working in a law firm are vital to the success of the organisation as the revenue generators, but they are not the only employees. The vast majority of law firms around the world will employ staff to perform other roles that are important to the success of the business. These can range from business managers, IT specialists and accountants to secretaries and messengers. Some firms call these groups 'support staff'; others call them 'business services staff'. Many of these people directly facilitate the delivery of legal services and so play an important role in supporting the quality of the services that the lawyers provide to their clients. Many are highly qualified professionals from other disciplines whose skills – for example, in business management, financial management or technology management – complement those of the lawyers working in the firm. It is therefore just as important to consider this group when looking at talent management in law firms; this chapter examines the development of both lawyers and support staff.

The chapter describes the steps in a typical talent management structure, starting with determining the skills that the organisation needs from its staff and then looking at ways of developing and managing people in line with those identified skills.

The chapter looks at talent management generally, without focusing on a particular kind of firm.

2. Managing whose talent?

It is understandable that many law firms will put the bulk of their talent management investment into the careers of the lawyers who work for the firm (at all levels). These are the revenue generators and so investment in their development is likely to produce the biggest returns.

However, in many firms, talented and capable as the lawyers are, they do rely on other professionals to support them. These may be highly qualified professionals such as accountants or expert support staff such as secretaries. The firms could not function efficiently without these support staff and so they have to be included in each firm's people strategy.

Not so long ago, many firms provided limited training to their support staff. However, as partners increasingly see the benefits of having highly professional staff to help them run their businesses, the trend is towards investing in the development of this group within the workforce.

The detailed development offered to support staff may justifiably be different from that offered to the lawyers. For example, a secretary may need to be taught about an IT package or an internal administrative procedure to perform some task which is not cost effective for a lawyer to perform. However, many support staff working in law firms are just as much a part of the fee-earning teams as the lawyers; they just perform different tasks. For example, the administrative support that a secretary provides to a lawyer working on a significant case can be a key element in the delivery of quality service. Therefore, there will be circumstances when the practical training of lawyers and support staff can usefully overlap.

This may be particularly evident for secretaries working directly with lawyers, but may be less obvious where support staff provide 'back room' services (eg, the accounts function). However, training can be used to encourage all employees to see themselves as part of one team, with a common goal of delivering on the firm's vision.

Even in the best-run firms that recognise this 'one team' concept, it is sometimes said that lawyers have careers, while support staff have jobs. Is this true and how can it be managed?

The nature of law firms is such that there is a clear career path for the lawyers who work in them – graduate recruit, associate and partner (whatever titles and intervening stages may exist in particular firms). At the risk of over-simplification, there is a broadly similar career path for most support staff roles in law firms, in that the individual may start as a junior team member and progress to a more senior, usually managerial level.

The issue of whether support staff have 'jobs' rather than 'careers' is not, therefore, whether the path for their particular role (or indeed their personal aspirations) is progressive. Rather, it is whether there are opportunities for progression within the law firm in which they currently work. The reality for many support staff is that while there may be opportunities for progression, these can be limited. Therefore, their career path may mean that they progress by taking more senior roles in a number of different organisations, rather than progressing to a senior level in the same organisation.

The extent to which support staff will move in this way will vary from firm to firm and from role to role. However, the issue for the firm where movement is the route to progression is how to treat the support staff in that category. One argument may be to provide them with sufficient training to enable them to perform their current role effectively, without any regard to whether this will enable them to seek a more senior role elsewhere. That might make business sense, in that the firm will get no return on its investment in helping the individual progress to a higher-level role with another organisation. However, it overlooks the fact that the development may enable the individual to perform his current role more efficiently and perhaps to take on a wider range of tasks, to the benefit of the firm's business. Furthermore, a firm that is known to provide good developmental opportunities will be attractive in the market, so the quality of applicants for open positions should be higher.

Firms can make a virtue out of the necessity of dealing with the departure of support staff seeking career progression by benefiting from the different past experience of new recruits in fluid recruitment markets. A recruit who has worked in several organisations (perhaps in different sectors) may be able to bring valuable new ideas and approaches to the firm.

3. Steps in a talent management structure

3.1 Competency framework

Competency frameworks have been in place in large corporates for many years. They give clarity regarding the expectations of the employing organisation. Increasingly, law firms have created competency frameworks that underpin all of their talent management processes. Therefore, it is worthwhile to consider the definition of a 'competency framework'.

It is a description of the knowledge, skills, behaviours and attributes which an organisation needs its workforce to possess in order to meet its business needs. Once identified, it supports all the stages in the talent management process, from recruitment through development and progression to departure.

Many consultants around the world can advise on identifying a competency framework suitable for an individual firm. The purpose of this section is to give some guidance on how partners can develop either their own competency framework or a clear idea of what is required should they seek external advice. It also highlights the challenges involved and the barriers to introducing these frameworks.

What does a competency framework look like? In many larger organisations, the framework will be a matrix made up of the headline knowledge, skills, behaviours and attributes (or 'competencies') that their workforces need to possess, broken down into 'seniority levels'. From that generic framework, the organisation can identify the relative importance of particular competencies for a specific role.

For smaller organisations, it need not be so complicated and the framework can be identified by reference to the particular role being considered. For example, if a firm is looking to recruit a secretary, the core tasks may be to type at a certain speed and to have knowledge of a particular word processing package. However, are these all of the tasks which the secretary will have to perform? Will the secretary work for one person or many? If the latter, the ability to prioritise may be important. Will a secretary simply type, or does the role involve some liaison activities inside or outside the firm (in which case, communication and interpersonal skills may be needed)? Will a secretary work alone or, if the intention is to work in a team, what is the secretary's role within that team (team-working skills may be needed)? Is the role fixed or is the expectation that the holder will take on additional tasks as his experience grows?

The same thinking can apply to a lawyer's role. The core activities of the role may be obvious, but further analysis may reveal more nuances in what is required to function effectively. For example, if a two-partner firm wants to recruit its first associate, the partners may decide that they want someone with a certain level of academic achievement and the ability to do research to support the work of the partners. Is research the only task (in which case, perhaps a research assistant may be appropriate)? Will the associate work for one partner exclusively or for both (in which case, again, prioritisation skills may be needed)? Will the associate work exclusively on the partners' files or will he be given his own caseload? Are there different expectations of the associate after working for the firm for one, two, five or more years?

The answers to these kinds of questions for differing roles can produce a variety of outcomes as to what is required. If the analysis is done effectively, it can maximise the chances of success for the recruitment process. It will also give the partners clear sight of any skills gaps that emerge during the recruitment process which need to be filled if the jobholder is to perform effectively.

Looking at individual roles can achieve a highly targeted framework (with all its associated benefits of transparency), but can be time consuming to develop. This can be a significant barrier. However, opting for generic descriptions rather than very detailed ones can mitigate such difficulties.

Therefore, this section now describes possible competency frameworks for lawyers and support staff.

Starting with lawyers, the first step in determining a competency framework is to recognise that to be an effective lawyer, the individual needs both excellent legal knowledge and skills and a wide range of personal, interpersonal and managerial business skills. What can be covered in these two categories?

Looking first at the legal-technical skills of lawyers, firms have a choice: they can opt either for a comprehensive listing of all skills and knowledge that the lawyer needs to perform his role effectively or for a more generic list of knowledge and skills. The former has the attraction of clarity, but the disadvantage of being time consuming to develop and keep up to date as circumstances change. The latter has the disadvantage of lack of precision, but if the analysis is effective, it will be recognisable to the lawyers of the firm and so be helpful. The trend is towards a more generic approach.

It is not possible to illustrate the former approach in any detail here, but it would cover all of the law relevant to the lawyer's role, as well as all of the relevant practice.

The latter approach is easier to illustrate. One possible list of headline descriptions could be:
- identification of legal issues;
- knowledge of the law;
- application of the law to the issues; and
- drafting.

How is 'knowledge of the law' in this generic approach different from the comprehensive listing? It is a matter of either keeping the description at a headline level (so giving the partners freedom to decide on the knowledge required) or spelling it out in detail. The end result should be the same (in that it is clear what knowledge the lawyer needs to perform his role), but the competency is easier to describe and requires less maintenance to reflect changing circumstances.

While the trend may be towards 'less is more', the challenge lies in giving enough detail for the competencies described to be clear to both sides.

The second element of a competency framework is the business skills. These will be the non-legal skills and behaviours that the lawyer needs to perform his role. An illustrative list could be:
- commercial insight;
- client awareness;
- business management;
- ethical behaviour;
- team leadership and people management;
- relationship building and networking; and
- communication skills.

Again, individual firms will identify the business skills that their own lawyers need to deliver on business objectives, but the key is to identify objective skills and attributes, rather than subjective characteristics. The former ensures that the firm's workforce has the right mix of skills to support its vision and should avoid unnecessary prescription in the 'type' of employee. The risk with a more subjective list of requirements is that the firm may have a workforce that has significant strengths in some areas, but is relatively weak in others, so that the firm lacks the breadth of skill needed to support its business. For example, requiring all recruits to have gained masters degrees in a particular area of law may make perfect sense when that area of law is producing a lot of work. However, this requirement may be less helpful if that work dries up or cannot be done profitability.

This is not removing a requirement for a high level of legal knowledge or skills. Rather, it is suggesting it can be phrased by reference to, for example, the ability to analyse problems, research issues, produce effective solutions to the client's problems, negotiate and communicate effectively.

While much of the competency framework will address the personal and interpersonal skills that the firm wants its people to develop, it can also cover the development of business management skills. An organisation depends on its people working together to deliver its strategy. One aspect of this is understanding the organisation's business drivers (perhaps particularly the financial drivers). Therefore, 'business management' (as included in the list above) can cover law firm economics, methods to improve efficiency in delivering service, contributions to know-how and so on. By emphasising these business management issues, the firm can ensure that the entire workforce contributes to its success. Building these messages into the developmental steps followed by the firm's staff can be more effective than merely explaining the business drivers, as it ensures that employees behave in a way which supports the firm's strategy.

The next stage in determining a competency framework is to decide how much detail the framework should contain underneath the broad headings, however many of those there may be.

A legal competency framework should recognise the fact that all lawyers develop their knowledge and skills over time.

Lawyers will (and should) devote considerable time and energy in the early years of their careers to gaining the core legal knowledge of their chosen area of specialisation. Thereafter, they will spend the rest of their careers refining and developing this knowledge, adjusting to changed circumstances, as appropriate. In contrast, lawyers will develop their pre-existing business skills (eg, the ability to communicate) in the context of a legal practice. As they become more senior, they may need to master a wider range of business skills, such as financial management, client development or people management.

Bearing this progression in mind, many competency frameworks will reflect such transitions through defining particular skills by reference to what may realistically be expected of the lawyer at a particular stage in his career. By way of illustration, a newly qualified lawyer may use his communication skills to write straightforward letters of advice or to brief the partner for whom he works on the outcomes of a research task. In contrast, a more senior lawyer may need to make a pitch to win work or to dissuade a client from a particular course of action because of some legal requirement. How many gradations the competency framework needs will depend on the circumstances within the firm, but at least four levels are required – junior associate, middle-level associate, senior associate and partner.

Further to the last point, a competency framework can be used to support the talent management processes of all lawyers of the firm, both associates and partners.

Clearly, for a firm-wide competency framework to have any real impact, it needs to be communicated to and understood by everyone in the firm. The firm needs to be transparent about the content of the framework and the support available to help its people develop in line with the framework.

Including partners in the framework has the advantage of making it plain to associates what is expected of them if they are to progress to partner level and obviously can support the talent management processes which a firm uses for its partners.

Looking at a competency framework for partners, a single level for all partners may work in many firms, but the role of a partner can and perhaps should develop over time:
- A newly appointed partner will need to establish or further develop his practice and build his reputation in his particular market.
- An established partner may have developed a strong practice with a good flow of work and it may be in the firm's best business interests for him to continue in this mode for the next one or two decades. However, it may also be beneficial to the firm if that partner develops broader and/or deeper relationships with key clients, brings on associates into the partnership, helps newly appointed partners to develop their practices and so on.
- A management partner will be involved in the management of some part of the firm and so perform important tasks that are distinct from his legal

practice. A successful business needs effective management and – whether all partners should progress over time into this type of role or only some – the need for and benefit of partners taking on these types of roles should be acknowledged.
- While some partners will remain in their post for life, in many firms there will come a point at which partners leave. Ignoring those who leave by reason of underperformance, the firm should give thought to what is expected of partners in the period running up to their retirement. What may appear in the competency framework will depend on the circumstances, but one issue which can be covered is the retiring partner's obligation to transition his practice to other partners at an appropriate stage.

While the first two and the last stage of the partner's career will follow in chronological sequence, the third stage (the management partner stage) can overlap with all of the others.

These principles can apply equally to support staff and it is possible to devise a competency framework for support staff that broadly follows the same pattern as that for lawyers. It can have two strands – the technical skills needed to perform the support staff role and the business skills needed. Inevitably, the list of technical skills should be tailored to the particular professional expertise of the support staff and so may look different from the headlines set out above for lawyers. The list of business skills set out above may be more easily applied to support staff, but again it will need to be tailored to ensure a 'fit' with the organisation.

Finally, it is worth remembering that a carefully analysed and tailored competency framework can define the culture in the firm. This is not with a view to ensuring that all employees are 'clones'. Instead, it can ensure that the entire workforce shares common values and attributes which will enable employees, in their many and varied ways, to help the firm achieve its business objectives.

3.2 Performance and talent management processes

An effective competency framework underpins all performance and talent management processes in the organisation.

First, it gives clarity to employees as regards what is expected of them, so that they understand not only the standards that they have to achieve, but also the support they can reasonably expect to be provided to them. Managers can measure performance against agreed firm-wide standards for the purposes of progression, dismissal, compensation and so on, and also understand the learning and development infrastructure that they have to put in place.

This section now looks at the appraisal or review processes that are commonly in place in law firms (here, the term 'appraisal' is used to cover all formal performance discussions).

The lawyers will receive (and indeed demand) feedback on their performance on client work as their careers progress. That coaching, mentoring and supervision process is vital to their development and can help them to progress in their careers very effectively. However, in addition to this ongoing feedback, many firms have a more formal regular appraisal process in place. Typically, a formal appraisal meeting is held once a year, at which performance to date is reviewed and objectives for the future are set. This is subsequently complemented by some form of quarterly or half-yearly review meeting(s), to discuss the lawyer's progress against the objectives set. These review meetings give the lawyer the opportunity to flag whether opportunities promised at the formal annual appraisal meeting have not been provided.

There are many approaches to these discussions, but prior to the formal annual appraisal, a typical preparation structure might be as follows:

- The lawyer is asked to conduct a self-review of his performance against the objectives set at the previous appraisal and to give thought to the next stage in his career (using the competency framework for guidance, as appropriate).
- In parallel, the lawyer's manager will review past progress and future development.
- As part of the information-gathering process, many firms include feedback from colleagues of the person being appraised. This can take many forms. It could be from colleagues identified by the person being appraised with whom he has worked over the previous year, so that the appraiser has the views of outsiders. In larger firms, the appraiser will consult his peers not only to get feedback on the person being appraised, but also to facilitate an appropriate comparison between all of the people being appraised, so as to ensure that the business objectives of the group are met. Some firms go further and arrange upward feedback (where feedback is given on a senior, including a partner, by all members of his team), or 360-degree feedback (given from all angles – seniors, peers and subordinates). Whichever feedback process a particular firm adopts, it is useful as it gives '3D' information for the benefit of both parties to the appraisal or review. However, depending on the particular process that the firm uses, care needs to be taken to ensure that it is effective and this requires a degree of trust across the organisation. For example, if the person being appraised can choose who will provide feedback, there is the risk that he will choose only people who will give good feedback. The upward or 360-degree feedback process can be very effective in terms of giving real clarity on performance, but there is the risk that justifiable negative feedback may not be given if junior employees think that this may cause problems for them with the senior in due course.
- The feedback (however collected) is collated and then discussed at the formal appraisal review meeting, at which past performance is reviewed and objectives for the future are set. As regards past performance, there should be no surprises. Good or bad performance should not be raised for the first time at this annual meeting; rather, it should have been flagged at the right time during the year and it can then be built into the appraisal discussion. The objectives set at the appraisal review meeting should fit with the competency framework, as well as with the firm's business objectives.

Of the range of options of information gathering outlined above, what is the most common? The challenge with the more extensive upwards or 360-degree approach is that it is time consuming to manage. Therefore, in many law firms, the information gathered is limited to the views of the partners for whom the individual lawyers work.

Some firms will combine a performance review with a salary or compensation review; others keep these two discussions separate. One common approach is to give some form of grade (eg, 'Exceeds expectations' or 'In need of development'), which in turn determines the level of salary or compensation increase and/or bonus that the individual is subsequently awarded.

Turning to the objectives set at these meetings, the factors that are taken into account in deciding what are appropriate topics are:
- the business needs of the firm;
- the current skills levels of the person being appraised; and
- the likely career progression of the individual.

The objectives could therefore cover acquiring or developing a particular area of expertise, working for specific clients or in particular teams, undergoing some specified training and so on. When preparing the objectives, the common acronym SMART should be borne in mind, so that the objective is:
- specific (eg, 'work on XCo's next M&A transaction');
- measurable (which the illustration above is);
- achievable (the objective will fail this requirement if, for example, due to the economic downturn there is no chance of XCo undertaking a corporate transaction in the foreseeable future);
- realistic (which means it must be feasible for the person being appraised to achieve the objective; the illustration ticks this box if, for example, the person being appraised or reviewed is an M&A specialist with the right level of expertise); and
- time bound (there must be a timeframe within which the objective is achieved; in the illustration, the timeframe needs to be added).

This approach is applicable to everyone in the firm at all levels, both partners and associates, and both senior and junior support staff. Clearly, the level of challenge that the objective represents will vary, depending on the individual involved. The objectives of a newly qualified associate may be limited to building his legal-technical knowledge. The objectives of a senior partner could be to achieve challenging billing targets, acquire a relationship with a major client in a particular target sector or requiring the partner to make a wider contribution (perhaps in terms of management responsibilities) to the firm, on top of his existing fee-earning activities.

The process described in this section has benefits to both the firm and the individual lawyers, but is clearly not simple to implement.

The process requires a considerable investment of time on the part of the firm and busy partners may have difficulty making the time to design and implement it. Furthermore, giving comprehensive, critical but constructive feedback can be a challenge. What if the lawyer is upset by the feedback and leaves the firm? This is potentially a problem in a busy practice.

However, on the other hand, the lawyer will want feedback on performance and progress. By not giving that feedback, will he develop to his full potential? If not, the business of the firm will be prejudiced.

3.3 **Managing performance and the shape of the workforce**
The outcomes of the appraisal or review process can be either positive or negative. The process obviously can support an associate moving towards partnership by helping him to develop the right skills and knowledge at the right pace. It can be negative in the sense that if an individual is underperforming, the process can make that plain; though, aside from very serious shortcomings, the individual should be given the opportunity to improve.

While the appraisal will not be the only vehicle for managing the shape of the workforce, it will play an important part.

People businesses such as law firms will have a business model based on a particular approach to leverage of partners to associates/paralegals. It is important for the firm's business health to manage that leverage properly, though doing so poses challenges.

On the one hand, a senior and experienced associate can be an invaluable resource to a partner, in that the associate can handle cases with limited supervision, so removing a burden from the partner. However, the downside is that having a senior associate doing the work (no matter how well) may in fact be less profitable than if it were done by a more junior and capable (but cheaper) associate. Furthermore, the senior associate doing the work may deny more junior associates development opportunities, to the detriment of themselves and the firm's business.

Clearly, this issue is not a serious problem if the senior associate is progressing to partner level, but it becomes an issue where the senior associate is deemed to have plateaued and is unlikely to be a partner candidate.

As a result of this dilemma, some firms have a policy of 'up or out', in that there is a clear understanding on both sides that the associate will leave the firm if he does not make it to partner. Other firms take the view that while the leverage model requires associates to move on, a strict 'up or out' policy may not be entirely for the benefit of the firm (eg, because of the loss of client relationships, expertise, team management or other activities). From this flows a 'grow or go' policy, which encourages constant development, but with the recognition that if the individual does not continue to achieve agreed objectives, that person will move on.

The turnover of lawyers inherent in any leverage model can be seen as a reason for withholding investment (on the basis that while the individual must be trained well to complete his current range of tasks, there is little point training him to perform a role which he may not perform with the current firm). This point has already been addressed in part, in that an organisation that offers a range of developmental opportunities will make itself more attractive in the recruitment market and so be able to recruit the best people. Once in the firm, identifying and supporting the key talent (eg, the future partners) to achieve their full potential will aid long-term retention.

Another angle is that, given that a certain proportion of the workforce will inevitably leave the firm, taking advantage of this makes good business sense. Where will they go? It is true that some will join competitor firms, but even that can have business benefits. Working with a friend in another law firm on a difficult transaction may help to move the transaction forward (without, of course, suggesting under any circumstances that the former employee would do anything other than look after the interests of his client to the best of his abilities). Similarly, if the lawyer who has moved firms finds that he is conflicted from acting for a particular client, he may refer that client to his old firm. In any event, the nature of modern lawyering is such that there are often opportunities for different firms to work together. Another option commonly seen in the larger commercial firms (but not only there) is for lawyers to leave the firm to go in-house. Depending on the lawyer's new employer, he may become a 'work giver' to his old firm and so be a very profitable contact.

3.4 Learning and development approaches

The learning and development process for lawyers has been based on the apprenticeship model for hundreds of years. Lawyers learned their skills on the job, under the supervision of an expert 'senior', and acquired the necessary legal knowledge through research, whether to address a particular client problem or by reading around the subject.

This approach of on-the-job training remains the basis of most lawyers' development and is highly effective in training a lawyer to deliver the services required by the clients of his firm.

However, as time has gone by, legal education has become more formalised and, aside from the wider variety of university law degrees which are available, lawyers in many jurisdictions have access to a plethora of training courses on a wide variety of legal-technical and business skills topics. The growth of these courses aimed at qualified lawyers is, in some jurisdictions, driven in part by the continuing professional development or continuing legal education obligations imposed on lawyers by the local bar association. While it is important for lawyers to meet the regulatory obligations imposed on them, they should undertake developmental activities in any event, to ensure that they are up to date on the law and practice relevant to their areas of specialisation and to enable them to service their clients efficiently, as well as to run their businesses profitably.

When looking at the best ways for a firm to ensure the development of its lawyers, or for an individual lawyer to manage his own development, there are a variety of options.

(a) *On-the-job training*

This is the principal way that most lawyers acquire the bulk of their knowledge and skills.

From the firm's point of view, it should look at ways of providing its lawyers with a spread of work, so as to develop their skills in line with the business's objectives.

There is an inevitable tension between providing junior lawyers with a spread of work versus giving them a narrow range of tasks. The former develops their skills across a (relatively) broad range and can be motivating (thus aiding recruitment and retention). However, the junior lawyers' supervisors will have to devote time and effort to training them on the new tasks and the cost of this may not be fully recoverable from the client.

As regards the latter, it gives the firm the benefit of having lawyers with deep expertise in a particular area of work, who can perform their tasks cost effectively with minimal supervision. However, the junior lawyers who acquire a narrow specialisation as a result may become demotivated and may have difficulty moving into new areas if their specialist work dries up for some reason.

Therefore, it makes sense (as far as possible) to achieve a balance between helping a firm's lawyers to develop specialist knowledge and enabling them to build their skills across a reasonably broad range.

The key to managing this is proper work allocation processes (involving analysis of the work that is coming in and the allocation of tasks to lawyers with suitable skills and/or developmental objectives), coupled with effective supervision processes.

The latter will involve appropriate delegation of work, coupled with comprehensive feedback processes to help the lawyers to improve.

This approach to training is the most cost effective, in that the lawyers learn what they need to learn to handle their clients' cases. The challenge is to supplement this to a sufficient extent to ensure that they have a sound underpinning to their knowledge, going beyond what they may need to handle a particular case. This is where more formal training structures come into play.

(b) *Formal training*

Following on from their university studies, most lawyers are comfortable with learning in a formal classroom setting. This can be efficient, in that an expert can impart knowledge and skills to a group.

While receiving face-to-face training in a classroom is an approach with which many lawyers are familiar, training is increasingly available online. This can either be provided by a commercial training organisation or, in some firms, created in-house (whether by videoing in-house lectures or creating tailored online programmes).

However, academic research indicates that the level of knowledge retention from these processes can be limited and is usually less than for on-the-job training. The limitations of classroom training can be ameliorated by creative structuring of training sessions (favouring interactive, practically based events over 'talking heads').

(c) *'Just in time' training versus 'just in case' training*

On the basis that knowledge retention is maximised if the knowledge is used quickly after it is received, it is often more efficient to deliver training on topics which the lawyers will use in the short term, rather than training them on topics which they might use at some point in the future. The fast-moving pace of legal practice is such that it is not always possible to opt for the former approach, but it is worthwhile bearing the concept in mind when planning the development of a firm's lawyers.

Bearing these options in mind, a firm should give thought to the training structure that best fits it. Smaller firms with limited resources may rely on on-the-job training (perhaps supplemented by some formal classroom training, especially where that is required to meet local regulatory obligations). Larger firms may put in place a more highly structured learning and development programme.

A typical structure would be to create two strands – one covering legal-technical knowledge and the other covering business skills topics.

The precise nature of the legal-technical programme will depend on the practice of the particular firm, but ideally it will give new entrants an understanding of the key law and practice that they need to deliver quality work to their clients, and will be coupled with appropriate updating sessions when the law changes, to reflect new approaches and so on.

A business skills curriculum will reflect the skills identified by the firm in its competency framework and will help its lawyers to develop these skills progressively over their careers with the firm.

Formal training sessions can be supplemented by induction or 'on-boarding' sessions for new arrivals and updates from the firm's management, all of which can contribute to developing a consistent firm-wide culture.

While this section has referred to the lawyers' development, the same principles apply to the development of support staff.

Perhaps the greatest challenge in running a formal face-to-face training programme is releasing the delegates from their client work to attend the courses. The balance is between delivering effective client service today and ensuring that the lawyers are developed so that they can service tomorrow's demands. While this option is not open to all firms (as it can be expensive), the trend in some larger firms is to make use of online training. This can take the form of both video recordings of in-house lectures and specially produced e-learning courses (with both being made available to the lawyers in the firm via the in-house intranet). The former is relatively inexpensive, but the latter can be costly. Much online training is freely available on the Internet, which may mitigate the cost.

4. **Conclusion**

Talent management as explained in this chapter is not a 'nice to have'; it is a business essential.

Most firms operate in a competitive recruitment market, and being able to attract (and retain) the best recruits by offering them excellent learning and development opportunities contributes to the success of the business.

Similarly, ensuring that the firm's lawyers and support staff can deliver a top-quality service to clients is vital to its business health.

Ensuring that everyone in the firm understands its business drivers (eg, by including business management in a competency framework) and can contribute to delivering work profitably is a significant factor in the continuing success of the organisation.

Coaching

Jonathan Middleburgh
Simon Pizzey
Huron Legal

---

1. Introduction

Ruth is a 35-year-old senior associate in a medium-sized law firm. A first-class graduate in history, she specialised in tax early in her career. An acknowledged technical specialist, Ruth has struggled to build an independent client base. Having recently failed to make partner, she has been offered coaching with an external consultant.

Stephen is managing partner of a leading international law firm and is two years away from an agreed date for retirement. His senior colleagues have urged him to plan for the future. Stephen has admitted to a couple of close colleagues that the future terrifies him. At the suggestion of the firm's senior partner, the HR director has set up coaching for him.

Jason has six years' post-qualification experience in a 10-partner firm. He has excellent client-handling skills, but recent appraisals have flagged issues with delegation and people management. Jason's manager, Heather, has tried to help him address these, but without any real success.

The above situations are doubtless familiar to anyone who has worked in a law firm. Perennial problems present themselves – how does a technical specialist redefine himself as a winner of work? How does a successful lawyer transition towards retirement? How best to help someone who struggles with delegation and people management?

Coaching claims to provide a solution to these problems. But does it? Does it offer a panacea or is it just an expensive placebo? How do coaches measure their impact? At a more fundamental level, what is coaching and how does it claim to shift entrenched behaviours?

This chapter provides an overview of coaching principles for those new to the field, as well as a discussion of issues of interest to those more familiar with coaching but perhaps unconvinced as to its efficacy.

Starting with a working definition of 'coaching', the chapter sets coaching in its context among other approaches to professional development, such as technical skills development, training courses, postgraduate qualifications such as MBAs and reading management books.

The chapter goes on to discuss how to get started: setting up a coaching contract, agreeing on the number of sessions and ensuring that the relationship does not end up with the the coaching client (or 'coachee') being dependent on the coach.

Using three case studies (adapted to preserve confidentiality), the chapter illustrates how coaching actually works and how it drives outcomes. The chapter describes how the coach works with the coachee to set goals, typical topics covered during coaching and what common outcomes look like. Coaching is distinguished from other approaches, in particular from mentoring.

The chapter further highlights key elements of the coaching approach that make it particularly suitable for lawyers.

The difference between external and internal coaching is also addressed. For example, if a law firm hires an external coach for one of its lawyers, how will that relationship work? The chapter explains how internal coaching relationships work best and how using a coaching approach when managing others can be more effective than traditional 'hands-on' management.

Coaching is a developing field; like any relatively young field, it continues to define and redefine itself and will doubtless do so for many years to come. Alongside some excellent, skilled practitioners there are inevitably people who claim to have coaching skills, but who in reality fail to deliver a proper coaching experience. This is likely to persist until coaching becomes globally regulated and routes to accreditation are more widely understood. With this is mind, the chapter considers how to find a coach, what to look for, what questions to ask and what accreditations to seek out.

2. What is coaching?

There is no widely accepted definition of 'coaching'. Nonetheless, many definitions contain similar elements.

Tim Gallwey, author of the best-selling *Inner Game* series of books which he began writing in the 1970s, defines 'coaching' as: "The art of creating an environment, through conversation and a way of being, that facilitates the process by which a person can move toward desired goals in a fulfilling manner."[1]

Philippe Rosinski similarly defines 'coaching' as "the art of facilitating the unleashing of people's potential to reach meaningful, important objectives".[2] Anne Scoular, co-founder of the well-known Meyler Campbell coaching programme, aptly describes coaching as concerned with "pulling out the capacity people have within".[3]

For practical purposes, most definitions encompass the following elements:
- Coaching is a learning activity.
- The coach does not teach the coachee.
- The coach facilitates a learning process.
- This process typically involves the coachee acquiring additional understanding or insight into his or her actions or behaviours.
- The learning process is frequently goal oriented – that is, successful coaching will help the coachee to get closer to the attainment of his stated goals.

Of these elements, the second is one of the most important to grasp. The coach does not teach the coachee. Coaching can be more or less directive or non-directive, but all coaching starts from the premise that:

---

1 W Timothy Gallwey, (2000), *The Inner Game of Work*, Thomson, p177.
2 Rosinski, P (2003), *Coaching Across Cultures*, Nicholas Brealey Publishing: London, p4.
3 Scoular, A (2011), *The Financial Times Guide to Business Coaching*, FT Prentice Hall: Harlow, England, p7.

- the coachee has to take responsibility for the outcomes of the coaching process; and
- the focus is on the coachee acquiring insight and learning, rather than the coach dispensing knowledge to the coachee.

Take the example of Stephen, the managing partner approaching retirement. A coach will not tell Stephen how to plan for his retirement or provide him with financial advice or strategies for how to spend his newfound leisure time. What the coach will do is help Stephen to think through his goals for the next stage of his life, acknowledge and address his anxieties, and then plan for the future.

Or take the example of Ruth, who is struggling to build her own client base. A good coach will not advise her where to look for clients or tell her how to network. Good coaching will help Ruth to reflect on any obvious blockers to her obtaining new clients – for example, lack of confidence or reluctance to sell herself. A good coach will use a variety of tools and techniques to help Ruth overcome her confidence issues and develop strategies for networking and building her own brand.

Coaching creates a safe environment where the coachee can reflect on the goals that he brings to the coaching. It is a space for reflective learning, where the coachee can receive and process feedback from both the coach and colleagues. But coaching is a purposive, goal-based activity and a good coach will not have done his job if he does not help the coachee to move towards the attainment of those goals.

Contrast coaching with more traditional forms of learning and the differences stand in sharp relief. Traditional skills training for lawyers is usually aimed at the acquisition of technical skills. The prevailing teaching technique is 'chalk and talk', and the teaching method is the transmission of 'knowledge' from teacher to learner. 'Chalk and talk' has its place, of course, especially where the learner needs to acquire some defined knowledge. Even in that case, however, research into effective learning suggests that we remember only roughly 20% of what we see or hear, 50% of what we both see and hear and 70% of what we see, hear and discuss. By contrast, we remember 90% of what we see, hear, discuss and practise. Coaching is active learning, in the sense that coaching always involves practice, both within and outside the coaching sessions.

Above and beyond this last point, 'chalk and talk' cannot help where the goal is the acquisition of insight, the development of understanding or the need to make behavioural change. Consider the example of Jason, whose delegation and managerial skills are poor. Does Jason have a granular understanding of where his skills are lacking? His performance appraisal might have flagged a broad area for improvement, but he may need to get more detailed feedback from relevant colleagues. Having received that feedback, what is he to do with it? Does he have the tools or insight to become a better delegator or manager? 'Chalk and talk' might cover the basics of delegation and provide some useful frameworks for becoming a better manager, but it will not address or meet Jason's individual needs. It cannot help Jason to obtain clarity as to his own development needs, still less to practise a changed mode of behaviour. Coaching can help to do all of this, and more.

The same points can be made about all conventional training courses and MBA-type courses. They all have their place and some are highly interactive and provide plenty of opportunities for skills practice and development. But few, if any, provide an individualised learning experience akin to coaching, unless an element of one-to-one coaching is built into the learning process.

Coaching shares some similarities with the concept of mentoring. Mentoring, like coaching, has grown in application in the business setting over recent years. The International Bar Association (IBA) has recently promoted a mentoring scheme as part of its service to members. The programme is designed to provide small and medium-sized law firms, especially those in developing countries, with the opportunity to access advice on various management issues in their practice from mentors who are experienced law firm managers, such as former managing partners.

3. How to get started

A relationship with an external coach typically starts either when an individual feels that he has a need for coaching or when an organisation recommends coaching for an employee.

An individual does not always know what he needs. He may know that he needs help, but not know what that help looks like; he might have heard about coaching from a colleague or friend, but not know the full extent of what it might involve. An organisation recommending coaching may be a sophisticated purchaser of coaching services and the coach may be known for it. The potential coachee, by contrast, might have little or no prior experience of coaching. In either case, it is the coach's professional responsibility to explain what the potential coachee can expect from the coaching process.

Very early in the coaching engagement, preferably before starting work, the coach needs to discuss the ground rules for the coaching. Who is paying? Who owns the information coming out of the coaching? Is all that information confidential – that is, to go no further than coach and coachee? If there is to be feedback to a third party – for example, a line manager or someone within HR/learning and development of a sponsoring law firm – what are the rules around feedback? It is important for the coachee to know that anything personal will 'stay in the room' – that is, not be shared by the coach with any third party. This is vital if the coach is to develop a relationship of trust and confidence with the coachee. Most paying organisations will want some feedback – to know what the coaching is achieving – and it is therefore important to set rules around specificity of feedback.

The nature of what is agreed will vary from case to case. For example, in a situation where the coaching has been set up to assist a partner approach the prospect of retirement, one would expect there to be complete confidentiality, unless that partner should choose to share the outcomes. On the other hand, where the coaching has been set up to assist development of, say, a group of department heads, the full value of the coaching will become apparent only if there is a degree of sharing what has been learned. In a more general situation, such as coaching for performance development with the use of psychometric tests, it might be agreed that the data will remain confidential to the coachee, but that a report on the coaching outcomes will be produced.

As long as the ground rules are discussed and agreed at an early stage, problems rarely arise in practice. Most coachees understand that if a law firm is paying for expensive coaching, it will require some high-level feedback. Problems typically arise only if there has not been a clear conversation about ground rules. It is essential that these ground rules be recorded in writing and signed by all parties involved.

Personal chemistry is paramount in choosing a coach. In theory, the coach himself might decide that the chemistry is not right or that the coachee is not ready for coaching. Sometimes the coach will discern that the paying organisation is foisting coaching on an unwilling individual. In that situation a sensible coach will decline to proceed, as an unwilling coachee will not engage constructively with the coaching process.

Assuming that coach and coachee both decide to proceed, they will need to agree on the number and frequency of coaching sessions. These will depend on the presenting issues. If the issues are complex, there may need to be at least four to six sessions. If the issues involve a need to make behavioural change – as they often do – it is important to recognise that changing behaviours takes time. It takes a long time to form habits and behaviours, and sometimes longer to unpick them.

Equally, however, a good coach will want to avoid allowing the coachee to develop a dependency on the coaching relationship. Stereotypes about dependent therapeutic relationships abound (viz Woody Allen and his decades in therapy). Coaching itself can develop into a dependency and it is incumbent on the coach to avoid this happening. Any coach who suggests a long-term coaching relationship may not have the coachee's best interests at heart.

4.   **How does coaching actually work?**

Once all preliminaries have been dealt with, the coaching itself can begin. It is important to stress that every coach has a distinctive style and approach. That said, there are certain typical ways to coach. The approach described here is the well-known GROW model of coaching.[4] 'GROW' is an acronym for the stages of the coaching process:
- goal setting;
- reality checking;
- reviewing options; and
- identifying what will be done.

In the first stage of this process, the coach explores what the coachee wants to get from the process and helps the coachee to formulate goals. Typically, the coach will ask the coachee a range of questions aimed at defining these goals. A skilful coach will use a combination of insightful questioning (usually starting with open questions, then probing as needed) and active listening.

Take the example of Stephen, the partner who is two years away from an agreed retirement date. Stephen might initially formulate quite limited goals around planning for his leisure time in retirement. Insightful questioning from the coach might elicit that Stephen is feeling anxious about retirement and frightened about

---

4   Whitmore, Sir J (2009), *Coaching for Performance* (4th Ed), Nicholas Brealey: London, p55.

his future; that he is not sure whether he actually wants to retire; that he is worried about his financial future or about atrophying in retirement. The coachee might suggest that Stephen should frame some wider goals for the coaching. Very different goals might emerge – for example, identifying what Stephen ideally would like to get out of his life over the next five to 10 years and determining whether, in fact, he wants to retire or would rather explore the possibility of some alternative role within the firm.

In the second stage of the process, the coach explores reality with the coachee. In Stephen's case, this might cover a number of areas:

- What motivates him? Where do his core interests and values lie? Is working a fundamental motivator for Stephen? Could he envisage a lifestyle where he is no longer working? Is he putting off retirement because of fear?
- What is the financial reality for Stephen? Can he afford to retire? Are fears about the cost of retirement simply a proxy for some deeper anxieties about the future?
- How much of Stephen's view of himself is invested in his work and current status? Lawyers often underestimate how much of their sense of self-worth is invested in their professional status. Relinquishing this status can be challenging, not just from a financial perspective.

Often, the coachee will want to move swiftly from reality checking into reviewing options. Lawyers tend to prefer action planning rather than reflection, but coaching is a reflective process and it is often the reflection that underpins a breakthrough. How can someone really plan for retirement if he does not yet know what he wants to get out of his retirement? Reflecting on values, motivators and interests is an essential precursor to action planning and many coachees find unfacilitated self-reflection difficult or impossible.

Coaching is not just about reflection – it is about shifting from reflection to action. The skilful coach will stimulate reflection but, at the right moment, shift towards action. This third stage of the process – reviewing options – typically involves the coach working with the coachee to generate a range of options which are then explored.

In stage two of the coaching process, for example, Stephen might recognise that he is not ready to give up work entirely. He may have seen retirement in black-and-white terms, but might now move towards viewing it as a mix of work (some paid, some voluntary or less well remunerated) and leisure.

Stage three might then initially involve generating a range of possibilities for Stephen:

- finding a new role within his existing firm, such as a business development or ambassadorial position;
- finding a similar role within a different firm;
- doing consultancy work on a part-time basis;
- seeking a non-executive role within a client or another company;
- deepening existing leisure interests;
- trying out a new leisure activity;

- taking on voluntary work; and
- spending more time with his grandchildren.

Quite often, the coachee initially finds it difficult to generate options. Sometimes it takes a while to get going, but then the options flow. It is key at this stage for the coach to open up the coachee's thinking (the coach will use various techniques to do this). Once a range of options have been generated, these can be examined and whittled down. Some will be unrealistic – not working at all may not be an option because of family commitments or insufficient pension provision. Some will be fanciful – travelling might seem attractive, but when interests are discussed in more detail, Stephen might conclude that he would prefer to take one long and two shorter trips each year. A skilful coach will help the coachee to review the options and test them out. This might take more than one session – the coach might suggest, for example, that the coachee research the practicability of certain options for further discussion in the next session.

The fourth stage involves action planning – identifying what will be done and when, and committing to a plan of action.

It is important to correct any impression that the process is simple or linear. It can sometimes be circular and often iterative. For example, Stephen might have formulated limited goals at the beginning of the process, focused purely on planning for a non-working future. Once he starts looking into options, he might realise that he wants to broaden his goals – for example, by considering whether he really wants to stop working or whether he might contemplate a part-time position. Our other coachee, Ruth, might focus on business development outcomes at the start of the coaching process, but gradually realise that she needs to make behavioural changes in order to build a reputation as a trusted strategic adviser, rather than a back-room technical specialist.

5. What makes coaching so suitable for lawyers?

Traditional training can be a challenge in areas of development apart from the acquisition of technical legal knowledge, because of the characteristics that many lawyers share. Lawyers tend to be fiercely independent and highly autonomous. They often have strongly held views and generally think that their own ways are best. This manifests itself in a desire to be in control and to have freedom in decision making.

Lawyers are trained to be critical and to look for potential problems in any matter or transaction. Indeed, the well-known US psychologist Martin Seligman builds a powerful case that negative thinking or pessimism is a strong predictor of success when it comes to technical lawyering skills.[5] However, the personality characteristics which serve lawyers so well in their early careers come back to bite when the lawyers advance into managerial or leadership roles. A lawyer's immediate response to any situation, whether it involves potential legal issues or not, is often to point out what is wrong with it, a reaction that is not always productive when leading others.

---

5 Seligman, M (2002), *Authentic Happiness: Using the new positive psychology to realize your potential for lasting fulfilment*, Free Press: New York, NY, p178.

Moreover, lawyers are busy people, often facing significant pressure to meet client demands. They tend to prioritise client work and will quickly object if they feel that their time is being wasted on something of limited perceived value or relevance.

A combination of key ingredients within the coaching approach make it an ideal solution to address these challenges. Arguably the most important of these factors is that the lawyer remains in control of the agenda, sets direction and spends time on his own priorities. The process is focused on the uniqueness of the coachee and his situation, rather than on the intentions of the coach. One can therefore expect that objectives will be different for each person, even if he is part of the same firm, department or work team. For example, in coaching two associates within the same firm on the topic of partner promotion, each may come to the sessions with completely different approaches and ideas. A standardised, structured partner development training programme – without a one-to-one coaching component – would not meet the needs that they can articulate within the confidential setting of a coaching environment.

The classic GROW model provides a disciplined means of ensuring that the coachee directs the agenda. The starting point of a coaching conversation is to invite the coachee to articulate his goals. This emphasis on setting clearly defined goals works particularly well with lawyers. Lawyers are used to the need for precision and tend to focus on outcomes. They often have no difficulty in framing goals (in contrast to other clients, for whom articulating goals can be an enormous hurdle). The risk is that lawyers might jump straight to a conclusion without giving sufficient time for reflection and testing. In this respect, the second element of the GROW model has a significant role to play, requiring the coach to test the reality of the proposition.

Interestingly, some of the associates whom we have coached found the freedom to set their own agenda to be unsettling. This seemed to reflect the fact that the opportunity to do so was uncommon. However, having overcome these feelings, they ultimately found coaching to be a profoundly rewarding experience.

The second key factor that so readily marks out coaching as suitable for lawyers is the emphasis on the coachee finding his own solution. Fundamental in this endeavour is that coaching is about listening, not telling. This is grounded in the belief that "clients are naturally creative, resourceful, and whole and are capable of making the best choices".[6] The coach does not take responsibility for the outcome and is not there to advise. Rather, "the coach's role is to develop the client's resourcefulness through skillful questioning, challenge and support".[7] Advice giving is believed to create dependency – the very opposite of the coachee staying in control and maintaining responsibility for the outcome.

The third key factor which makes coaching so suited to lawyers is the action-based approach. Lawyers, perhaps like others, are generally averse to commitments,

---

6   Whitworth, L Kimsey-House, K Kimsey-House, H Sandahl, P (2009), *Co-active Coaching*, (2nd Edn), Davies-Black: Boston, p19.
7   Rogers, J (2008), *Coaching Skills*, Open University/McGraw-Hill:Maidenhead, p7.

but equally are often pragmatic, goal focused and competitive. Lawyers frequently find the fourth stage, action planning, the easiest as it comes naturally to many of them. They like the certainty that comes from having an agreed set of actions.

Lawyers often become reflective more readily than coaching clients in other organisations. They tend to grasp the concept of coaching very rapidly. For example, they often quickly understand the intellectual ideas about emotional intelligence – however, they then want to move on to other topics, sometimes at breakneck speed, without necessarily reflecting fully and applying the learning. Clients in other organisations can be slower to grasp the intellectual content, but can be more reflective and may spend more time on practising and making the necessary behavioural changes.

A stumbling block within some legal organisations has been the tendency to perceive coaching as a response to a need for some identified remedial improvement. However, attitudes on this have shifted significantly over recent years. For example, many leading law firms in the United Kingdom now offer coaching to senior partners as a matter of course. Heads of HR and learning speak of a new view of coaching as a positive opportunity. A helpful analogy is that of leading sports players using coaching to continually make small improvements in performance.

6. Is coaching an expensive placebo?

Prospective clients often question whether coaching is anything more than expensive conversation. How can one measure the impact of coaching and does the outcome justify the cost?

These questions are entirely understandable. Coaching is a 'soft' process and outcomes are typically intangible. However, a growing body of science demonstrates the efficacy of coaching outcomes, and lawyers can be shown hard data providing evidence that it is not just a placebo.[8]

Nevertheless, the reality is that one cannot 'prove' the efficacy of coaching in the same way as that of a medicine or vaccine. The nature of the coaching process means that it is impossible to conduct blind trials with control groups or to conduct rigorous experiments. For example, other variables may impact on the coachee's development – the coachee might receive helpful input from a line manager during the coaching process or read a useful book that causes a breakthrough.

That said, the growing body of scientific research is complemented by other softer data. Coaching has grown exponentially within the corporate world over the past 10 to 20 years. Companies are not known for spending money without weighing carefully the return on investment. Their willingness to invest hundreds of millions – if not billions – of dollars on coaching[9] is a powerful indicator that they are satisfied that good coaching drives good outcomes.

---

[8] See for examples: De Meuse, K P, Dai, G, & Lee, R J (2009), "Evaluating the effectiveness of executive coaching: Beyond ROI?" *Coaching: An International Journal of Theory, Research and Practice*, 2, 117-134; Evers, W J G, Brouwers, A, & Tomic, W. (2006), "A quasi-experimental study on management coaching effectiveness", *Consulting Psychology Journal: Practice and Research*, 58, 174-182; Grant, A, Curtayne, L, & Burton, G (2009), "Executive coaching enhances goal attainment, resilience and workplace well-being: A randomised controlled study", *The Journal of Positive Psychology*, 4, 396-407.

Anecdotal data, moreover, is not to be discounted or disregarded. Many business leaders have written or spoken about the benefits of coaching[10] and their comments also provide helpful evidence as to its efficacy.

In practice, it is relatively easy to track whether coaching is making a difference. One straightforward way to measure impact is to obtain 360-degree feedback data on the areas to be addressed in the coaching process before starting in earnest, then to repeat this during or at the end of the process.[11] For example, Ruth's firm could obtain 360-degree feedback on her impact and influence before starting coaching. This could include rating her on a one to 10 scale on various dimensions related to her impact, influence, gravitas and so on. The firm could then obtain ratings on these same dimensions during or at the end of the coaching process.

If the coaching is helping Ruth, one would expect to see a significant improvement in these ratings. If the ratings are relatively unchanged, it is reasonable to conclude that the coaching is not helping her. This might be due to a range of factors: Ruth's failure to engage with the coaching process, her inability to change or the inefficacy of the coach. Whatever the reasons, one could say that the coaching is not making a significant difference. Conversely, if the ratings show a significant improvement, it is reasonable to assume that the coaching is having the desired impact.

7. **Internal versus external coaching**

This chapter largely focuses on external coaching, primarily reflecting the fact that the authors provide coaching as external consultants to their clients. What, though, of internal coaching? Does it offer similar benefits to external coaching?

First, it is important to define who will provide internal coaching. It can be provided internally by an experienced, qualified coach – for example, someone in the law firm's learning and development department or a HR professional – or, less frequently, by a line manager (ie, a lawyer) who is qualified as a coach. Often, when law firms talk about internal coaching, they are describing less formal 'coaching' provided by a line manager who has acquired some coaching skills through internal or external training.

In theory, if internal coaching is provided by an experienced, qualified coach, outcomes should be broadly similar to those outlined above. However, internal coaches rarely have the range of experience of an external coach, who will typically have worked with a wide variety of clients and may well have coached lawyers in a range of law firms. Moreover, even if the internal coach is highly experienced and well qualified, an additional difficulty presents itself. Lawyers often feel reluctant to open up to internal coaches in the same way as they will to external coaches, regardless of assurances as to confidentiality. Lawyers are typically concerned that

---

9   See www.coachfedration.org/includes/media/docs/2012icfglobalcoachingstudy-executivesummary.pdf. This 2012 study estimated global spend at c $2 billion, with signs that this amount will increase in the future.
10 See, for example: www.n2growth.com/quotes-coaching.html and www.abetterperspective.com/Quotes.html.
11 See Goldsmith, M (2007). *What got you here won't get you there: How successful people become even more successful*. Hyperion: New York, NY, p111.

personal information may leak or that data gleaned during the coaching process might influence other internal processes, such as performance management reviews. These concerns are usually misplaced, but they are a reality. Lawyers typically feel more comfortable undergoing coaching from someone external.

When coaching is provided by a line manager, the term 'coaching' often denotes a style of supervision or management, rather than the provision of a series of coaching sessions as described above. Sometimes, line managers say that they are 'coaching' more junior lawyers, but have at best a limited understanding of what 'coaching' actually means. Indeed, some will say that they are 'coaching' more junior lawyers when they are in fact micromanaging them.

Certainly, adopting a 'coaching' style of supervision or management can be extremely helpful to both supervisor and supervisee. A coaching style of supervision embodies the elements summarised at the start of this chapter and sees the supervisor ask many questions, alongside giving advice. Rather than teaching what needs to be done, he endeavours to help the supervisee to learn.

Take the example of Heather, Jason's manager. She has, to date, failed to achieve any real success in helping Jason to improve his delegation and managerial skills. She may have attempted to help him previously by telling him what to do or by giving him hints and tips regarding better delegation. By contrast, a coaching style of supervision might involve Heather exploring with Jason how he has gone about delegating in the recent past, asking him to consider instances when delegation has succeeded, prompting him to reflect on why delegation has failed previously and so on. Heather is likely to share some of her own insights based on the answers that Jason provides. This alternative approach is centred on helping Jason to develop his own insight, rather than on teaching him what to do.

It takes time and practice to develop these skills. Many lawyers think that they are very good at asking questions. The reality is that they are often very good at asking closed or leading questions. This means they tend to be looking for particular answers and therefore are not truly listening to what the coachee is trying to communicate. The development of an effective coaching style requires training, practice and feedback. But the dividends, in our experience, justify the effort.

8. **Finding and selecting a coach**

Having identified coaching as an appropriate solution for a specific development need, the first step is to find someone suitable. This can be a daunting task, raising questions such as: "Where do I look?" "How do I know that those claiming to be business coaches are properly trained or adequately experienced?" "Are there particular skills that would be useful for the coach to possess?"

The Internet will provide an overwhelming number of hits, even if searches are limited to a particular city or region. It may be insightful in terms of seeing the extent of what is available, but is unlikely to assist in selecting a trusted coach

Undoubtedly, the best approach is to seek out personal recommendations. People within the legal community are generally willing to share experiences and make introductions. Professional networks and groups such as the IBA should be good sources of contacts.

However, a coach who works well with one group of people in a particular situation may not necessarily be the best fit with another group, which may have different personalities and issues. It is therefore important to use recommendations only as a helpful starting point.

There are a number of professional associations for coaches. The difficulty is that because there are so many, there are no commonly accepted standards. Nevertheless, professional associations may be a useful starting point and their websites can be informative. Perhaps the best known is the Worldwide Association of Business Coaches, which accredits training organisations such as Meyler Campbell and certifies their graduates. Other bodies include the Association for Coaching, the International Association of Coaching and the International Coach Federation. There are also many good and experienced coaches who are not accredited by one of these associations but hold other professional qualifications – for example, in occupational psychology.

As with any other procurement, it makes sense to be clear about the desired outcomes and to invite a number of prospective coaches to explain how they would approach the assignment. Inquire also about their level of experience in dealing with similar situations. Depending on the number of coachees, there may be benefits in working with a specialist organisation, rather than with just one individual. It is unlikely that one person will be the best match for all of the firm's coachees; an organisation should be able to provide a number of alternatives. One benefit of working with an organisation is that its coaches should share core coaching values, so that all coachees receive a broadly similar experience.

It will be important to be clear how the coach or organisation addresses issues such as confidentiality, initial chemistry meetings with potential coaches (are they free of charge?) and reporting. Cost is an obvious factor in the procurement process. This can vary considerably, depending on the number of sessions per coachee and the time allowed for each session. It may be sensible to try a pilot project first. Certainly, if the investment of time and money is likely to be significant, an early review will ensure that the coaching is progressing as planned.

9. Conclusions

This chapter has articulated some of the benefits of coaching for lawyers. It has explained how the coaching process typically works and why it therefore meets the particular development needs of legal practitioners.

A growing body of research supports the scientific efficacy of coaching. It is difficult to argue credibly that coaching is a mere placebo – a body of evidence buttresses the experience of seasoned coaches that coaching can achieve transformational outcomes. That said, the practice of coaching is as much art as science, and finding a suitable coach involves both research into his pedigree and qualifications and a feeling that the chemistry between coach and coachee is right.

Looking for the right coach can be a voyage into the unknown – our concluding hope is that this chapter has provided some helpful guidance to the uninitiated as to where to go and what to look for, so that firms can see their lawyers develop into successful partners with enhanced aptitudes for leadership and management.

Leading lawyers through change

Amber Sharpe
Psychologist
Robert Sharpe
Psychologist

1. **Introduction**

   Implementing change in law firms, whatever their shape or size, is guaranteed to provide a cocktail of challenge, pushback, factionalisation and mischief, as well as reasoned debate and effective amendments. From my experience of law firms, from Magic Circle to high street, the phrase 'herding cats' is applicable to only one profession more so than law – and that is psychology. What follows is true of all of professions; and the reflections on the legal profession presented in this chapter can be doubled and more for my own, psychology. At least lawyers have managed to accommodate like-minded souls together, with varying degrees of comfort, under the umbrella of a law firm. Few psychologists have managed the same marvel of cohabitation!

   I write this chapter as both a 'participant observer' (in the anthropological sense of the term) and a trusted adviser who has been invited into 'the thick of it' to facilitate major change in unprecedented circumstances. Prior to the early 1990s, no one had ever experienced the expansion of a law firm from one office to over 40 globally. The 1990s saw several law firms achieve this through remarkable – and still unrivalled – feats of human engineering. Equally, no one had experienced the tsunami of internet-delivered, commoditised legal advice that threatened to remove the bread-and-butter legal work of high-street firms. Many smaller firms rose to the challenge and are flourishing today as a result of radical changes in management style, structure and legal focus.

   This chapter is offered with sincere respect for the pioneers who 'broke the mould' and rode the globalisation wave, and with admiration for the flexibility of those local firms that re-launched themselves or invited non-lawyer commercial leaders to guide them through two decades of professional change. Weaknesses addressed in this chapter are identified against a backdrop of awe-inspiring growth and development of the global legal profession, and are intended to assist with its stellar evolution!

   The observant reader will have noted that while this chapter is under joint authorship, the style of first person singular is adopted, which refers, where it is used, to Robert Sharpe. Amber Sharpe, who holds qualifications in both psychology and law, has provided much valuable 'young lawyer' research and first-hand observational input to ensure that this chapter is fully current. However, the first person singular has been retained both for readability and as an indication that any

Leading lawyers through change

views that might occasionally be seen as radical are attributable, at least primarily, where they belong.

2. **Managing expectations**

Change occurs within a context. This context includes tradition, ritual, promises, expectations, threats, opportunities and predictions.

The perception of change occurs within a mindset. This mindset includes motivational drivers, self-confidence and self-esteem, personal values, sense of active participation and control.

Handling change depends primarily on how the individual's mindset has evolved. This evolution includes natural predisposition, family attitudes, teaching methods, job training, leisure activities, compensation and promotion criteria.

There is no 'one size fits all' formula for leading lawyers through change. All change carries with it a degree of discomfort. That discomfort can give rise to a wide spectrum of individual responses, from exhilaration in the case of a stimulus seeker to fear in the case of a risk avoider. When this response spectrum occurs within a population of lawyers – whose purpose is to apply a sceptical mindset to any given proposition – leading them through change can be expected to be paradoxical and challenging. This chapter aims to shed light on why change is often difficult to implement within law firms, and to suggest changes to training programmes and law firm management that can facilitate successful outcomes.

By setting out some psychological fundamentals concerning how minds work in general, and lawyers' minds work in particular, this chapter establishes a background of psychological know-how against which to discuss practical issues of change. First, however, it is important to consider the hopes, dreams and contexts experienced by today's lawyers.

3. **Aspiration and the law firm context**

In an increasingly complex and compliance-driven legal environment, which is contemporaneously commoditising and deregulating, significant challenges face lawyers entering into and already practising in the profession.

In many parts of the world, the legal profession no longer commands the automatic respect with which its clientele once greeted practitioners. Accelerating commoditisation, barrack-room internet law and do-it-yourself legal document packs have all conspired to reduce the perceived gap between client and professional from the client's standpoint. This has happened similarly in other professions. Fifty years ago, a house was cleaned from top to bottom before a doctor was allowed to visit. Now doctors attend self-defence classes to learn how to handle patient violence and struggle frequently against Google-assisted self-diagnosis while attempting to get the patient well. Of course, demystification of the professions is to be applauded, since an informed clientele usually uses its advisers more effectively. However, an unfortunate but common consequence is a reduction of the perceived value and status of professionals. So, then, who would become a lawyer?

Some study law because they come from a 'legal family'. Others do it for the money (although not as many as might be thought, from what they tell me). Then there are those who want to help make the world a better place through their legal efforts. Still others want to find out how it all works. But whatever the deeper motivations, every postgraduate entering training with a firm knows that he is preparing himself for the day when 'the buck stops here', having entered a profession with the ultimate objective of providing the 'last word' on legal matters. Postgraduates have not entered their professional specialisms to make decisions by committee as, for example, the design team for a new car or washing powder might. While a lawyer may seek a colleague's view, this is very different from personally signing off on an advice or agreement whose integrity may have far-reaching and expensive implications.

In short, being a lawyer is not a team sport, but rather a group activity in which individuals play out their roles on cue, according to their skillsets and regardless of the other players who make up the rest of the group. This is the basis of the self-reliance upon which, quite appropriately, any professional's status, reputation and success are built.

Lawyers get together in firms of widely varying shapes and sizes for company, economies of scale, opportunities to cross-sell to clients and a mutual understanding of each other's peculiarities. They do not gather together for homogeneity of viewpoints, values or *modus operandi*. Indeed, 'fighting their corner' against opposing views is the basic attribute of lawyers; this makes it notoriously difficult for law firm management to implement changes which challenge colleagues' currently held views.

But while a law firm may appear to clients to be a 'brand', with team-like cross and on-selling, to the lawyers working with in it, it may be more like a cooperative of self-contained individual practitioners. If a law firm really were a 'team' structure, then change by 'command and control' might work efficiently. However, top-down edicts may face guerrilla opposition in the 'group cooperative', flat, individualistic structure that actually exists within most law firms, where far more individual canvassing and reassuring are likely to be needed to make change propositions acceptable.

4. Left, right and limbic

The first component of the promised psychological know-how is a fundamental understanding of the way in which the main parts of the brain function together, as background to a discussion on lawyers and change. That may well sound as daunting to a lawyer as completing a corporate merger would sound to a psychologist. For both, the truth is that it is easy when you know how. The following thumbnail sketch says all that we need to consider and has become the route map for thousands of lawyers, from trainees and partners to coachees and seminar attendees. Most of the rest of the discussion follows logically from the fundamental axioms.

The three brain areas that produce our thoughts and actions are the left and right cerebral hemispheres and the limbic system.

The right hemisphere is responsible for creativity, interpersonal behaviour, artistic and musical appreciation, dreams, ideas, possibilities, 'blue-sky' thinking and innovation; it is generally the brain's playground. As such, it is where we have most of our fun and where we experience 'thinking outside the box' – that is, insights and invention. Right brain activity is often referred to as 'divergent thinking' – we start with the seed of an idea that explodes into many possibilities, some of which are considered for feasibility and handed across to our left hemisphere for further work. Importantly for this discussion, it is where the consideration of 'change' takes place and especially where positive connotations of change occur.

The left hemisphere is the seat of convergent thinking. It takes those right hemisphere ideas that have made it through the strategic evaluation centre and forms them into a reality. The left brain calculates, applies logic, project manages, costs, structures, completes and finishes the end product ready for deployment. It looks on 'change' largely as an annoying departure from its well-honed methods, algorithms and techniques that have made it such a safe, sure calculator – unless, that is, its right hemisphere neighbour provides it with a new possible algorithm to add to the collection.

The limbic system is the seat of emotion. While it also manages the body's homeostasis – maintaining a stable state of temperature, digestion, circulation and so on – this is of little psychological importance. The limbic system is responsible for all of our emotional expressiveness, from joy to anger to fear. This part of the brain 'appreciates' what the other two parts have dreamt up and created and gives us the impulse to find other ideas to bring to fruition.

Essentially, this cooperation of brain areas is the entire explanation of what we call 'motivation': getting an idea, making it happen, rejoicing in the finished product and deciding to do it all over again. The more harmonious and integrated these brain areas are, the more the individual behaves and feels comfortable with his actions and thoughts. At its height, this harmony is the basis of what sportspeople, musicians and actors refer to as being 'in the zone': a transcendental state of 'flow' where the performer feels completely 'at one' with his actions. This is where great performances, world records and other memorable acts occur. Virtuoso cellist Rostropovich's genius, for example, was that he was in a permanent state of simultaneous left-brain-right-brain-limbic activity. He could co-compose, perform and cry openly with sadness or joy – all at the same time. Most of us have to make do with doing things one by one: salutations, Maestro Rostropovich!

Parenthetically, this trilogy of brain areas also provides a framework for understanding and responding appropriately in any verbal exchange. Speech patterns can contain facts or opinions (from the left brain), desires or possibilities (from the right brain), and emotions or feelings (from the limbic system). All utterances can be analysed into one or more of these groupings and responded to appropriately. A formulaic example could be: "I can see you're [insert emotion recognised: 'angry', 'excited', 'worried' etc] about [insert occurrence, prospect etc] and want to [insert objective, vision, possibility etc]." While this looks more like maths than psychology, it has a name – 'reflective listening' – and works like clockwork in bonding with, enlisting and persuading colleagues or clients. So, as a prerequisite of leading lawyers through change, listening effectively to their reactions to change propositions is likely to encourage them to find new ways of looking at what could otherwise be worrying prospects. Maths, after all, has many and varied uses.

The formal – and most of the informal – training received by lawyers is exclusively left-brain dominated. The right brain is often treated as something to fit in if there is time and limbic activity is seen as at best an annoyance, at worst toxic. Focused teaching modules on building social skills, developing self-esteem and confidence, being good fun to be around or motivating self and others are rare or non-existent in legal colleges or firms. Yet all of these are right brain or limbic attributes and they are all characteristics that firms appear to seek keenly. "We've got any number of good technically able types," as one senior partner put it, "but few whom we feel confident to expose to clients." The inevitable conclusion is that most law firms' training and recruitment philosophies value the 'safe intellectual' type over the 'adventurous entrepreneurial' type – and that this preference will dictate the culture of future law firm generations. It is now easy to see that leading safe, intellectually calculated lawyers through change is likely to be significantly more demanding than leading adventurous, entrepreneurial lawyers who would be more likely to envision opportunistic possibilities through change via their more practised right hemispheres.

I have spent thousands of hours with trainees, associates and partners, facilitating their right brain and limbic activities, especially in the context of mentoring and preparing partner-track associates. Invariably, working with lawyers on practical ways of involving their creative and emotional functioning leads to the qualities of fun and flexibility that are as much of a friend to 'change' as logical analysis can be its enemy.

The advice from all of this, therefore, is to train and encourage the whole brain if you want lawyers who can accommodate and embrace change as well as perform due diligence, draft and process. That said, one would not entrust one's Jaeger LeCoultre to a motor mechanic, even though both he and a watchmaker use screwdrivers. Developing a lawyer's psychological attributes requires professional technical competence – a one-hour chat with a life coach of indeterminate provenance in a law college or at an associate development away-day is not sufficient. Lawyers who would not let a lay practitioner loose on their own children's minds and attitudes should be similarly discerning with the minds of their fee-earners. Just as qualified lawyers are arguably best placed to practise law, so trained, qualified and regulated psychologists are best placed to practise psychology.

For the avoidance of doubt, psychologists are not just there to be called in to treat illness or impairment; they can also profile, coach, mentor, develop, facilitate, mediate and otherwise expand the opportunities and options of those they advise. Where law firms have engaged psychologists to work with them on both internal and client matters, they have anecdotally reported significant gains. In one case, the successful psychological profiling of the opponent and analysis of the claimant's *modus operandi* (neither of which had anything to do with 'the law') resulted in a 'dropped hands' outcome, saving the defendant a minimum of £50 million in damages. In another, the successful profiling of a complex psychopath employment law claimant in a £500,000 'work-related depression' damages suit against his employers similarly resulted in a dropping of hands. The inclusion of psychology in these two cases alone clearly illustrates where the viewpoint of one profession can profitably see what the viewpoint of another may not.

5. Rationalisation and compensation

Rationalisation is our second fundamental psychological building block. Without it, we would cease to function; there is a basic human need to form an understanding of our environment, however individual or eccentric this understanding may be. Rationalisation works in a self-justificatory and circular fashion. On the one hand, we make sense of events by fitting them into our personal belief framework ('rationale') of how things work. On the other hand, we build and strengthen our beliefs in our correct understanding of the world by harvesting new experiences that support this rationale.

We usually rationalise after an action or event (*post hoc* rationalisation), though we can also rationalise something we are about to do (*a priori* rationalisation, often dignified with terms such as 'strategic'). Through this process, we justify our actions and proposals to ourselves and we tend to interact with others who share our rationale, justifications and views. As we age, we become progressively more certain about our 'viewpoint' and increasingly resistant to change.

This phenomenon is closely related to the '*Einstellung* effect',[1] now more commonly referred to as 'mindset'. Mindset is the biggest enemy of change, 'thinking outside the box' and the 'thought leader' protagonists. Essentially, we repeatedly resort to trusted problem-solving methods – even when shorter or more effective solutions are available – and robustly push back against change or challenges to the established ways of doing things.

As a prime example, a firm's compensation model can be as axiomatic and unquestionable as a religion. A firm might adjust its model by putting in a new bonus tweak, just as a car manufacturer might show off this season's saloon car's new fastback. But it is rare to see radical changes, unless the firm – like the car manufacturer – gets sold or merged. Yet with firms adopting a wide variety of compensation schemes, from lockstep to 'eat what you kill', there is no clear winner so far as the legal industry is concerned.

Adherence to a compensation model clearly reflects the power of rationalisation. Having decided to join a certain type of compensation system, the individual will need to become comfortable that he has made a sensible choice. He will thus seek out evidence that his is the best of the systems on offer and will become a 'believer'. Once a person has moved from empiricist – or evidence gatherer – to converted believer, he has made the serious mental commitment of rationalisation.

This process strengthens important business requirements such as organisational culture, brand and unity. Problems arise, however, if a firm's top strategists wish to make radical changes to the core processes in which the culture has invested its trust. Now, the very belief that for so long had been a major ally can become a major opponent. The 'party line' is a double-edged sword.

Beliefs are rationalisations that have become spurious axioms – personal 'truths' that are psychologically fundamental. Lawyers are, by nature and training, both analytical and rational, reaching judgements readily and strongly and becoming

---

[1] Luchins, AS (1942), "Mechanization in problem solving – The effect of *Einstellung*", *Psychological Monographs*, 54 No 248.

adherents and believers within their chosen structures. 'Party line' and 'values' can become synonymous in the hands of corporate culture consultants keen to help firms to engender an emotional as well as intellectual buy-in from their staff. While their techniques are often effective, later adjustments to the party line can be seen as a *volte face* and fuel for opponents' derision.

When using management 'buy-in' techniques to embed some particular mindset, law firm leaders might therefore consider how to avoid over-tightening the nuts and bolts of organisational culture. Tight cultures can work in a pyramidal corporate structure because change can be implemented, usually quite acceptably, by fiat. The flat management structure of a professional organisation denies this luxury. For a professional workforce to be amenable to change, it may be advisable not to screw its members down to a party line too tightly in the first place. Caution may be advisable to avoid carving well-intentioned sentiments of today in stone, when these may need to be revised tomorrow.

6. Drivers and the 'lawyer's mind'

All humans – and most animals – manoeuvre through life under the influence of two drivers. These are the prospect of success (winning or 'response reward') and the avoidance of failure (not losing or avoidance of 'response cost'). Carrot and stick, success and fear – these drivers can act singly or in combination, and provide our third psychological building block.

As a general psychological rule, behaviour patterns that derive from a 'prospect of success' or reward basis tend to be more flexible and adaptable, especially to change. Such people can usually see the opportunities that change can bring. Behaviour patterns based on a 'fear of failure' model, by contrast, are generally more rigid and resistant to change, with such people tending to see the pitfalls and problems associated with change.

All professions are based on a 'fear of failure', risk-averse model of training and an intolerance of error. Law, like medicine, accountancy and construction, requires a specific ability to make correct binary judgements – right/wrong; in/out; good/bad – and to stand by those judgements. Such qualities are considered professional, principled and reliable, and provide the basis for the training and subsequent mindset of the professional. With successful work usually drawing little comment and errors attracting lengthy post-mortems, malpractice suits or professional exclusion, progress as a lawyer relies on observance of the rule: thou shalt not err.

Excellent sports teams and profitable corporations, by comparison, have a culture that is reward seeking and success-focused – the 'carrot'. The effective sports team manager holds lengthy debriefings after match wins to help the players to gain insight into how they achieved their success. After a loss, they mostly forget the match, go home to sleep and start 'success-hunting' afresh the next day. Such a culture contrasts sharply with the almost universal absence of the celebration of professional victories and the enervating post-mortems that accompany professional mistakes.

Thought leadership and lateral thinking seem to preoccupy law firm management as desirable qualities among their lawyers. By definition, to be innovative and brilliant, a solution or process must involve doing something that is not tried and tested. However, this means that such an innovation would not be easily justified if it were to fail. Innovations might well be seen as risky to propose or carry out; if they work, they may be mostly ignored and uncelebrated. Little wonder, then, that they appear to be so elusive.

Firms on recruitment drives have learned to make themselves look more appealing to hire prospects by espousing appreciation of the unusual and innovative, since innovation is usually fun and attractive. If this appreciation is well grounded in reality within their firm, their prospects of talent retention and adaptability to change may increase significantly. If it is not, then a costly lateral hire may fail rapidly and expensively.

A poignant sentiment I have often heard during lawyers' exit interviews or retirement processes is of the type, "Well, at least I can look forward to making a real contribution now…". On one such occasion, the speaker was oblivious to the irony that he had led a 20-lawyer, cross-border, bank-syndicated acquisition worth $5 billion only a year ago. Just another banal routine matter for that law firm then… and for the lawyer, apparently.

Law firms must 'walk the talk' when it comes to appreciating flair, daring and innovative creativity. These qualities are unlikely to flourish if they are not trumpeted, celebrated and referred to in compensation terms at every opportunity. If encouraged, they are likely to promote thought leadership and innovative behaviour, which are close cousins of change acceptance.

7. **Self-esteem and the lawyer**

"But wait a minute," says our lawyer, progressing well through seven or eight years of qualification. "I've stuck to the rules and the established methods and now I'm being told I have to be a thought leader (won't that be a risk?); I have to get myself board consultancies or appointments (but boards will not want someone who is always telling them why their ideas might be hazardous); and I have to merge myself into a team (when I've been taught that ultimately I should only rely on my professional judgement). I'm also being told that my chances of partnership and my compensation are determined not only by how good my legal skills and fees yield are, but also by how good a salesperson I am; how inclusive and facilitative I am with my colleagues; whether I can contribute to a system where my group's file is the measure of my success rather than my individual earnings; and an array of similar 'soft skills attributes' that my law college didn't have in its curriculum. Help!"

For this lawyer and the majority of his peers, a significant element of personal development has been omitted – the building block of self-esteem. Superb training in the technical elements of law is rarely augmented with mentoring aimed at gaining insight into how lawyers can blend legal competence with interpersonal skills and innovative thinking – a practice that is fundamental to a strong sense of self-esteem and confidence. Where this happens, it usually does so informally and through the 'luck of the draw' of early work experiences with a senior role model who has mastered this blend of talents. Clearly, luck should not be the determinant for such an important blending process. Instead, firms might encourage appropriate role model lawyers to mentor juniors more widely on the development of a style that suits their personality and blends interpersonal skills with legal competence.

Self-esteem is closely related to, and dependent upon, rationalisation, through which our environment makes sense to us. From this rationalisation stems a common belief that if we do things well, we will develop self-confidence and self-esteem. Sometimes this happens – though usually by chance. Most often, there is a gap between doing things well and self-esteem, giving rise to the coining of the term 'impostor phenomenon'.[2] While first researched as a particularly female issue, we have discovered that there are just as many men – maybe more – as women making their way through professional life thinking, "When are they going to find me out? Do they realise I'm only...well...me?"

Self-esteem is developed not just by doing things well, but by working out how we do the things that we do well and relying on that knowledge to feel confident that we can do similarly well on future occasions. This makes future successes more likely and we come to feel comfortable that we can replicate the use of our underlying skills and attributes in the future. Those firms, companies and organisations who swap, "Well done, now here's another task to do" for "Well done – how did you do that then? Can you see how to apply that in the future?" foster robust senses of self-esteem and confidence in their staff and support an innovative culture of pride in a job well and cleverly done. That single move from "what I did" to "how I did it" is the most important determinant of high self-esteem – and it is very inexpensive to implement.

A resilient self-esteem means retaining self-belief, self-confidence and self-worth, notwithstanding the risk or commission of errors. If a lawyer's self-esteem is based on risk avoidance and error-free performance, it will be threatened by the prospect of change, with resistance to change being likely.

So, risk aversion and fear of failure frequently produce a mindset of technical excellence within a vulnerable self-esteem framework. The more vulnerable an individual's self-esteem, the more resistant he will typically be to change, with its attendant risk of failure.

For many lawyers, their individual billings are their most direct measurement of their worth and largely underpin their self-esteem. Before leaving this subject, therefore, it is worth paying a visit to the popular old chestnut of 'individual billings' versus 'one-file billings'. In this long-running debate, senior management strives to develop greater team playing and client development by changing from a 'he who opens the file claims the billable hours credit' model of individual lawyer appreciation to an 'it is immaterial who opens the file: many lawyers might work with this client and their reward lies in how facilitative they have been of each other's input' idealised model.

There are many difficulties with making this change – not least of which is that most firms will have selected their young lawyers in assessment centres where candidates perform as gladiators in points-scoring group discussions, where the

---

2   Clance, PR and Imes, SA (1978), "The Impostor Phenomenon Among High Achieving Women: Dynamics and Therapeutic Intervention", *Psychotherapy Theory, Research and Practice* 15 ≠3.

objective is to defeat as many of their opponents as possible to secure the job. It is unsurprising that lawyers selected by such methods will be reluctant to join a lawyerly collective where their glory is shared and diluted. Already professionally sceptical, lawyers working in a firm changing to a 'one file' culture will additionally look with predictable scorn upon the de-equitising or dismissal of colleagues whose 'personal numbers' are low and be unlikely to believe, going forward, that individual file 'brownie points' do not matter. Lawyers are, after all, persuaded by evidence rather than rhetoric, making unambiguous and consistent actions far more persuasive than anomaly and opaque expediency when delivering messages from the top.

The advice here is, first, to pay attention to the lawyer's successes, victories and problems solved. Paying attention means finding out – from them or others – how they achieved their success. What attributes, skills and talents did they discover and can they rely on in the future to ensure repeated success? "Good show, Carruthers" and a glass of champagne may suffice for a 30-minute 'fix' at a matter completion, but long-term esteem building requires work – interested, focused exploration of that lawyer's core resources. Such interest will facilitate the strengthening of self-esteem and confidence, making the introduction of change likely to be less threatening and, consequently, less resisted.

Second, if major changes are proposed that affect compensation, or even the criteria upon which job security is based, then senior management would do well not to act in ways that can be interpreted by their colleagues as ambiguous. Lawyers do not react well to ambiguity at the best of times, let alone where their livelihood is concerned.

8. Change, recruitment and partner selection

Very successful lawyers – financial and professional 'rainmakers' – are not usually successful simply because they are good lawyers. A few years ago, a study was conducted of several Magic Circle high-fee-earning partners. The objective was to produce a video, *Winners in Law*,[3] which was completed with fascinating results.

Star lawyers or rainmakers succeed because they are personable, attentive collaborators – with their clients, with their partners and with their associates. This has nothing to do with law and everything to do with collegiality. Winners in any endeavour are necessarily good at creating and sustaining *ad hoc* teams. They rapidly gain the trust and respect of those they need to work with, 'rolling up their sleeves' with client, partner or associate on an equal footing. The law comes somewhere second, often implemented by others in the *ad hoc* team – others who may not be so fluent in these collegiality attributes.

It was stated most elegantly by a senior figure, who said: "Up until we make an associate up to partner, we have been employing them for excellent legal technique. When they become partners, we suddenly expect them to push most of that downwards to their associates and become marketers and business builders – which many find quite difficult. The partner who adapts most easily and successfully to that

---

3   Sharpe, R (2003), *"Winners in Law"*, video publication, Dr Robert Sharpe

is the one who, as a student, realises they are actually an entrepreneur or marketing person; subordinates that for 10 years while they do a law degree and go up the ladder; gets their partnership; and then lets their underlying natural personality burst through."

What this wise senior was saying is that anyone entering the legal profession thinking that he is going to spend a lifetime just 'doing law' is courting disappointment. With deregulation, commoditisation and the Internet, most of the jobs that a lawyer would have settled for happily a generation ago are increasingly being done by trained clerks or computer software.

There is little doubt that a generation from now, we shall see a different kind of law career entrant applying to and being recruited for membership of the legal profession. This will probably require a change in traditional selection criteria for future trainee or lateral hire lawyers and should be of major concern to law firm partners. They should be in a position to justify the selection criteria that they and their HR departments use to recruit key professional personnel – criteria such as mid-adolescence exam results; ability to handle role-played conflict with an actor in the interview process; or candidates out-talking several others around a group discussion assessment centre table.

In the case of academic achievement, many law firms in the United Kingdom still rely on the arbitrary exclusion of candidates who have not excelled in mid-adolescence examinations, notwithstanding that they may have achieved a master's or PhD degree at postgraduate level. This takes no account of the growth and development potential of candidates and, psychologically, discounts those individuals who may not have flourished in a school environment, but accelerated rapidly once they entered further education. Such selection criteria may thus exclude those with significant potential for personal and intellectual development, selecting arbitrarily along left-brain criteria and completely ignoring right-brain creativity, innovativeness, fun, collegiality and limbic emotional intelligence in the initial 'rough grading' of applicants. Many 'star' lawyers had average to dismal mid-adolescence exam showings, while others did the old-fashioned 'articles' in order to qualify. Neither historical landmark appears to have handicapped them *en route* to rainmaker status.

In the case of trainee or partner candidate assessment centre exercises, it is usually the quiet operator who listens and waits for the right moment that is most effective in real life. Yet he will almost certainly be marked down for such behaviour at an assessment centre group discussion exercise, while the bombast grabs the 'points' and doubtless gets the job, even though he has failed to demonstrate collegiality – supposedly a modern-day prerequisite.

Candidate assessment 'measures' of the type just described have as much *a priori* bearing on the real-life qualities of candidates as horoscopes. The assessors in these contrived situations are invariably professionally unqualified in the measurement of what they are viewing, often even resorting to asking role-play actors for their opinions on candidates' efforts! This is a questionable approach to selecting the firm's most valuable assets – that is, its future custodians and ambassadors. As for the candidates, in such an instance there is little that could be more demeaning of their countless hours of professional advancement than being judged by a jobbing thespian. They may, however, be comforted by the plethora of blog posts that give detailed advice on how to use interpersonal techniques that will score well – ironically, regardless of how candidates behave in real life.

Raising the stakes yet higher, many of the larger law firms are beset by even more complex cultural issues surrounding partner selection assessment centre procedures. This was expressed most eloquently by an Italian international lawyer, who observed: "Anglo-Saxons think in black and white, whereas Italians think in shades of grey. We both get to our end goal most of the time, but in quite different ways. The problems come when trying to judge which approach is 'right', especially in recruitment and partner selection." In role-plays conducted in an Anglo-Saxon-centric partnership assessment centre, points are awarded for identifying the problem, elucidating the other person's point of view, implementing a solution and facilitating the other person in retaining their dignity – all within 20 minutes. This rarely happens in real life. So the Italian candidate would simply be unable to demonstrate the value of his approach: how he would likely take a long lunch with the other party, discuss many non-work interests, talk around the problem and part company as new friends, agreeing to talk the next day to agree on a solution – thus weaving the particular interpersonal magic which retains that client or enlists that colleague for life.

Frequently described by partners as "a ridiculous way to select trainees and partners", the use of such selection criteria and procedures has a clear bearing on leading lawyers through change, especially internationally. By selecting and promoting the firm's lawyers on the basis of quasi-measurements that inevitably miss many of their personality attributes, law firm leaders may allow themselves to assume a homogeneity of views across their colleagues that simply does not exist. It is obvious from the Anglo-Saxon-Italian example above that leading British lawyers through change will be an entirely different prospect from leading Italian lawyers. Multiply this by as many nationalities as any one firm includes in its global reach and it then ceases to sound implausible to suggest considering the hiring of outside applied anthropologists to pave the way for major change proposals.

Interestingly, although these questionable selection procedures proliferate, I have never seen any personality disorder screening interviews carried out among candidates – this notwithstanding that the legal profession and judiciary have been represented by Dutton as carrying a greater than average percentage incidence of psychopathy,[4] lying second in his rankings (with the clergy not far behind). Dutton's research and views have inevitably attracted criticism – though Hare, with several decades of experience in the subject, concurs.[5]

Personality disorders, of which psychopathy is one, are likely to cause disruption in the workplace and more so during periods of change. Distinguished by the common elements of insightlessness, lack of empathy and emotional flatness or inappropriateness, the estimated 10% of the general population with personality

---

4   Dutton 2012, *The Wisdom of Psychopaths: What Saints, Spies, and Serial Killers Can Teach Us About Success.*
5   Babiak P and Hare RD 2006, *Snakes in Suits: When Psychopaths Go to Work.*

disorders (2% being the estimated incidence of psychopathy) are disproportionately attracted to professional and senior executive positions that hold obvious opportunity for control and influence. Their disruptive characteristics encounter little hindrance because the professions tend not to censure their own and senior executives tend to rise above straightforward disciplinary action.

Such personalities are unlikely to do well where interpersonal skills or collegiality are concerned: once 'dug in', they may become self-aggrandising, tyrannical or unaccountable, and will often absorb a disproportionate amount of management and HR time. To ignore such a selection criterion is to dismiss a large body of psychological research as irrelevant. It also further calls into question the selection, from an assessment centre group discussion exercise, of the 'thought leader' impositional contestant, who will often have shown clear evidence of an absence of empathy, insight or emotional competence. To add a final layer of misdirection, an accomplished psychopath – sometimes called complex psychopaths – can demonstrate the most charming and charismatic attributes during a selection process, simply by learning to mimic the socially acceptable behaviour of genuinely collegial people. Navigating through such convolutions is challenging for psychologists experienced in the subject; expecting lay assessors – even other professionals – to detect these personality attributes is probably unrealistic.

Law firm seniors should consider carrying out audits of the quasi-measurements captured in parlour-game-based assessment centres to examine exactly what they think they are measuring. Psychologically, assessment centre processes are sufficiently obscure as to be worthless as predictors of suitability (though they may well reveal characteristics of undesirability), and demeaning of the candidates who still bewilderingly submit themselves to the ordeal. Of course, the games and snapshots are far easier to employ than psychological rigour and the evaluation of evolving intellectual patterns, which are likely to cost law firms in partner time and professional advice. Time thus spent, however, brings partners into first-hand contact with this fundamental process and is much more likely to result in staffing up with flexibly minded, inspirational and effective lawyers, rather than technically efficient lawyers of indeterminate collegiality.

In addition, international law firm leaders should ensure that their firms' selection processes and assessors have sufficient cultural intelligence to encompass the rich diversity of alternatives by which interpersonal challenges can be addressed. If respected, such diversity can be of significant assistance in change implementation, but can equally be costly if ignored.

9. The change paradox

Two frameworks currently co-exist – uneasily at best, clashing at worst. On the one hand, the lawyer has been trained and developed to be reliable, planned, unsurprising and unsurprised, conservative in respect of tried methods, risk averse, stable and left brained. On the other hand, just like other organisations, law firms are finding that they must compete for market share, demonstrate daring and creative innovation, experiment with management styles and generally behave in a more extravert, right-brained fashion than they used to.

For many lawyers, the firm that they joined a decade ago has altered dramatically today. It is little surprise that many talented lawyers leave the profession when they see shifting goal posts, narrowing bottlenecks to partnership and little by way of celebration of their successes and excellence. And little wonder that change engenders such personal strain and resistance (albeit mostly unconscious) among lawyers at all levels.

Here, in a nutshell, is the paradox: the discipline that has made for a good technical lawyer is premised on a fear of failure. Failure is minimised by adhering to old ways of doing things. Adhering to old ways of doing things is facilitated by resisting change. But resisting change also means missing opportunities for growth and risking being surpassed by agile competitors.

The components that make up the professional experience of lawyers can thus be summarised as follows:

- They are trained to know and remember the due processes and precedents by which previous lawyers have succeeded in addressing their clients' matters (*Einstellung* effect).
- Their method of training has been based on the intolerable nature of error and on the corollary that errata are anathema to a career (response cost effect).
- Little is ever made of intellectual or interpersonal triumphs on the way through a matter or deal, by either colleagues or the individual themselves ('banality of brilliance' phenomenon).
- The focus is always on the 'what, when, who' of the matter's completion and rarely on the 'how' (self-esteem factor).

This results in efficient problem-processing technicians who function well unless confronted by either an intellectual accident (error) or the prospect of a change that could heighten the risk of such an accident (change aversion).

This chapter has addressed the challenge of leading lawyers through change by considering those elements of the lawyer's professional journey that conspire to produce change resistance. The implications are that if lawyers of the future are to embrace change – in respect of innovation, business needs, team file assessment, boardroom consultancy, and trusted advisory and thought leadership – then law college curricula and law firm induction, training, appraisal and compensation need to adjust significantly so as to include professional training, as distinct from cursory reference, in these areas.

From student to practising lawyer, legal professionals can be encouraged to undertake activities that are likely to facilitate right-brain and limbic thinking, including:

- collegiality skills building at law college;
- regular internal teach-ins by those displaying excellence;
- 'how did you do it?' debriefings after all completions;
- at least one funny story garnered from every matter;
- innovation break-out lunches;
- 'stand-up' comedy training days (yes, really);

- solution-focus workshops (rather than problem-seeking meetings); and
- training in handling difficult people.

As a final piece of advice, there is a golden rule in psychological intervention, whether in treatment, mentoring or training. Before attempting to implement change, first break existing ritual moulds and barriers. Ideas such as those above are designed to do just that and, by loosening up the thinking culture, provide a better chance of successfully implementing change.

'What got you to here won't necessarily get you to there' is a useful guideline for those about to lead lawyers through change – applicable as much to themselves as to those they are leading.

Facilitating fast and smooth transitions from law school

Sarah Hutchinson
The University of Law

Every law firm wants its trainees and new associates to hit the ground running. This chapter examines how law firm management teams can best prepare for the transition of their future lawyers from law school to the workplace. It describes how this preparation supports and empowers law students to make a successful transition from law school to practice.

1. **Early-stage indicators of success**
   Before outlining the strategies and tactics to facilitate transition, it is necessary to define what a 'successful transition' means. The University of Law has worked closely with our international law firm clients to establish their views on what defines a successful new lawyer. We asked them to describe the most successful behavioural patterns demonstrated by lawyers in the early stages of their careers. These early-stage indicators are a good predictor of long-term successful integration into practice. The most commonly identified features are summarised below.

1.1 Personal attitude
   Many law firms state that it is important for a new lawyer to be keen and confident, but not arrogant. In practice, this means the following for associates:
   - showing an interest in all aspects of the law;
   - showing a keen interest in clients and understanding their concerns and issues;
   - demonstrating a determination to learn;
   - demonstrating the ability to take on board any setbacks and regard them as learning opportunities; and
   - behaving with confidence and maturity.

   All law firms encourage associate behaviours such as respect, discretion and commercial acumen.

1.2 Client-handling skills
   New associates need to develop excellent listening and interviewing skills in order to elicit information from clients. However, a law firm will also want to see these skills in evidence when dealing with internal colleagues – for example, when a partner delegates a piece of work to an associate. The new associate's response to a delegated task is a good indicator as to whether he will behave professionally when taking client instructions.

A new associate will often be asked to attend networking events with clients and colleagues and to represent the firm at various events. The associate's handling of these situations will create a significant impression in the minds of the law firm partners and will play a part in successful transition. Does the associate appreciate the commercial objectives of the event? In more extreme circumstances, does the associate behave appropriately and act professionally to ensure that the firm is not brought into disrepute?

Client service skills are also vital. Has the associate researched whether the firm has service level agreement standards that underpin the client relationship? Has the associate identified the client's issues and ensured that the matter is dealt with quickly and efficiently?

1.3 Research and problem solving

A new associate's first assigned task is often a piece of research for the supervising partner, and the quality of the associate's work will be important in setting first impressions.

The associate or trainee will have deeply ingrained research methodologies, skills and research report writing techniques from his academic training. This can lead to a disconnect between the partner's expectations and the associate's work. The firm may need to work with the associate to refine such skills to be appropriate in a professional context. For example, does the firm have a preferred research style? Does the associate seek out the preferred house style and ask for guidance on the partner's expectations?

1.4 Commercial and business awareness

The need for commercial and business awareness is frequently highlighted during the recruitment process, but new associates are often surprised at the need to time record.

The extent to which an associate understands the basics of law firm finances is critical to perceptions about his commercial skills. It may sound simple – understanding how the charge-out rate is determined and keeping the client updated as to costs that have been incurred and the likely costs of taking a matter forward – but it is a skill that law firms expect associates to develop and demonstrate at an early stage. The law firm can best instil this skill by a thorough induction into its system of charge-out rates, and by establishing standard updating procedures to ensure that the client is kept up to date on costs throughout the matter.

Cross-selling is another key part of client management and building new business, which also draws on client-handling skills. An early adoption of cross-selling will inevitably embed the associate into the practice and encourage positive behaviours more widely. It shows that the associate:

- is offering good client service, as he has listened to the client and communicated a solution;
- has gained a new client for a colleague; and
- has impressed the partners with his ability to bring new work into the firm, which will increase the longer-term likelihood of being retained.

Trainees and associates who actively develop the firm's business through involvement in events sponsored by the firm – such as marketing events or involvement with the local community – are highly prized. Being seen at events helps to raise the associate's profile within the firm, the client base and community. Ultimately, this may lead to new work and an enhanced client base for that associate.

The associates who typically make the most successful transition are those who demonstrate a combination of the above behaviours and make the earliest contribution to the law firm's profits.

2. Working with new recruits

It is in the best interests of both the law firm and new recruits that the transition is as efficient and smooth as possible. This is particularly important for those trainees or associates who are embarking on their first meaningful experience in a working environment.

There are many tools that a law firm can employ to help new recruits, from a thorough induction programme to more flexible support mechanisms, mentoring and coaching. These are covered in other chapters of this book. This chapter considers three specific aspects of transition management:

- setting and managing expectations;
- a suggested competency framework; and
- troubleshooting.

2.1 Setting expectations

Many lawyers enter the profession with limited understanding of the law firm as a business. The new lawyer will require guidance on the expectations of his colleagues and clients and on his role within the firm. Ensuring that the lawyer or trainee has a clear picture of these expectations can provide a solid foundation in overcoming the challenges of transition.

As with most professional service firms, the majority of law firms have established guidelines setting out the their expectations of the individual, depending on his function within the practice. This can take the format of a competency framework or a statement of roles and responsibilities.

At the University of Law, we have worked with our law firm clients to create a generic set of competencies for young lawyers, which now underpins students' preparation for the world of practice. This competency framework is described in Appendix A and is reproduced with the kind permission of the University of Law.

Typically, a competency framework establishes the key attributes expected of a new lawyer, including:

- business skills – for example, business development, client relationships, commerciality;
- legal technical competence and development of specialist practice technical skills;
- self- management attributes (commitment, workload and diary management, professional responsibility and personal development); and
- working with others (team working and communication skills).

2.2 **Managing induction and matching performance to expectation**
Having created a clear statement of expectations for new lawyers, it is critical that the process now addresses how and when the lawyer will be measured against such expectations. A competency framework in isolation is inadequate for all but the most self-motivated and accomplished lawyers.

The law firm manager needs to ensure not only that expectations are clear and understood, but also that there is opportunity and motivation for the lawyer to practise and demonstrate how he meets the set criteria.

Establishing opportunities to develop and practise these attributes is a key part of the manager's role. A self-evident example is that of a new lawyer who must demonstrate the ability to work in a team: he should be given the opportunity to participate in a case or matter requiring multi-disciplinary team activity.

It is useful for the lawyer to complete a self-reflective log, in which to record tasks and events that demonstrate a competency and can be used as the basis for self-reflection or appraisal. Using a self-reflective log during a programme of study has assisted students at the University of Law to identify their strengths against a competency framework and identify areas requiring development or improvement.

In a non-judgemental environment, this helps both the individual and his future employer to create opportunities to maximise his potential as a successful lawyer.

Finally, a reasonable timeframe for assessment against expectations should be agreed in advance, to enable the lawyer to plan the period of development and evidence-gathering.

3. **Strategies to facilitate a smooth transition before arrival of new recruits**
It is essential that the 'pipeline' from legal education through to the 'ultimate consumer' (ie, law firms) is direct and clear. It is incumbent on law schools to play an integral role in this process by actively engaging with the profession. This is evidenced by the many ongoing reviews of legal education (including by the American Bar Association and the United Kingdom's Legal Services Board).

Individual law firms and lawyers also play a critical role in the pipeline between law school and employment in law firms. Senior members of the profession inform and oversee this transition at both an organisational and individual level.

A future employer can work closely with law schools in the following ways:
- Engage with law schools to ensure that the firm's expectations and requirements are translated into students' education and experience. This could take the form of:
  - providing input on the curriculum;
  - sitting on advisory boards or committees to give professional advice on legal education strategy, policies and practices that will facilitate transition; and
  - working with the law school or a cohort of students to tailor the learning experience in order to ease the transition from law school to employer.

The International Bar Association (IBA) is leading the way, through its LLM in international legal practice. This is a collaboration between members of

the IBA, the University of Law and individual lawyers. The curriculum has been created for students and junior members of the profession, and is tailored to meet the skills and practice areas required by IBA member firms. It incorporates know-how and case studies created to prepare the next generation for modern practice.
- Engage with students in law schools to create awareness of the firm's expectation in practice. Examples of useful activities include:
  - giving talks and delivering skills workshops (eg, engaging with law students to enhance their commercial awareness and client focus);
  - taking part in online discussions, webinars and law fair speaker panels;
  - joining mentoring schemes and taking part in 'extracurricular activities' involving members of the profession (eg, acting as judges in mooting, negotiating and debating competitions);
  - engaging with careers services and law faculty careers tutors to inform their careers advice; and
  - offering work placements, vacation schemes and open days to give prospective lawyers a flavour of what working at the firm would be like.

Engagement with law schools and students brings additional benefits for law firms. They enhance their profile with the lawyers of the future, thus securing a strong pipeline of talent for recruitment. In addition, they have an opportunity to identify prospective talent, enabling them to make recruitment decisions based on performance over a longer period of time, rather than solely at interview.

4. Troubleshooting at the outset of a lawyer's career

The University of Law undertook research with our law firm clients to establish the main areas where new recruits do well and those areas where some tend to underperform during their initial period in the office.

Overall, most of our law firm clients report that their trainees and new associates adjust quickly to the workplace. How they adapt seems to depend on their maturity (through experience, not necessarily age). A classic example, particularly for those who have been consistent high achievers in school, is the limited experience of new associates in managing situations that they cannot control. As soon as the work starts to pile up, such new associates may need to take time out to cope. The extent to which the pressure of work or the culture of the working environment can accommodate this pattern may be critical to the transition from law school to the workplace.

How trainees and new associates apply themselves and their attitudes to practice are the key to making the leap from study to work. Areas of weakness highlighted by law firms include:
- expectations – understanding what the firm and its clients expect of a trainee or new associate;
- pressures – awareness of the typical stresses facing lawyers;
- personalities – understanding what drives lawyers; and
- career management – being proactive by anticipating caseload, preparing for the workload, networking and presenting well at all times.

4.1 Lack of awareness

New associates are sometimes slow to grasp what their firm expects of them. The firm needs to ensure that expectations are clear and well understood. It is worth explaining to new associates that they are expected to demonstrate a keen interest in clients, cases and matters, with an eagerness to learn and a commitment to deliver excellent client service.

4.2 Pressures

Time limitations and the need to prioritise tasks according to their urgency and importance are major sources of pressure in the workplace. In a law firm, new trainees and associates will also need to work out how to handle competing deadlines for work from several partners. Other potential sources of pressure include:

- social pressures during corporate entertainment events;
- managing support staff to ensure that work gets done, despite being at the bottom of the corporate hierarchy; and
- work-life balance – for example, resisting the pressure to work longer hours than required because the partner puts in a long day.

One solution to improve understanding of such pressures is for the law firm manager and new recruit to consider several theoretical case studies of 'sticky situations' during the induction phase. They can work together to decide what they would do and how they might prevent such a situation recurring in the future. It may also be helpful to examine when and why some solutions would not work.

In addition, time management training helps new associates to analyse the importance of a particular task and to estimate how long it might take, adding in a margin for unexpected eventualities.

4.3 Personalities

One element of getting it right in the transition from law school to law firm is an awareness of what drives or motivates a typical law firm colleague. Lawyers are often highly driven, with a keen competitive spirit, and they speak and act quickly. The typical lawyer values punctuality accuracy and commitment to meeting agreed deadlines. Lawyers set and strive for high standards and are critical, especially of themselves.

While trainees are not required to score highly on all such traits, they will be more readily accepted into the practice and will make a smoother transition if they adopt some of these typical behaviours.

4.4 Career management

(a) Proactivity

Some law firms report that new trainees do not manage their careers actively enough. For example, when moving into a new area of practice or taking on a case or file, the trainee should be encouraged to talk to the previous lawyer or associate as a matter of course. This can help familiarise him with the nature of the work, the types of people involved, important client background information, the work style of his new supervisor and how best to get work and seek feedback.

Some new recruit induction packs include a useful 'getting it right from the start' checklist. While this appears to contain commonsense actions – such as 'what to do when you get it wrong' – it is a good tool for those who are relatively new to the fast-paced workplace of a law firm.

Part of being proactive in career management is to request and to receive regular feedback. Many larger commercial practices operate mid and end-of-year appraisals.

(b) *Personal image and dress*
In many UK law firms, the dress code has moved from the traditional 'suit and tie' culture to 'smart-casual'. To the new recruit, this can present a significant challenge. What the smart-casual code means can vary between age groups and practice groups – some dress down (eg, jeans and T-shirts), while others opt for more formal attire. The new recruit is well advised to err on the side of caution: if in doubt about whether something is appropriate to wear, it should be avoided.

5. Practical tips to ensure a smooth transition

5.1 Ensuring that new associates understand the firm
Time recording and billing are vital parts of time management training and the sooner the new associate can be familiarised with such processes, the smoother the transition. Such familiarisation – or perhaps more formal training in these critical processes – enables the new recruit to understand how the firm makes money and can also act as a reminder that he may, for a limited period and on a net basis, be taking money out of the firm.

5.2 Email etiquette
Appropriate use of email is an integral part of working life, but for many lawyers straight out of law school this may be their first experience of using email in a professional context. Suitable email guidance could include the following:
- Ensure that emails to clients and senior colleagues are well structured, rather than a 'brain dump' of material.
- When forwarding emails, check that all messages included in the final email are appropriate and should be seen by all recipient(s).
- Think carefully about the list of recipients – who needs to know? What actions are expected of different recipients? In many law firms, if actions are assigned to a specific individual it is usual for such actions and recipients to be written in bold.
- Get the tone right – it needs to be clearer than if the associate were to use the phone or meet face to face, which confer the advantage of non-verbal cues. Many new associates tend to lack confidence and so escape into the safety of email. The associate should be encouraged to ensure that he does not always substitute face-to-face contact and phone calls with emails; sometimes direct contact is more appropriate

- Reply immediately – if only to acknowledge he has received the email. Otherwise, the sender may assume that the associate is ignoring the email.

5.3 Differences in values

Common differences between trainees or new associates and their supervisors are manners and grammar. For example, trainees do not always consider the need to inform others that they are unable to attend a meeting or that they are running late. Punctuality is a common trainee weakness and can be perceived by many established lawyers as a lack of courtesy or a casual attitude towards commitments.

As surprising as it seems to established lawyers, it may be necessary to raise this issue explicitly with a new lawyer.

Many grammatical errors made by new lawyers are caused by ignorance of relatively simple rules that are frequently broken, such as the placing of apostrophes. Some trainees fail to appreciate that correct grammar is a necessity in law, in addition to the requirement to deliver excellent client service.

One useful tip in raising such issues with newly recruited lawyers is to ask more established young lawyers to reflect on their own period of traineeship and to share with new recruits their hard-earned learnings – that is, what they know now that they wish they had known then.

6. Preparing the next generation of talent in law schools

Alongside many leading law schools, The University of Law works closely with our law firm clients to prepare our students for life in the office. Without losing the focus on technical legal excellence, it is possible to develop the skills and know-how that will better prepare the next generation to succeed in practice.

Some of the principles we have adopted at the University of Law include:
- making students aware of the expectations of future employers through the development of the competency framework (see Appendix);
- enabling students to evidence skills and attributes through the use of practical exercises, portfolios and self-reflection;
- setting and maintaining discipline in anticipating and meeting deadlines, time keeping and attendance recording;
- raising awareness of the differences between being a student at law school and being a trainee or associate in a law firm, and making students aware of the types of personality that they will meet in the office; and
- supporting students in adapting their behaviour to ensure appropriate office etiquette.

A useful tip to encourage good client-handling skills and listening techniques in future lawyers is to integrate a systematic '4W' approach in the classroom when tackling new case studies:
- Who – what do you know about the client and the firm's involvement to date?
- What – do you have all the information you need, in the correct format?
- Why – how does this piece of work fit into the larger picture?
- When – what are the deadlines for delivery?

We encourage students to adopt a solution-focused mindset, ensuring that they research the relevant points of law, apply these points to the legal problem and recommend a solution.

7. **Conclusion**

The transition from law school to the workplace is a critical stage in the development of lawyers and law firms are investing significant resources into integrating their new recruits. Firms increasingly recognise that the cost of recruitment and induction is substantial – effective management of this process can have a lasting impact on retention.

Appendix: The University of Law's Competency Framework
Reproduced with the kind permission of the University of Law

Background of competency frameworks

For law firms, the use of competency frameworks first emerged in recruitment of qualified lawyers and in career progression structures.

As a recruitment tool it became a sound staple, enabling decisions to be made against an objective background and sometimes mitigating the risk of partners making gut-feeling judgements on lawyer recruitment. As used for career progression purposes it was something of a revelation, breaking away from the established expectations that all lawyers progress at equal pace, and that you can expect every lawyer (whether at one, two or three years post-qualification) to be equally knowledgeable and skilled simply based on time-served in the office.

With this change in approach, career development plans, as well as remuneration, could be based on merit, providing an incentive to strong performers and honing a concept that ultimately became labelled as talent management.

Upstream of qualified lawyers, the world of the training and education in law schools in the UK had also been developing, but perhaps in a way that many law firms, whose partners had experienced more didactic teaching methods, had not appreciated. Students were being faced with case studies and scenarios that mirrored real life practice and forced the students to engage as prospective practitioners delivering a service to clients.

A Holistic Approach

The concept of commercial awareness and the requirement to build this in to the professional legal training of new lawyers is well established. Valuable this is, but it focuses on only one element of the lawyer's performance. From this starting point the University of Law developed its Competency Framework.

Making it Happen

The first step was to draft a framework, which was undertaken by a small cross-disciplinary lawyer team from a range of practice backgrounds including lawyers with experience in major corporate practices and legal aid experience lawyers.

The next step was to market test the draft framework. For this the University of

Law assembled a small external panel comprising senior people in law firm HR and training roles, together with two General Counsel. The view of the latter was highly relevant for us, as the in-house lawyer views the performance of the law firms.

The exercise turned out to be remarkably straightforward. Perhaps the most telling piece of feedback was the advice not to try and make the framework too complex.

How did the University of Law achieve the integration of the Competency Framework into its education? In design and delivery terms this was achieved by integrating reference to a set of competencies into all teaching materials and sessions, so tutors refer to relevant competencies in workshops and students improve their self-awareness.

The integration of the framework commenced in September 2011.

The Framework Explained and Reviewed

The Competency Framework is divided into four principal competency areas: Law, Self, Working with Others and Business. In each area there are between two and four headings, and each area then has between six and fifteen sub-headings. The competencies are expressed as for achievement by trainee solicitors, giving the University of Law's students objectives to aim for. The Framework could equally be adapted into the workplace and thus enable law firm managers to adopt as a basic starting point such competencies, whilst improving upon them by using the firms' own formulations.

Here are the competency areas in turn:

Law
It might be thought unfashionable to start with Law, but let us remember that this is the core of the job. The new recruit may end up as one of the great rainmakers of

```
                    Complacency: Law

        Technical                        Development
        competence
            |                                |
    Undertakes research             Develops professional
    tasks competently,              skills and technical
    using appropriate               ability, keeping up to
    technology and                  date with current
    information resources           legal issues
            |                                |
    Manages own fee-earning         Takes responsibility
    matters competently             for own learning and
            |                       development
    Demonstrates
    problem-solving
    capability
```

the profession, but unless the lawyer is technically competent, then he does not have a career.

Recognition of the need for continuing development figures heavily here, but also basic competence on work tasks within the new lawyer's capability and further the beginning of getting results – the problem-solving competence.

Self

If one did not start with law, one would perhaps start here. Learning to manage oneself is critical, as well as is commitment and taking responsibility.

Succeeding as an associate requires toughness of mind, so being resilient under pressure is a key quality. Other aspect may include delivery of work product with enthusiasm, tenaciousness and attention to detail, whether the task is challenging or mundane.

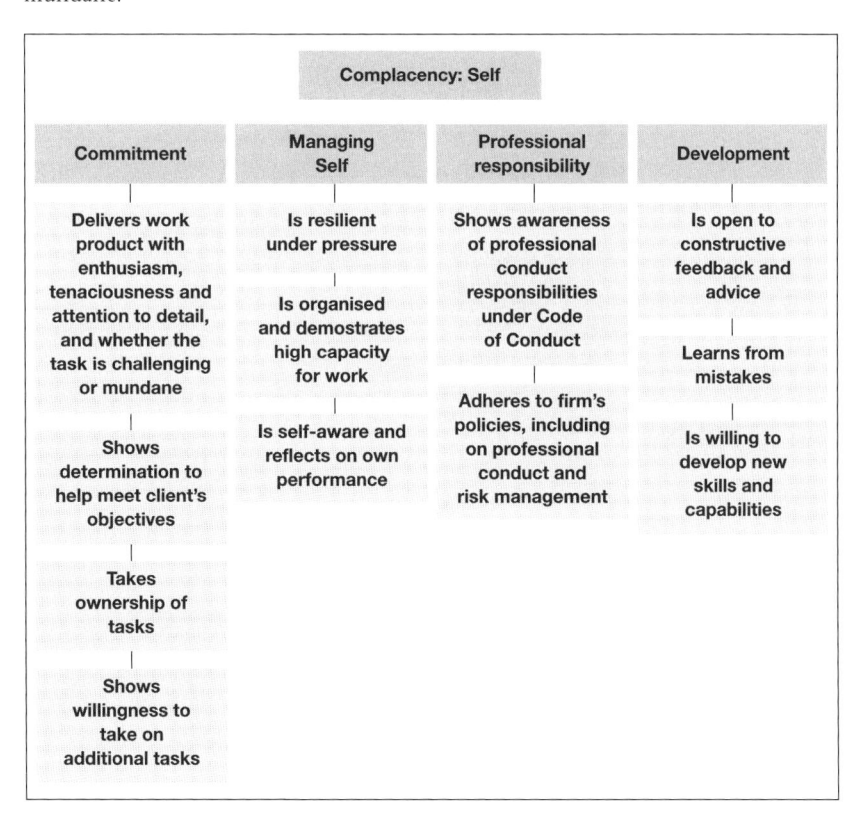

Complacency: Self

Commitment	Managing Self	Professional responsibility	Development
Delivers work product with enthusiasm, tenaciousness and attention to detail, and whether the task is challenging or mundane	Is resilient under pressure	Shows awareness of professional conduct responsibilities under Code of Conduct	Is open to constructive feedback and advice
Shows determination to help meet client's objectives	Is organised and demonstrates high capacity for work	Adheres to firm's policies, including on professional conduct and risk management	Learns from mistakes
Takes ownership of tasks	Is self-aware and reflects on own performance		Is willing to develop new skills and capabilities
Shows willingness to take on additional tasks			

Working with others

At a senior level in practice, after the ability to bring in the work, the ability to run a successful team is usually the next most prized competence. There is a good economic reason for this – although gearing ratios may vary according to the nature of the work, a solid core of profit in any firm is generated from the lawyers who do not have an ownership interest in the business.

Aspects that could be picked out here range from simple communication – undertaking tasks logically, articulately, concisely and tailored to the needs of the recipient, to the maturity of acknowledging task contributions made by others.

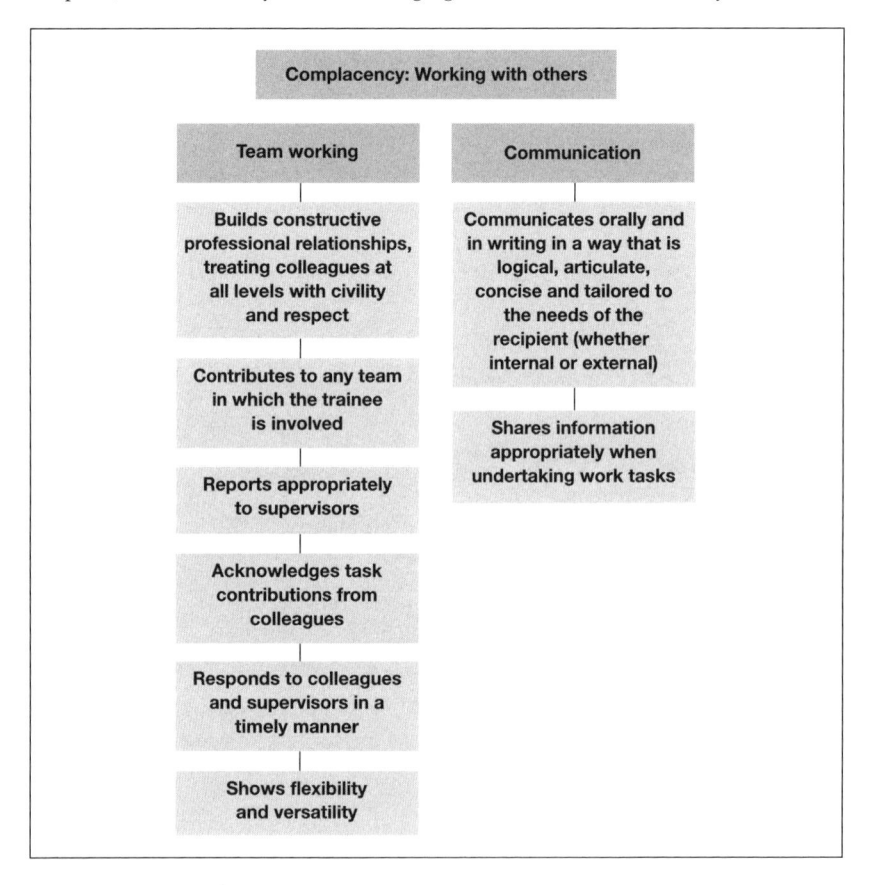

Complacency: Working with others

Team working
- Builds constructive professional relationships, treating colleagues at all levels with civility and respect
- Contributes to any team in which the trainee is involved
- Reports appropriately to supervisors
- Acknowledges task contributions from colleagues
- Responds to colleagues and supervisors in a timely manner
- Shows flexibility and versatility

Communication
- Communicates orally and in writing in a way that is logical, articulate, concise and tailored to the needs of the recipient (whether internal or external)
- Shares information appropriately when undertaking work tasks

Business

This area contains the core competence of being able to handle client relationships, critically starting with looking at life from the client's point of view. What can the client expect of the individual or the firm? How much effort should the lawyer be making to understand how a client's business works and in what way that should influence how the firm delivers its service?

The concept of business development often bewilders junior lawyers. How can the new recruit make any contribution when s/he has such little experience? As a starting point, a trainee you can hone research skills in briefing more senior lawyers on developments in relevant industries or regulatory changes that create opportunities.

Complacency: Business

Business development

- Shows awareness of market and competitor activity
- Is aware of the firm's business development strategy
- Assists in business development tasks where required
- Is aware of the skills and techniques required for effective business development

Client relationships

- Meets client expectations for trainee role performed on fee-earning matters when direct client interaction is appropriate
- Shows understanding of clients' service applications
- Makes an effort to empathise with client culture and to understand client organisation, structure and business drivers
- Develops rapport with members of client team at equivalent level

Commerciality

- Understands what services are provided by the firm
- Understands the commercial environment within which clients work and the need for advice to be tailored to that environment
- So far as appropriate to client base, shows an understanding of multicultural issues and business practicies
- Delivers a work product that is commercially as well as technically sound
- Meets deadline committments to clients
- Is aware of the significance of WIP and proactively manages own WIP
- Records chargeable time accurately

'Generation Y' – key talent management drivers

Sally Woodward
Sherwood PSF Consulting

1. **Introduction**

    They're overconfident – arrogant even, and impatient; they don't want to work hard but they still want the success that goes with it. They are disrespectful of authority, expect too much of my attention and are politically naive.. the sooner they realise it's a tough world out there, get their heads down and stop expecting the earth, the better it will be for all of us – including them..

    [As a group] they are much more confident than we were at that age; maybe a little too outspoken at times – but ....I find most of them to be hardworking, enthusiastic, committed, optimistic – even in today's uncertain climate, and hungry to learn. They often have good ideas – especially about making better use of the technology. They do question the status quo – I have heard them described as the 'Why' generation'. But that's no bad thing. I think we need to engage with and learn from them rather than expecting them to adjust to our ways...

    These quotes are from two different 50-something-year-old partners in two global law firms, in response to my question: "What do you make of young lawyers as a group – the under-30s, so called 'Generation Y' or 'millennials'?"

    What is this Generation Y of which academics, consultants, business people and lawyers speak? Does it really exist? Who does it comprise? What do they want? Do we have to – should we want to – adapt our firms to suit these 'millennials'[1] or can we simply sit tight and wait for them to 'grow up'?

    The term 'Gen Yers' (as the UK media label them) refers to individuals born during the last 20 years or so of the last century – exact date definitions vary between commentators – who are thus now aged between about 20 and 33. Like preceding generational clusters, members of Generation Y are said to share important characteristics that reflect key influences of the environment in which they were brought up, including significant geopolitical forces and events, social norms and economic conditions, technological change, and especially parental and educational styles.

    If you believe the headlines in the popular press (or business books), 'Gen Yers' are confident, ambitious – albeit not necessarily for the same things as their predecessors – collaborative rather than competitive, technologically savvy,

---

[1] 'Millennial' is a term that is more widely used in the United States to refer the same phenomenon, along with others – more or less judgemental – labels, such as 'the IPod generation', 'me firsts', 'generation why' and 'digital natives'.

dismissive of hierarchy and keen to make a positive difference in the world. According to many of their bosses (not just in law firms), many lack emotional intelligence, a work ethic and even a sense of personal responsibility. How representative and valid are these views and how much is media hype?

Even if Gen Yers as a population group emerge from their youth with some shared differences compared to previous generations, is it possible or helpful to generalise about them in the workplace? Are Gen Y medics, marketeers or entrepreneurs anything like lawyers who happen to be born during the same period? Or do the shared values of their chosen careers subsume those of their formative years?

In short, are the young lawyers of today so very different from those who are already at or near the top of established law firms and in-house departments? Or is this just an example of the perennial generational divide, such that as they mature they will put aside their childish or rebellious ways?

Moreover, if generational groupings are a response to environment, how does this manifest across cultures? Is Generation Y a phenomenon mainly associated with the so-called 'old world' (on which much of the existing research is based)? Are alleged 'Y values' as evident in Laos as in London, in Capetown, Rio or Mumbai as in Chicago?

More importantly, how should those currently in leadership roles respond to Generation Y values, aspirations and expectations? Is the generation gap an irritating challenge to be managed – even minimised – or an opportunity to be harnessed?

1.1 The evidence for generational differences

This chapter looks beyond anecdote and hyperbole to provide an overview and synthesis of selected, quality research on the Generation Y phenomenon, so as to separate the myths from potentially useful working assumptions. It is intended as background to the practical case studies and specific advice on talent management for Gen Y lawyers that are contained elsewhere in this book.

The chapter looks at three generational groups that now co-exist in the workplace – the 'Baby Boomers', 'Generation X' and Generation Y – with the main focus on the latter.[2]

Section 2 draws ideas about Generation Y from a wide range of research that is focused on individuals with a high level of educational attainment who hold jobs at the graduate trainee or junior professional/managerial level. These ideas are not specific to the legal sector and mostly derive from UK and US sources, where the majority of research has been done so far. Limited, but recent, evidence suggesting the global significance of some Generation Y themes is also covered briefly.

Section 3 discusses new research findings from a 2013 survey on "The 21st Century Lawyer", commissioned by global law firm Eversheds. This research investigates the attitudes, aspirations and perceptions of nearly 2,000 young lawyers,

---

[2] The so-called 'silent generation' born before World War II are mostly retired (in the traditional sense of the word). Those born in this century have yet to enter the workplace and their worldview is still being formed. Although they have yet to acquire a settled name and identity, labels such as 'the Facebook generation' are beginning to emerge.

in-house or in private practice, in over 300 organisations across the world. While not focused exclusively on Generation Y lawyers or designed specifically to test alleged Generation Y characteristics, it offers fascinating insights into, and at least indirect support for, many of the propositions that emerge from cross-sector generational research.

While even sector-specific research cannot provide specific answers, it may be a useful starting point for your own reflections and for developing a framework for further enquiry in your firm or legal department. The talent management issues and responses discussed in other chapters by those with frontline specialist experience in different contexts in part reflect – even if not explicitly – many of these generational differences.

2. Generational theory

Generational theorists suggest that there are characteristics shared by a body of people that reflect formative influences of the era in which they are born, and which are more than simply the characteristics that we tend to share and display as we proceed through different life stages of youth – early adulthood, midlife and old age.

This social theory has developed since the early 20th century and explains the apparent impact of the increasing pace of social and cultural change, along with a number of 'shocks' to the status quo, on the attitudes and behaviours of those who experience them during their formative years (ie, from birth to early adulthood and especially during early childhood and teenage years).

These include world wars and subsequent regional conflicts, excessive swings of the economic cycle – especially its increasingly wide impact, given the globalisation of trade – and a significant amount of social, geopolitical and technological change. Another major influence is changing fashions in parenting style. For example, contrast the approach of Boomer parents – who were themselves teenagers in the 'Swinging Sixties' and who exhibited a 'hands off' parenting style – with that of their Generation X children – whose so-called 'helicopter' parenting style is experienced by many Gen Yers in the form of tight parental control over both their educational and leisure activities

Generational theory seeks to explain why and how it is that young people of today not only rebel against the older generation – as they have done throughout history – but how they do so in very different ways from their parents. It suggests that succeeding generations are not younger versions of their parents, but have different attitudes and beliefs that together constitute a distinct worldview that, to a large degree, continues to exist throughout later life – albeit moderated by progression through the normal life stages and ongoing changes in the society in which they live.

The theory further suggests that during the last 50 years at least, the global nature of many key influences has resulted in many shared characteristics crossing geographic and national cultural boundaries, so that a teenager in China (at least in those parts that are more open to external influences) has more in common with his equivalent in Brazil, London or New York than with his parents.

The theorists do not purport to suggest that everyone of a similar age who has been exposed to the same historical and cultural experiences processes his environment in an identical way – there are still plenty of individual differences that reflect both genetic factors and the specific 'nurture' received. However, when making policies about recruiting, managing and developing key talent, understanding shared generational characteristics is arguably a useful starting point.

2.1 Dates and boundaries

Academics and consultants argue about the precise dating and names of different generational boundaries. These debates reflect the different times that key 'shocks' and other influences affected different parts of the world. In any case, those born around 'boundary years' – sometimes called 'cuspers' – are likely to experience influences of both eras. Some researchers suggest that cuspers choose which generation they want to ally with, rather than showing characteristics of both. Such inconsistencies may be irritating to lawyers used to precision in definition – generational research is definitely not a precise science.

Does the evidence support the theory? And what does it say about Generation Y?

If you focus on any one of the hundreds of bestselling books or articles and research reports available on the Internet, you could easily conclude that the answers are clear. Here is a conclusion from one 2009 report:

Generation Y, those born after 1980, are a confident, empowered generation with a sense of self-worth and responsibility. They communicate differently, they socialise differently and most importantly they expect to work differently than previous generations. They are used to an age of instant gratification – be it media, music or work. As a result, organisations are struggling to cope with the demands they make, and to engage and get engagement from Generation Y.[3]

Further enquiry suggests that the situation is not quite so clear-cut – even within a single country.

The table below[4] summarises some of the alleged characteristics and attributes of different generational groups, as gleaned from a wide variety of research reports.[5] These represent a sample of items appearing most often in the sources – a mixture of consultancy reports, outputs from popular writers on the subject (who claim to be basing their comments on more than anecdotal evidence) and research from business schools and university social science departments. It is not a scientific 'meta-analysis': the underlying survey data varies in sample size, methodology and hence, probably, validity.

---

3   By Deloitte and Touche, Ireland.
4   Synthesised from a number of sources selected according to perceived relevance to the themes of this book. Question marks refer to attributes often cited, but not backed by the Ashridge surveys.
5   Three Ashridge reports cited in detail in later sections of this chapter, a 2008 report published jointly by Penna and the Chartered Institute of Personnel and Development, reports by KPMG and PwC and the 2013 PwC report available here: www.pwc.com/gx/en/hr-management-services/publications/nextgen-study.jhtml.

	Boomers	X	Y
Born between; now aged	1940-1960 (the 'boom times'); 50-plus.	1961/5-1980; 35-50.	1981-2000; <35.
Defining themes in their formative world	A time of growth, development, infrastructure building, hope and a degree childhood freedom in nuclear families; followed by the 1960s and the 'permissive age' (in the western world at least).	Unsettled times during youth, as good times gave way to the uncertainty of the 1970s and 1980s; scarcity of work; freedom in teen years (sometimes called 'latchkey kids') ; globalisation; technological boom; fall of the Berlin Wall; end of apartheid.	Post-communism era and emergence of global terrorism and new conflicts; protected childhood – 'helicopter parents'; formative years of economic growth, consumerism and achievement culture created high expectations; difficulties of the recession; competition from new economies.
Attitude	Live to work – "if you have the money, show it".	"Whatever"; enigmatic; work to live – "it's just a job".	"Let's make the world a better place"; work and live to be self-fulfilled.
Likes	Winning; leading; success; being in control; money and status; working in the office for as long as it takes.	'Chilling'; being with friends; sceptical of authority and 'favouritism'; desire to be judged on results; competitive at work; working from home and only when necessary.	Interesting and challenging work; technology; managers who mentor/coach; lots of feedback; collaboration, not conflict; questioning; multi-tasking; flexibility.

continued overleaf

'Generation Y' – key talent management drivers

	Boomers	**X**	**Y**
Dislikes	Ageing!	Bossiness; inauthenticity; feedback – it is unnecessary.	Dishonesty; ostentation; hierarchy; working hard, rather than smart; long hours; rigid rules.
Key drivers/ what keeps them in an organisation	Money and money; possibly status.	Security and salary; work-life balance with increasing age.	Interesting work early on, then work-life balance; personal relationships; flexibility.
Key values/ attributes	Work ethic; personal growth; talkative, inquisitive and competitive; sensitive to feedback; team orientated; uncomfortable with conflict.	Autonomy; impatient for answers; multi-tasking; self-reliant; pragmatic, individualistic; risk-taking; informal; global outlook; somewhat cynical and pessimistic.	Independence and autonomy; risk-taking; team-player; 'street smart'; ambitious; sociable; tenacious; adaptable; innovative; confident (even arrogant), albeit with potential insecurities; impatient for personal growth and progress; optimistic (potentially naive).
Technology	A useful tool, mainly for others! Uses email at the office and perhaps Google at home.	'Digital immigrants': create own documents; use smartphone for email and laptop for web browsing, shopping etc.	'Digital natives': allegedly very technologically 'savvy'; use smartphones, iPads and social media; 24/7 – always connected.

continued overleaf

	Boomers	**X**	**Y**
Preferred form of communication	Memos; telephone; email for short interactions – mainly for work.	Email, then instant messaging; prefer email to face-time at work.	SMS and Facebook or face to face, socially; face to face and email at work. Not telephone!

2.2   **Making sense of it all**

The inconsistencies within, and overlaps between, these groupings highlight the difficulty of relying too heavily on any single source of research findings and demonstrate the limits of any attempt to reduce the complexity and diversity of human nature to a set of descriptive labels.

Reports originating in the United Kingdom appear more in agreement as to the differences between Boomers, and those born after the 'Swinging Sixties' began. The distinctions between the X and Y groups are harder to delineate. Although the former do seem to have developed more self-reliant behaviours and appear to be more concerned with security than their successors, this could simply reflect their life stage – the Xers have more children and mortgages. Yet at the same time, both X and Y groups are becoming less willing to sacrifice their life for their work than were their Boomer parents. Gen Xers are sometimes described as 'inbetweeners' – they are more easily defined by what they do not have in common with either their predecessors or successors than by any coherent set of shared attributes. That said, the Gen Xers do seem to have longer time horizons than their Gen Y successors, typically 'putting in time' to build experience and a career path in one or two organisations, rather than moving quickly from place to place if their expectations are not being met, with no apparent career goal or path.

The view that the biggest divide as regards values and beliefs is between the Boomers and those born in or after 1960/5 reflects my own experience of working with three generations of lawyers over the last 30 years. It is also supported by "The 21st Century Lawyer" research commissioned by Eversheds; the respondents in this report span both Generations X and Y.

It is possible that X and Y differences are clearer in those countries where the political upheavals of the 1980s and 1990s had an even greater impact on youth worldview than did the earlier social changes of the 1960s and 1970s. Cross-cultural comparative research on generational issues is still relatively scarce, save for the newly available Ashridge and PwC research cited later in this chapter.

Despite reservations, there does seem to be evidence of some shared differences in mindset and behaviour between the Boomer generation that is still largely running larger, more established businesses (including law firms) and later generations. Certainly, an increasing sense of dissatisfaction with 'traditional' ways of working – as established in the second half of the 20th century – is evident; this will not be reversed with increasing maturity.

2.3 **Relevant research: from the Ashridge Business School and PwC**[6]

The conclusions of three Ashridge Business School research reports, as well as a recently published PwC global generational study, are particularly illuminating. These focus on the highly educated subgroups of our society that are most likely relevant for our purposes. The commentary that follows draws mainly on the findings presented in these reports.

"Generation Y: Inside Out", published in 2009, and its 2011 follow-up, "Great Expectations – Managing Generation Y",[7] adopt a more nuanced view of the nature of generational differences. "Culture shock! Generation Y and their managers around the world", published in 2012, tests the applicability of Generation Y themes across cultures.

The first Ashridge survey – involving nearly 700 respondents from some 59 UK-based organisations (including one international law firm) – has the added advantages of:

- being multigenerational (ie, including both self-perceptions of different generations and also their perceptions of others); and
- using a variety of survey methods – both focus groups and online questionnaires. Online surveys run the risk of respondents interpreting terms such as 'ambition' or 'work-life balance' in different ways, – whereas qualitative research methods allow for greater clarification and probing of responses.

The follow-up 2011 Ashridge survey covered more than 2,000 Generation Y graduates, in professional/ trainee or junior management roles for less than five years, within a variety of sectors within the United Kingdom. Unlike the earlier survey, it takes account of the impact of the current recession on Generation Y employees. I have heard more than one Boomer or older Generation X manager confidently assert that the recession would change everything. While the recession appears to be having some small effect on Gen Y behaviour (based on the Ashridge 2011 results and other recent surveys), there is little evidence that it is, as yet, changing their worldview or career aspirations for if and when things improve. This said, the 2011 research does suggest a renewed concern with money among the younger Gen Yers, as compared with the pre-recession findings.

The 2012 Ashridge report adds a hugely valuable international dimension to the discussion about drivers of Gen Y talent and, since it was conducted in the last quarter of 2012, takes full account of regional economic differences by including results both from economies still in recession and those that are growing fast. It combines qualitative research developed with recent graduates and their managers from the United Kingdom, the Middle East, India, Malaysia and China – with online survey data from nearly 1,800 Generation Y graduates and more than 1,000 managers (mostly male, except in the United Kingdom) from a wide variety of countries, including from North America and continental Europe. Unlike previous

---

6 For further details, see www.pwc.com/gx/en/hr-management-services/publications/nextgen-study.jhtml.
7 Published jointly by Ashridge Business School and the Institute of Management and Leadership.

reports, most of the managers were Gen Xers rather than Boomers, thus providing an additional perspective on potential differences between the X and Y generations in the workplace.

The recent PwC report (which uses the term 'millennials', instead of 'Generation Y') is limited to its own employees, but represents 4,000 responses from both millennials and non-millennials across the whole PwC professional services network – including tax, advisory and accountancy – and within 18 global regions. One might thus expect there to be considerable transferability for law firms. The survey was explicitly prompted by PwC's concerns about the high level of early leavers, including much of the brightest talent. As it was carried out in conjunction with London Business School and University of Southern Carolina, it benefits from a measure of rigour and independence.

(a) *Describing 'Generation Y' – the 2009 Ashridge report*
The first Ashridge report criticised what it called "media hype" for having "produced a largely untrue negative stereotype of Generation Y, which may be restricting their potential in the workplace and society", and went on to state that, "just like any other group of human beings, Generation Y is made up of individuals. There are wide variations in their attitudes and behaviour".

This said, the survey does lend support to some key Generation Y characteristics, including the following:
- challenging and demanding;
- ambitious – albeit more for self-fulfilment than for job titles;
- friendly – they expect to have informal, open communication with all ages;
- not intimidated by the boss; and
- optimistic, as compared to their Generation X counterparts (at least at the time of this survey).

However, in comparison to earlier findings on Gen Yers, Ashridge researchers found little evidence that their sample group were risk takers: if anything, they self-reported as less adventurous than Gen Xers and were more focused on spending time with family and friends. Nor did this report find much evidence of the team-playing ethos previously attributed to Generation Y. Interest in, and skill levels with, technology varied (beyond the use of smartphones). The sample group did not appear to be driven by global environmental concerns and few respondents seemed to be seeking a meaning or purpose to their work. Neither did they appear to have a global outlook – although this result might reflect the fact that the vast majority were raised in the United Kingdom or United States, while respondents to earlier Generation Y surveys were from more culturally diverse backgrounds, albeit subsequently living or working in the United Kingdom or United States.

(b) *Generation Y graduates in the workplace – the 2011 Ashridge findings*
This later Ashridge research focuses on the expectations of Gen Yers in the workplace. It is less concerned with establishing general worldviews than with identifying and explaining sources of apparent tension between recent graduates and their current

bosses. The findings indicate a greater degree of shared values and beliefs among the young than some of the broader-based surveys – at least as regards their attitudes towards their work and careers – and thus have potential relevance to the subject of this book.

The survey revealed a significant disconnect between the aspirations and ambitions of those in the first five years of their career and what they were currently experiencing from their work, especially in relation to their stated top priorities of:

- challenging and interesting work;
- rapid career advancement;
- freedom and independence to complete tasks without being micromanaged;
- flexibility in their use of time;
- managers who are coaches or mentors, and friends rather than 'bosses'; and
- work-life balance.

Moreover, most managers surveyed (both older Gen Xers and Boomers) significantly underestimated the importance of these factors to their Generation Y staff – especially the desire for work-life balance, an aspiration also shared by the younger Gen Xers in the survey.

The researchers found little evidence of a 'team player' culture among the graduates, except in the sense that they were happy to collaborate with each other to get things done. As one put it: "My line manager sees his job as one to make the department better, whereas my view is to benefit my own personal goals – and if they fit in with the department's, then even better."

A major issue for participants in this sample, as indeed for those surveyed in other reports mentioned here, is the dislike – shared with later Gen Xers – of the 'long hours' culture and the impact of this on their work-life balance: "[My manager] has no life other than work and spends all evenings and most weekends in the office, gets much stressed and cares far too much. I do none of these things."

Nor did this sample of Gen Yers appear to want or need a lot of feedback, although a 'coaching and mentoring' boss was seen as very important (and not often found). A key priority for these Gen Y graduates was their strong desire to give respect to, and to be respected and valued by, others – irrespective of age and status.

On the positive side, bosses reported high levels of enthusiasm, positive engagement with their work and a 'willingness to go the extra mile'– presumably, so long as this did not take up too much leisure time. But almost 60% of respondents said that they intended to leave their current employer within two years, 40% within a year and 16% as soon as possible, recession notwithstanding. Of those intending to leave immediately, the primary reasons cited were a failure to meet their desire to be treated with respect and to feel valued, as well as frustrations about the lack of, or speed of, career progression (although they indicated a possible willingness to defer promotion if other needs were being met).

(c) *The PwC "NextGen" 2013 report*

The PwC report echoes most of the more recent Ashridge findings – although in PwC at least, the desire to be part of a team-orientated culture at work seems to feature more highly than across the broader graduate population. PwC researchers also report fewer differences between X and Y generations than some of the media hype would suggest: the PwC 'non-millennials' were equally interested in work-life balance and there was a widespread demand for more flexibility as to when and where work could and should take place. Being tied to an office by a culture of 'presenteeism' was seen as a major cause of dissatisfaction and high turnover – and an unnecessary one, given the availability of the best technology. The demand for measurement by output, rather than by hours spent in the office, was a persistent theme.

Just as importantly, this PwC survey refutes the idea that the younger generation are not committed to their work and expect to get the rewards without putting in the effort. Professionals in PwC at least are realistic about the economic drivers of the business: a significant percentage claimed that they were ready to sacrifice pay or defer promotion in order to get the greater work-life balance and flexibility that they desire.

A consistent and important finding from all the research that I have read is the high proportion of Gen Yers who do not see their long-term future tied to one firm or even to one career. Ironically, this may be due at least in part to the actions of the Boomers themselves:unwilling or unable to 'retire' in the traditional sense of the word, many are now busy carving out a portfolio second career for themselves.

The (generally shorter) time horizons that most Gen Yers seem to have imply that they are looking for such a 'portfolio' approach earlier on in their lives. This is not purely a Gen Y phenomenon – many Gen Xers (now in their later 30s and early 40s) who share the 'work to live' value are already seeking to create a more family-friendly portfolio life, even after acquiring financial and family responsibilities. This trend tends to support the proposition that the worldview and values acquired in formative years continue to influence behaviour throughout later stages of life. In other words, if Gen Xers are not yet 'growing up' and becoming more like their Boomer bosses, it suggests that the current demand for more flexibility and work-life balance is not simply a function of life, or career, stage.

(d) *Generation Y themes across borders*

Until recently, there has been relatively little easily accessible academic research on the question of whether generational theories apply across cultures.[8] The two most recent reports suggest that broadly speaking, they do.

Both the Ashridge 2012 report and the 2013 PwC survey find alleged key attributes of Generation Y in respondents from across the world, especially their peer orientation rather than respect for authority – and their demand for flexibility and work-life balance. PwC reports a great degree of commonality between the United States and western Europe, although both reports also say that local cultural norms can sometimes trump inter-generational themes – for example, an enhanced focus on technology in India, a strong drive for international experience in Malaysia and

---

[8] This may mean simply that it is not available in English – I have not been able to conduct a full literature review.

additional inter-generational tensions in the Middle East (ie, over and above those deriving from more generalised Generation Y values). Perhaps unsurprisingly, both reports support the view – that, for many of those who choose to join an international business, getting international experience is an important priority, so it is crucial that employers deliver on promises made at the time of recruitment.

Key findings of earlier research about what Gen Yers want from their work and from their employers are also broadly replicated across the four regions surveyed, including the Gen Y focus on interesting and challenging work, career progression and bosses who mentor and coach, and who recognise and appreciate them as individuals. That said, in the Ashridge report at least, salary appeared higher up the list of priorities for many respondents. But the stated intention to move employers within a relatively short timeframe[9] appears to be a global norm, even in countries still in the depths of recession. PwC also found that the likelihood of early departure increases for those whose needs for support, appreciation and flexibility are not being met.

The 2012 Ashridge report also reinforces earlier findings that Gen Yers, wherever they are based, appear to lack 'people skills' or emotional intelligence when they first enter the workplace and are less willing to adjust to organisational culture and politics than preceeding generations – something that at least some of the Generation Y graduates quoted in the report seem willing to acknowledge themselves.

(e) *Addressing the disconnect*
The research supports some, though not all, of the negative stereotypes of Generation Y, although the authors of the latest report point out that, in the United Kingdom at least, Gen Yers' "unrealistic" expectations are in part the product of the upbringing provided by their Boomer parents and have probably also been reinforced by promises made to them by Boomer bosses during the 'war for graduate talent'.

The main conclusion is that, however unrealistic they may be, "it is no use viewing Generation Y's expectations as character flaws or as traits to be screened for during the recruitment stage or 'managed out'. They are part of Gen Yers' fundamental make up".

The authors of the Ashridge reports conclude that both parties need to adjust their view of the world and of each other, and that there is a need for compromise – including by Gen Yers in thinking carefully about what and how they communicate, demonstrating respect for relevant organisational norms and standards and being willing to become team players.

Conversely, PwC's conclusions are more challenging. Pointing out that by 2016 more than 80% of its global workforce will be born after 1980, the report states unequivocally that it is essential that organisations listen to and respond to what

---

9   Albeit with some significant regional variation, with about half planning to leave between two and five years – respondents in the United Kingdom, North America and India being the least loyal, and Malaysians the most loyal.

drives and motivates their people, and be willing to adjust their approaches to meet the needs of their staff and to make the workplace attractive to all generations

Some of the so-called 'disconnect', the writers argue, can be solved simply by surfacing and removing false assumptions about the new generation's needs and values. One example relates to feedback. The 'bosses' in the Ashridge survey had no doubt been exhorted and trained by their organisations to give clear objectives and specific feedback on task performance and assumed that this is what their Generation Y recruits wanted. In fact, the latter seem less concerned about getting regular feedback and more interested in having a manager who takes time to take a personal interest in them and their development (taking over, perhaps, where their helicopter parents left off).

Both the Ashridge and PwC reports contain a number of practical recommendations, many of which will resonate with the experience and recommendations of authors of other chapters in this book, in relation to lawyers.

These include the following:
- fostering two-way communication to understand each other better;
- encouraging transparency and realism around career prospects and progression;
- creating a more flexible culture as to where and when work is done – so long as the results are delivered on time –(as distinct from requiring that those who want a better work-life balance work part-time);
- increasing the opportunities for global mobility – or at least international experience and secondments;
- making greater use of 'contingent working' arrangements for those who want to take regular breaks (ie, lawyers are employed on a series of short-term contracts or for particular matters or cases, but remain associated with the firm for training and social purposes);
- making even better use of technology to support flexible working arrangements;
- adopting a more sophisticated and robust approach to managing performance based on 'outputs, not inputs' at all levels, – to support a more flexible working culture and contractual arrangements;
- developing the roles and skills of line managers as coaches and mentors and challenging rules that may have outlived their original rationale, such as those about working hours (a specific suggestion is to use 'reverse mentoring': in one example of this, a Gen Yer and a Boomer executive have succeeded in bridging the gap to mutual advantage by exchanging career guidance for coaching on how to use social networking tools); and
- investing time, energy and resources to listen to, and stay connected with, people at all levels in the firm.

The 2012 Ashridge report contains a wealth of detailed case studies and practical recommendations derived from the actions that leading organisations that rely on recruiting top graduates are taking in different parts of the world to address the disconnect between the generations – either to retain Gen Yers for longer or to be known in the market as successful developers of Generation Y talent. The report also highlights some important regional or national differences in Generation Y values and aspirations that global organisations will need to explore before seeking to develop organisation-wide approaches. It should be a useful complement to the Eversheds survey summarised below, as well as to the legal-sector-specific talent management advice given in other chapters of this book.[10]

Even with such adjustments, however, the Ashridge researchers hypothesise that we are seeing the beginnings of an irreversible shift in lifetime career patterns for many Gen Yers, with a period of up to 10 years post-university seen as as a time for experimentation and exploration, perhaps with periods of intensive work for different employers punctuated by sabbaticals that provide work-life balance. Age 30-plus thus becomes the time for settling down to a more consistent period of building a career, which may well be a portfolio career and one in which the predominant value is living a full life, rather than the 'live to work' value of their Boomer parents.

2.4 Applying these findings to law firms

Most recent research echoes the changes that I have seen in attitudes and aspirations of lawyers over the years I have worked in the sector. In fact, the demand for better work-life balance and flexible working culture is arguably even more vociferous in many leading law firms, as the pressure to maintain or increase profit per-partner meets the increasing demands of global clients for lower fees and the advent of new, technology-based competitors into the market from outside the profession. It is not just the Generation Y lawyers who are getting tired – literally and metaphorically – of the demands to be present, or at least available, 24 hours a day, seven days a week.

The solutions do not lie solely in the HR domain – that is, in changing policies and practices relating to measurement, promotion, rewards and working hours or location. Frustration results as much from bad management of matters or of people as from the challenges inherent in meeting clients' legitimate commercial needs. Lawyers have always been more comfortable with crisis management than with project management and, for many years, have claimed that it was impossible – and hence not sensible – to plan ahead, because every case is different and unpredictable. Now, at last, many firms are investing heavily in training and encouraging lawyers to borrow principles of good project management from many of their client organisations.

A recent exercise in one international law firm illustrates two of the key themes regarding flexibility or work-life balance and the desire for international experience. A group of Generation Y associates were invited to do some 'blue-sky' thinking to design their ideal law firm for Generation Y lawyers and their clients – without worrying about the challenges of how to move from the current model to the 'brave new world'.

One or two associates questioned whether the traditional law firm as we

---

10 Currently, only an executive summary of the Ashridge research on "Generation Y and their managers across the world" is publicly available here: www.ashridge.org.uk/Website/Content.nsf/wFARCRED/Culture+shock+Gen+Y+and+their+managers+around+the+world?opendocument. For further information and access to the full set of data, please contact Ashridge directly.

currently see it will continue to exist at all in 10 to 20 years' time. They argued that with many legal services being provided by large multidisciplinary firms, 'virtual' firms of self-employed individuals or smaller niche firms, there would be room for no more than a handful of very large law firms. Most doubted whether large offices, in which lawyers and support personnel spend most of their working time, would be necessary or economically viable for many firms.

The majority of associates thought that relatively minor changes would go a long way towards alleviating many of the frustrations of their generation. By 'minor', they meant relatively inexpensive, although they acknowledged that accepting the suggestions and making them work would imply a major change of attitude in many firms. Their suggestions include the following:

- Reverse what they saw as the prevailing presumption that 'working from home' means 'not working', and remove the need to 'make a case' to spend time out of the office. Some even suggested that the default presumption should be that work is done out of the office, except for scheduled client-work-related meetings, training, knowledge sharing or socialising events.
- Introduce an informal system of international short-term (eg, one to six weeks) work experience 'swaps' – akin to 'vacation house swaps' – whereby individuals could organise short-term exchanges of personnel with other locations of the firm, or even its key clients, so as to gain experience of another organisational or geographical culture. Depending on the projected value of each 'swap' to the firm, the time could be taken partly out of holiday allowance, or as a reward for high levels of performance. Usually accommodation could be swapped as well as role, thus reducing the costs associated with short-term visits.
- Provide a broader range of unpaid or part-paid 'sabbaticals' to travel, for further education or even simply to develop new skills or hobbies. Depending on the skills and experience acquired, these could be regarded as equivalent to time served in the firm, as regards promotion or reward criteria.
- Adopt a wider set of 'flexible working' options: many applauded the 'Lawyers on Demand' initiative of Berwin Leighton Paisner for creating more interest in different types of contractual arrangement.
- Facilitate more widespread mentoring – both formal and informal – and, most importantly, count participation in mentoring schemes towards chargeable time targets.
- Measure performance on the basis of achievements, not by hours spent in the office or recorded on a time sheet.
- Make effective management of people and of matters a precondition for promotion, rather than simply paying lip-service to such requirements.
- Adopt a 'zero tolerance' approach to people – however senior – who are at best ineffective and at worst destructive of confidence or morale in the way they interact with others.

These bear a striking resemblance to the recommendations of the Ashridge and PwC reports. Perhaps contrary to some fears of those currently in leadership roles, this particular group of associates was acutely aware of the need to ensure that client service was not compromised (while pointing out that their clients increasingly shared the same aspirations for work-life balance) and also of the need to make the changes economically sustainable.

This group also echoed the findings of the large-scale surveys about the relatively short-term career horizons of many young professionals: a significant number said that they wanted a variety of life and career experiences, before 'settling down' to build a career in any one firm. Ironically, such a model, albeit bringing its own challenges, could in fact relieve some of the current pressures on those law firms that are struggling to sustain the traditional model of partnership and career progression in difficult or unpredictable market conditions. The challenge may thus shift to become the employer of choice for recruits aged 30-plus, rather than those at 20, or perhaps to provide a career path that embraces and facilitates early flexibility for those top graduates whom the organisation wants to attract back into the fold once their exploration phase is done. The growing experience of many firms in establishing successful 'alumni networks' could help such flexible career paths to succeed.

3. **Eversheds' "The 21st Century Lawyer" survey**

Commissioned by global law firm Eversheds and conducted by RSG Consulting, a leading independent international consultancy, "The 21st Century Lawyer" project is the first comprehensive survey of the impact of generational differences in the legal profession.

The scale and scope of the sample give the findings of this report real value. The data comes from 1,826 respondents working across 73 different countries in over 300 organisations. The firms and organisations represented are categorised as 'global', 'international' or 'domestic', according to the number of countries in which they have offices, but all of them are leaders in their markets. About half the respondents are clearly Gen Yers (ie, under 30), while most of the rest – aged between 31 and 40 – are either cuspers or clearly in the Generation X group, depending on where you fix the precise date boundaries.

Due to be formally launched in Autumn 2013, Eversheds will publish a dedicated website that allows users to interrogate the data in a multitude of different ways, so as to see how particular groupings of lawyers in different types of firm and in different countries or regions responded to questions about their aspirations, expectations of employers, perceptions of how well or otherwise these are being met and plans for the future.

It should provide an invaluable tool to those readers who wish to benchmark data from their own firms against what will be a relevant and statistically valid sample or who would simply like to gain insights about what questions they might ask or ideas they might test out with their own group of Generation Y lawyers.

The survey is wide-ranging and offers a rich and flexible source of data on many of the questions currently exercising those responsible for managing talent in law firms around the world. These include the following:

- How does working as a lawyer compare with their expectations (the answers include reasons why it does or does not match expectations)?

- What are the career aspirations and intentions of 21st century lawyers?
- What factors make them choose or change firms?
- What do they most want from their employers?
- What would they most want to change about their workplace, if they could?

Unlike other published reports, whose findings reflect the authors' specific interests and hypotheses and often leave the reader with more questions than they answer, the Eversheds interactive microsite will allow enquirers to manipulate the data in order to explore whatever issues are of most interest and relevance to them. If you want to know the responses of lawyers aged 30 or over in domestic firms in Asia-Pacific to questions about what would make them choose or move firms, you can find them.

Here are some headlines about findings that were of particular interest to me in writing this chapter – especially in answering some of the general questions posed earlier about the degree to which generational differences appear to exist at all and/or apply across sectors, cultural and other boundaries:

- Clear generational themes are emerging that reflect many of those found in the Ashridge 2011 and the PwC 2013 cross-sector research – especially in affirming the importance of quality of work, a sense of autonomy, career progression (based on merit, not seniority) and the desire for more flexibility in working patterns and greater work-life balance. There is also, among these respondents at least, more evidence of a desire for social interaction and teamwork than was evident in the Ashridge survey.
- There seem to be no clear shared differences between responses from 26 to 30 year olds (Generation Y) and those in the 26 to 40 age group (Generation X). There are a few interesting differences, however, betweenresponses of the 26 to 40 age-group majority and those of the newest entrants to the legal workplace– that is, the 21 to 25 year olds. These mainly relate to money as a reason for both choosing and moving firms. It is unclear as to whether this reflects some intra-generational differences[11] or is simply a reflection of their career stage. It will be interesting to track whether, over time, the views of this youngest group become more or less like those of their older Generation Y brethren, for whom factors other than money appear to act as primary drivers of behaviour.
- The good news is that the majority of those surveyed – some 83% – say that they are broadly happy with their chosen career. This is, perhaps surprisingly, somewhat different from the views of the recent graduates surveyed in the Ashridge 2011 report. The youngest age group (<25 years) are the happiest of all – this might possibly reflect a more realistic set of initial expectations, moderated by their experience of the recession that hit during their student years
- As in the Ashridge sample, two-thirds of respondents think that they already get enough feedback. One might speculate whether this finding is a matter of

---

11   Some researchers have identified differences between early and later groupings within Gen X.

definition (eg, whether they interpreted the question in terms of task-related feedback, so as to get the job done), simply reflects their low expectations in this area, given the reputation that many law firms have for not being good at giving feedback, or mirrors the findings of the Ashridge survey that Gen Xers say they do not need feedback, while Gen Yers say they do not want feedback, but rather coaching and mentoring.
- The less good news is that less than half of the respondents consider that their current firms empower them to reach their full potential, and it seems that the majority do indeed have very different career aspirations and time horizons than the Boomer generation. In fact, one-third of all respondents in all age groups contemplate moving firms in the next 12 months, even if they are currently satisfied – this figure rises to 50% of those who report dissatisfaction with their current employer.
- Findings on specific issues that arguably reflect generational concerns do seem to cross geographical and cultural boundaries. While one might expect this to a degree among lawyers inside global and international firms, similar findings emerge from lawyers employed in domestic firms: it does not seem to matter which country or region they come from, with a couple of exceptions. One such exception is that the least satisfied lawyers overall work for North American or domestic firms. Also, responses from those located in the Europe, the Middle East and Africa region diverge from the majority in indicating a higher level of interest in monetary reward although this may possibly reflect the higher proportion of men in this group, since money is generally a lower priority for women).
- Generally, there are no signficant gender differences in answers to specific questions – including in areas where perhaps one might expect these, such as concern for work-life balance. But women are least satisfied overall with their career choices – possibly because the significance of their top priorities not being met may be greater. This is particularly evident in responses to questions about partnership aspirations, where more than 40% of female respondents (compared with only 30% of men) say they do not want to be partners in any law firm, not simply in their current one.

Top of the list of concerns and priorities for most respondents across ages, firms and boundaries revealed by this latest research are the following:
- interest and challenge of the work;
- shorter working hours or rather the desire for work-life balance (this was the highest priority for those aged 27 and over);
- flexible working;
- career progression;
- international experience; and
- law firm culture (eg, stress arising from the relentless focus on billings and profit or the competitive nature).

This last factor is, by definition, more sector-specific, although it seems to support the view that competitiveness is not a key attribute of the post-Boomer lawyer, something that larger firms, whose strategy depends on collaboration, could surely turn to their advantage?

The opportunity to gain international experience is a key driver for 60% of respondents outside the United States and Canada; it is even more important for the under-25 age-group, where two-thirds said it was essential, and more so for men than women. This might support the view that a global outlook is indeed a Generation Y value, or maybe it simply reflects the greater opportunities that exist in a highly globalised sector such as law.

3.1 Moving firms, partnership aspirations and longer-term careerplans

There is an interesting difference between the main reason given by younger respondents for why they would move firms – namely, a desire for a better quality of work and/or remuneration – and that given by those aged between 28 and 40 – namely, the search for work-life balance. This may reflect the fact that these two groups are at different stages of their careers and lives, but the responses of the youngest group may yet herald a shift of values back towards a more work-centred worldview, possibly triggered by the current global uncertainties, both economic and political.

Two-thirds of respondents overall say that they do want to become partners – although this hides some significant regional variations, from 80% in South America to less than 60% in North America (perhaps reflecting relative prospects). Given that one-third of all respondents say that they are thinking of moving firms within 12 months, there would seem to be something of a disconnect in evidence, in some firms at least – even among those who still aspire to partnership. Further, 80% of respondents think that the current partnership model is not sustainable and 60% suggest that the career path needs to be shorter.

Nearly two-thirds of respondents do not intend to spend the rest of their career in a law firm at all.

In summary, my preview of the findings from the Eversheds report do seem to mirror those that have emerged from the latest UK cross-sector Generation Y research, albeit with little apparent difference between answers from those who 'technically' form part of Generation Y and those who are later members of the preceding Generation X. The results also suggest that many of the aspirations and attributes identified in the UK and US research do indeed apply in other regions and cultures, albeit with some variations, and that many of the specific theme themes highlighted in the PwC global research do indeed transfer into the legal sector.

4. Conclusion

Across a wide range of knowledge-based businesses and, to a large degree, across the world, it seems that there are perceptions of a disconnect between Generation Y (and some Generation X) talent and the prevailing workplace culture, along with evidence that for many Gen Yers, the time horizon for staying in one firm may be as short as two to three years, even in times of recession. This allows employers little time to recoup the significant investment of time and money typically involved in recruiting top graduate talent. Cost savings apart, there must surely be a real and sustainable competitive advantage for the firm that can credibly demonstrate that it is a 'Gen Y friendly' place to work and in which to build a career (even if that career may well prove to be shorter than in the past or does not really 'get going' until aged 30 or later).

Bridging the generation gap will require an open mindset on both sides and mutual adjustment of both expectations and behaviours. This is made both necessary and perhaps more challenging for law firms in many jurisdictions by slowing growth, increasing competition for clients and relentless pressure for increased efficiency and productivity.

It may indeed be hard to give Gen Y young lawyers interesting work with plenty of autonomy, rapid career progression and a fair degree of work-life balance. Creative solutions – perhaps involving clients, who will be facing similar pressures within their own organisations – will be required, and it would be wise to learn from those law firms that have found effective ways to attract and manage the talent of Generation Y. On the other hand, giving each other respect and showing appreciation for individuals (from whatever generation) for the effort that they put in takes little time, no money and is recession-proof. Perhaps this would not be a bad place to start.

Into partnership: building sustainable client relationships

Kevin Doolan
Eversheds LLP
Moray McLaren
KermaPartners

1. Introduction

When asking a room full of senior lawyers, as we regularly do in our consultancy work, "How do you feel when you are selling your services?", the sense of discomfort is almost palpable. Some will find that their shoes or the clock on the far wall has suddenly become of great interest.

And if groups of successful lawyers – people whom we can congratulate for already building the profitable client relations required to sustain their legal career – find this so difficult to answer, it is even worse for those junior lawyers who are now expected to develop clients at an earlier stage of their careers. Let us start by considering the case of Jane.

1.1 The challenge

Jane has been among the high achievers at her law firm since the day she started. Not only was she the leading student of her graduation year, but since joining the firm she has flown through every challenge, becoming first an associate and then senior associate on schedule. After eight years with the firm, it was assumed that she would now progress to the top of her career via an invitation to join the partnership.

Today, however, her career expectations have been frustrated and Jane is struggling to understand why. The managing partner has explained that, despite exceeding expectations throughout her time at the firm, she will not be making partner as expected.

This scenario is increasingly playing out in law firms of all types, shapes and sizes. Jane is hugely disappointed and would be forgiven for feeling that the 'rules of the game' have changed – and they have.

Working long hours and delivering a good legal service to existing clients are important, but are increasingly unlikely to lead automatically to progression to partner. It is only when facing this new reality that the need for all partners (not just some select 'rainmakers') to achieve real growth has become so clear.

When making the case for partnership, existing partners are bound to ask Jane, "If you are such a great lawyer, why can't you give us a list of the new clients that you have brought in? Don't great lawyers attract new clients? And if you aren't going to do that, or create real growth from your existing clients, then why should we make you partner? Aren't we just then sharing the same-sized cake between more people?"

Even in countries where there is still market growth for legal services, existing partners would rather promote someone to partner who has demonstrated real business-building skills, rather than one who just 'does the legal work'.

1.2 New requirements

For all of the reasons explored in this book, Jane's career has hit an unexpected bump in the road. Against the backdrop of changing market conditions, law firms are reviewing the current skills requirements of their most senior lawyers – especially as they approach the gateway to partnership.

Lawyers now need to be more than good legal technicians: they need to be better managers, lead junior lawyers more effectively and get closer to clients and understand their needs better.

Building an effective book of business – once perhaps seen as a consequence of partnership – has now become a prerequisite. And while senior associates were previously expected to focus primarily on work output, they are now required to go out and develop client relationships.

Like a growing number of bright young lawyers globally, Jane now has a serious bridge to cross. She has to prove her ability to attract clients and build a profitable book of business before – not after – she makes partner.

1.3 Market changes

In our work with law firms over the last two decades, we have seen a universal and significant change in the legal market. At the risk of both oversimplifying and simultaneously stating the obvious, the pendulum is swinging in favour of clients and away from law firms. The client is increasingly now in control.

While the financial crisis of 2008 accelerated this change – as supply of legal services outstripped demand in many markets – it was not the cause. The new client mindset – the 'procurement' approach to legal services – is having a knock-on effect for all law firms. These new approaches are trickling down from the general counsel at international businesses into even the most traditional domestic companies. Even areas of the world that were previously unaffected by this change are now starting to see the effects.

Like many of the current challenges facing lawyers, this will not simply disappear with the rising tide of an improving economy. This particular train has now left the station.

2. Sales without selling

At its simplest, 'sales' or 'cross-selling' may be the requirement outlined by her managing partner, but Jane is not overly excited about this new prospect. There are two good reasons for the aversion that most lawyers feel towards selling. First, they became lawyers to practise law – if they had wanted a career in sales, they were pretty unlikely to have chosen law. Selling is not something that they actually want to do – for the majority of lawyers, satisfaction comes from delivering a great legal service, meeting the challenges that the work throws up and feeling a sense of achievement from a job well done.

Second, selling is about risk. Increasing the level of sales activity inevitably means increasing the risk of rejections, which can lead to a personal sense of failure.

2.1 Stop selling

During our sessions, we ask lawyers at all stages of their careers, "Remember a time that you were recently sold to by someone else – how did you feel?" Almost all of them can remember a salesperson trying to push some unwanted offer onto them. They recall the unpleasant feelings that they experienced – at a deep, instinctive level, people do not like being 'sold to'. The seller was pushing something that was in his interests. And when we ask general counsel, it should come as no surprise that they equally dislike being sold to.

It is an interesting place to pause and reflect. Lawyers do not like selling and clients do not like being sold to. So why not stop selling?

How does this help Jane? While many law firms have invested in sales training programmes for their lawyers – at all stages of their careers – we strongly believe that selling is not the answer. The magic that will help all lawyers, including Jane, is at the same time both simpler and more complex than the average 'selling for lawyers' programme would suggest.

We believe that the answer for the vast majority of lawyers (excluding the natural-born rainmakers who develop their own successful and comfortable style) is to approach the problem from the opposite direction: to ask not, "How can I improve my selling skills?", but instead, "What would make this client want to buy more from me?" and (for a potential new client) "What would make this target client switch from their existing law firm to mine?" Our experience has shown that in both of these cases, it will not be because the client has been 'sold to'.

Our approach – let's call it 'sales without selling' – requires a deeper understanding of individual clients' needs and has the fortunate foundation that it actually plays to the lawyer's core skills of investigation and analysis, of their desire to help their clients to be more successful, rather than trying to train them in a new and alien skill of 'selling'. We think that this has been the real secret behind its success – rather than trying to change lawyers in some fundamental way, our process asks lawyers to use their core skills in ways that win more work.

For this to be effective, lawyers need to understand that they are looking at two separate scenarios. Building more work from an existing client is very different from gaining the first piece of work from a new client, and a different thought process is needed to navigate each successfully.

2.2 Why would an existing client give Jane more work?

The key to unlocking more work from a current client is appreciating what inspires client loyalty. What makes them come back again and again? What might make them give Jane a whole new area of work (by 'cross-buying', not by Jane 'cross-selling')?

The clues can be found in our own behaviour when buying services from providers such as airlines, hotels and restaurants.

Any decent provider will offer the basic service. In fact, the overall standards for legal services are continually rising – clients (particularly the most valuable international clients) have high expectations. To hold on to them, lawyers need to provide a really good standard of service.

This is exactly what Jane may have been doing – and using up almost every available hour to do so. The problem for Jane in seeking to grow an existing client is that her competitors will also be providing that high level of service.

Think about it. If talking to any client, could Jane honestly claim that her key competitors (those whom she comes across repeatedly) could not do a good job on their legal work? The reality is that clients typically have a wide choice of firms for each type of advice that they need (only in the most specialised areas of work could anyone claim real rarity of skills), and other firms should all be able to provide a good level of service.

A client will want to buy more from Jane only if she differentiates herself and becomes more valuable to the client than her competitors – it will not be about her giving the client a hard sell (or even a soft sell) if her service is just the same as her competitors'.

2.3 Success factors

Our research with clients shows that success requires the following factors:
- The client feels that their lawyer understood their business.
- The lawyer delivered value outside of the core service.
- The lawyer spent time 'off the clock' and in person to better understand the client's needs.

This last point is particularly important. Jane cannot succeed unless she invests time in understanding the client better (not in marketing to them), and she cannot do this via email, no matter how good a lawyer she is – phone calls and meetings are essential.

3. Building personal relationships

Face-to-face time with clients is crucial for Jane, as she will be building relationships. Doing a great job but failing to invest time in this way will leave her in the second league – and will not inspire client loyalty.

One general counsel expressed it this way: "I have eight law firms on my panel and only one of them has ever tried to build any relationship with me and my team: coming over to have coffee, asking us great questions, spending time with us in our offices. The others seem to think that we are an anonymous, remote organisation – I'm really surprised. That one firm is continually growing its share of work because they actually seem interested."

It is important to think about this statement. The winning firm was not selling; it had not asked its lawyers to sell; rather to talk to clients about their businesses, to show interest and to learn 'off the clock'. As a result, this particular client was buying more from that law firm without anyone doing any selling.

In-house lawyers speak of the vulnerability that they feel when bringing external lawyers into their business and placing them in front of close colleagues. Building trust – on both sides – is key, and we know from the wave of current research on neuroscience that this is primarily an emotional response built around subconscious behaviours. We often do not even realise it is happening!

At its simplest, this means knowing the client better – both the business and the individual personalities involved – at the heart of which is having a better conversation with them. This is about their agenda, not Jane's – understanding their personal and business aims and how she can help to achieve them.

More than one general counsel has told us about those painful pitches and 'beauty parades' when even the most senior of lawyers feels the need to explain what sounds like the history and structure of their law firm. As one explained: "I had to say, 'Excuse me for interrupting, but we have selected you to come here today, alongside the other firms, as we already know you are all excellent lawyers and well qualified to help us on this assignment. But if you don't mind, we would just like to explain our needs on this particular project.'"

3.1 Listening, but not hearing

Effective listening is the starting point, but is perhaps the antithesis of what many see as being a professional – giving an opinion on what is right and wrong in a no-nonsense way. In fact, we all know excellent lawyers who are very poor listeners.

For most lawyers, building relationships requires being a good listener and having enough confidence to let the client lead the way. Jane needs to show that she is confident, but not pushy. Jane should not try to use these regular contacts to sell. It is very offputting. She does not need to – if she is helping a client, delivering a much more tailored service and better understanding the client's business, then she will differentiate herself and more work will flow.

The secret is about building a differentiated service – an enhanced legal service that goes beyond simply doing the job. Get in professional help, if needed, in order to produce a business growth model for key clients. Or brainstorm both with clients and with fellow partners. The important output is to produce 10 to 20 ways to work differently with key clients in ways that they value. Start thinking about how to make clients' daily lives easier, help them in their careers, make valuable introductions for them to others – show that it is not just about doing the work they have sent. Be a trusted friend, coach and adviser – not just another lawyer.

4. Winning work from new clients

So, why should a new client, who may not yet have met Jane, start giving her legal work? This whole area of finding new clients is one of the most troubling for many young lawyers. It is relatively easy to understand that impressing existing clients with a better level of service, understanding their business and adding value is a good route to growth. Problems with potential new clients fall into four specific areas:

- Why should a target client move their legal work to Jane? What is the benefit of change?
- What type of target client is most likely to use Jane's services? What are the best targets?
- How does Jane actually meet target clients and get face to face?

- Once Jane meets them, what would persuade the target client to give her legal work (given that usually the client will already be using other law firms)?

4.1 The benefit of change

The secret about meeting target clients is to have a distinctive value proposition to offer. If Jane's service is the same as other lawyers, then it is hard to think of a reason why it is of value for the target client to meet her. Jane's position is the same as that of any commercial business, and it is worth revisiting the 'generic competitive strategies' put forward by Professor Michael Porter at Harvard Business School in his 1980 classic *Competitive Strategy: Techniques for Analyzing Industries and Competitors*.

The three strategies that he describes are cost leadership, differentiation and segmentation (market focus). In law firm terms, this could be described as:
- cheaper (offering the same service as the client's current law firm, but charging less);
- better (giving the client a more valuable service than the current law firm – for example, by better understanding their business or having subject experts that their current law firm does not have and charging more); and
- more focused (being a niche firm specialising in the client's business area – for example, advising only on intellectual property or acting only for energy companies. For larger firms, this can be achieved by having a clear sector-based structure in the firm).

This is an important starting point that is often missed by lawyers who tend to focus on their own expertise, rather than on the realities of a client that already has lawyers and is being expected to move work away from them.

Unless the target client happens to be particularly unhappy with their existing legal advisers, it will not give work to a new firm unless there is a real belief that the new firm offers a more attractive service than their current lawyers. Here, it is useful to think along the lines of Porter's strategies – is Jane's message to the target client that she is cheaper, better or more focused? She needs to have this clear in her mind, because it should influence the way that she approaches and talks to that target client. If Jane is not clear about this, she cannot expect the target client to understand why they should change lawyers.

4.2 Best targets

Given that any lawyer can devote only so much time to seeking out new clients, it becomes crucially important to pursue the best targets – those that are most likely to say 'yes'.

There is a simple way that Jane can establish this. The best targets are those that are most similar to existing clients. The expression 'most similar' needs to be defined in terms of the legal service that is being offered.

For a labour lawyer, it might mean clients with over 5,000 employees, because this is his area of specialisation. For one M&A lawyer, it might mean owner-managers who are looking to sell out at the end of their career; for another, it might mean clean energy companies looking for major venture capital investments.

Without doubt, the best targets look very like an individual lawyer's existing client base. Of course, it is possible to gradually move up market – but this must be gradual. Too often, a lawyer can become excited about acting for a Fortune 500/FTSE 100/Ibex 35 multinational corporation because it is seen as a 'trophy client' that can help the lawyer's personal brand. But such companies may be aggressive on price, use tough procurement techniques and be demanding clients. If they are similar to that lawyer's other clients, then fine – but if not, they are unlikely to be the best targets.

In general, it is worthwhile to create a simple scoring sheet for target clients, which is based on the characteristics of the existing client base. A lawyer can then test target clients against this scoring sheet to help focus on the best targets; experience has shown that a small number of current targets – perhaps two or three – is the most effective. As a first step, it is useful to set up Google alerts on these target clients. Google will then generate email updates of news stories affecting the chosen targets.

4.3 Getting face to face

Unless Jane is providing the most routine of legal services, she will not win a new client without meeting them. But how can she get in front of such busy people who do not know her yet?

Without doubt, one of the best sources of target clients will be Jane's existing clients – she should start by asking them. If they are happy with her work, they should be happy to make introductions to others (if they are not happy, then Jane's time will be better spent in remedying this, rather than chasing new clients). For example, her existing clients may be able to directly introduce her to others and set up a coffee or lunch with them – they may even be happy to come along.

This type of warm introduction is valuable and should be seen as the best route to new clients, because it leads to an implied recommendation by the current client that is reassuring to the target client. Several general counsel have told us that they are surprised at how rarely they are asked to make these types of introduction by their law firm advisers.

The next best route is for Jane to network through other non-client connections, or to use a special focus to meet potential new clients. For instance, if Jane has a particular focus on the laws relating to food labelling, she can offer to give talks on this topic at relevant food industry events or write articles for relevant journals. She will certainly want to join all the food law groups on LinkedIn and join in conversations or pass on valuable hints and tips.

Jane will benefit from raising her profile and networking around potential clients. If she does not feel comfortable in networking situations, it is worth taking a colleague – even better if she can go to a relevant event with a client who can introduce her to other people. She should also consider having professional training in networking – this will make a big difference to her success and is not something that comes naturally to many lawyers.

The key point for Jane is never to sell when she meets a potential client. It comes over very badly and will rarely be of benefit or interest to them. Jane just needs to let them talk about themselves and their business, asking good questions, showing interest and using follow-up questions so that the conversation does not become an interrogation. For example, she could say, "That's interesting – tell me more about how that affected your business".

If Jane asks relevant supplementary questions and empathises from her own experiences in the potential client's area of business, this will be a good first meeting. Jane wants them to gain a favourable impression – this will not come about if she is talking endlessly about herself and her law firm. Jane needs to be interested in them rather than trying to be interesting about herself.

Jane's goal from a first meeting may be that the target client is prepared to stay in touch and perhaps come to group meetings (a roundtable that she is organising or an industry event) so that she can spend more time getting to know them.

It is essentially a courtship – the target client needs to feel safe that Jane is not going to switch into sell mode, that she has something of value and that she is showing genuine interest in them and their business. She cannot move too quickly.

During the period after the initial meeting, Jane should be in 'help' mode. Are there any articles that she can send to them relating to matters that they talked to her about? Does she have any guides or tips that she could email to them? Looking through her contacts on LinkedIn, is there anyone whom they might like to meet? If so, she should suggest arranging this. Keeping in contact and being helpful is all that Jane needs to do she as she builds up to the stage where she can have a one-on-one, face-to-face meeting with the target client.

Jane needs to earn the right to this meeting by being helpful, adding value and giving the client insights that they might not have thought about. That is effectively all that is needed for the 'sell'.

4.4 The compelling case

So why should this target client give Jane legal work? In practice, we have found that the principle of reciprocity gives the best chance of generating work from a new client. It is worth examining this in detail, as many lawyers have told us that they find this final stage – actually getting work – the most difficult part. Many have ended up in a friendly circuit of meetings and conversations that never seem to get anywhere. Certainly, there will be some cases where it is time to give up, but only after these fundamental approaches have been tried. Beware of endless conversations about sport, families or other non-work topics. These can be mutually enjoyable, but can push out conversations about business.

The subject of reciprocity has been well researched by Professor Robert B Cialdini and is described in his book *Influence*. It plays well with the core skill of lawyers – that of helping their clients. Cialdini's research demonstrates that if someone wants something from someone else, he or she must first give that person something.

If Jane gives, this creates an obligation of reciprocity – "Jane introduced me to an important contact; she gave me free advice on a matter that I was concerned about; she gave me some great ideas about how I might approach an issue that I was facing in my sector – so I owe her." Lawyers in highly specialised areas, or those who focus tightly on a business sector, can create this reciprocity by delivering thought leadership, insights and examples of how other clients are tackling an industry-wide issue.

Lawyers tend to feel comfortable with this concept – they feel happy about offering free help (while it has to be free at this early stage, this does not mean devoting whole days to deliver some substantial legal project for free, but rather providing small pieces of free help).

Cialdini's research shows that if Jane builds a new relationship based upon giving help, the typical businessperson will want to find some work to give her in return – something that might give them an opportunity to see her in action on a paid matter, so that they can judge whether they want to pass on more work in future.

4.5 The final step

If a target client is thinking of instructing Jane, it is important that she can minimise the risk that they feel in taking this step. At this stage, Jane is untested and the potential client might worry that she may not be as good as they thought – and this is on a paid matter. Every target client which is sending out instructions to a new adviser feels somewhat vulnerable.

Jane can reduce this worry in two ways. First, she should have some happy existing clients that a new prospective client can talk to, in order to find out what she is really like. This makes a significant difference, and if she does not currently have existing clients who would be happy to do this, she should focus entirely on current clients and leave new clients for later!

Second, Jane should try to ensure that the new client takes small steps before they think about taking a large step. If at all possible, they should try her out on something relatively small or straightforward before committing to transfer a whole area of work to her or giving her a 'bet the farm' matter. A good way to start off would be for her to be attentive for relatively small pieces of advice.

This is just as important if Jane has only major pieces of advice to sell – for example, if she is an M&A lawyer specialising in end-of-career sales by founders or managers, she needs to develop a smaller piece of advice as her entry point (eg, a workshop on "Preparing for Sale: 10 things you need to do in the year before you sell") to give the target client something small on which she can be tested.

This approach is supported by research. A specialist team which handled major pieces of litigation wanted to know what the main factors were when a client was deciding which firm to instruct on a large piece of work. The number one answer (for all but the most specialist areas) was, "The firm which has handled a mid-range piece of litigation for us really well." Rather than marketing 'bet the farm' litigation services to target clients, the team could make more progress by winning instructions on a mid-range piece of work (with a lower risk for the client in instructing a new law firm) and then performing on that work exceptionally well.

5. Making it happen

All of these ideas regarding 'selling without sales' are easy to use, but they are of value only if Jane makes time for them and repeats them regularly. To some extent, they need to become habits. How is she going to do this?

Jane will need to come up with a plan or system that works for her. For example, she may set regular time aside time to run through key clients and targets and think about what she has been doing that will create a differentiated service. At the start, she may benefit from specialist training, mentoring or coaching.

For Jane to invest time in winning new work, this needs to be aligned with the firm's remuneration system and performance management. She will inevitably sacrifice some time that could have been spent doing billable work in favour of investing time in building long-term profitability for the firm. Remember that in building enough work to become a partner, the aim is to maintain the same leverage (ie, profitability) of the firm, developing sufficient work – of the right quality – for her own new team of associates.

A balance must be struck between time spent on business development and time spent on work for clients. Jane will be expected to maintain high levels of utilisation on chargeable time. This makes it all the more important to ensure that time spent on business development is efficient and aimed at the best targets. However, there also needs to be an acceptance that doing a good legal job and focusing entirely on this is unlikely to create sufficient growth in existing or new clients to build a practice and a case for partnership.

The starting point is about making friends with the client, being there for them, helping them out when they need it and acting as a support and sounding board.

In parallel, Jane also needs to 'find her passion'. By this, we mean that lawyers who have found a sector or a specialist area of advice that fascinates and energises them, come across positively to clients. Enthusiasm is infectious, and it is worth Jane spending some time on finding the work type or area of business that really excites her. In order to build a successful career, we all need to find an area of work about which we are passionate and clients with whom we enjoy working.

If a young lawyer can tap into this and then spend time learning how to provide an enhanced level of service, then growing existing clients and attracting new clients is achievable without having to change into 'selling mode'. In our experience, this is some of the best news that any young lawyer like Jane can have.

Managing talent in global law firms

Jay Connolly
Dentons US LLP

1. Introduction

In any size of law firm, attracting, leading, developing, retaining and incentivising talent – the only resource – is critical. While these tasks can be more or less challenging for global law firms compared to smaller firms, in many cases they offer similar opportunities – albeit amplified by scale, geography, culture and expectations.

This chapter sets out some of these challenges and opportunities, along with tools and strategies that are used in many large global firms today. It shares insights into current practice and provides ideas that can be scaled to suit firms of any size.

2. Defining 'talent' in a global law firm

Talent management has long existed in large law firms, although the definition and focus that exist today are relatively new phenomena. Large firms in the 1970s and 1980s were significantly different in size and reach, and thus adopted far less sophisticated approaches to talent management. Existing talent at recognised legal institutions served as a magnet to attract other talented lawyers, and respected, challenging, career-building employment options, while beginning to grow in wider professional services, were not the same as exist today.

Fast-forward 30 years and the global legal market has developed significantly as a result of technological advances, changing client needs and law firm consolidation. In the last few years, large firms have struggled to come to terms with the so-called 'new normal' in which they now operate. This includes:

- a willingness of clients to disaggregate matters (ie, outsourcing);
- a growing interest in pricing alternatives;
- greater availability of detailed information about law firms and their practices; and
- a changing role for in-house general counsel and downstream impact on firms.

These market changes have increased the need to build talent within firms, not only to enable them to work within this 'new normal', but also to allow them to lead the way forward.

The changes in the industry have also affected the answer to the question, "How do you define talent in your firm?" Different answers exist to this question, including the following:

- Lawyers – in many firms, talent management is focused purely on the lawyers as revenue generators. The legal minds in any firm are necessarily a key part of the talent pool that needs to be nurtured.
- Potential partners – within the population of lawyers in any firm, either explicitly or implicitly, there will be some who are seen to be 'on track' for partnership. Many firms now have a competency model in place for lawyer development, which can make measurement of this clearer. Non-traditional roles also exist in firms today and, for example, staff associates often fulfil valuable, but non-partnership track roles.
- Partners – within some firms, the primary focus when discussing talent is on the partnership. This is more likely the case in areas of high specialism – and therefore typically lower-leverage environments. It is essential to build the legal skillsets and wider business development capabilities of partners in such firms.
- A firm-recognised sub-group – many firms have implemented talent development programmes targeted at defined sub-groups – for example, selection of senior associates against pre-agreed criteria for access to additional training or coaching.
- Everyone – many firms are realising that everyone in the firm is part of the talent pool. Firms have become more systematic about gathering feedback from key clients on their performance. Such feedback often includes comments on the rapport and relationships with other staff at the firm – for example, the partner's assistant who remembers the client and is proactive when the client calls, the reception desk staff or the conference support team who pay attention to detail and resolve any issues that arise on-site.

When you consider talent management, whom do you think of within your firm? Where are you focusing attention? Identifying talent is important, but the more important question is how to develop the variety of talent that exists in your organisation.

3. The impact of diversity

When considering talent and the focus for firms, it is also essential to consider diversity. The US and UK markets have seen a significant rise in the focus on this topic in recent years, albeit with limited changes evident in the profession thus far.

Clients are driving the diversity agenda, leading to an increased focus on this topic within law firms. Clients are taking an interest in diversity for a variety of reasons, such as the following:
- As they drive successful diversity agendas and goals in their own businesses, there is a desire to make an impact on their suppliers.
- In a sea of legal suppliers, clients find it difficult to distinguish between the offerings of different firms. Legal ability, finesse and skill are obvious prerequisites; clients have thus been looking beyond these criteria for a number of years and are now doing so in a systematic way.
- The path from senior associate or law firm partner to in-house counsel at a

client offers an opportunity for those frustrated with progress of the diversity agenda to help drive change by demanding it as a client.

It would be wrong to suggest that it is purely clients that have driven the change in focus in recent years. They have played an important role, but we have also seen change across professional service firms and from individuals within firms. Diversity committees, affinity groups and specific initiatives have moved beyond the event and sponsorship-planning stages and are engaging in the more challenging, meaningful debate about structural change. Law firm websites, particularly those in the United States and United Kingdom, highlight the importance of diversity. US organisations such as the Minority Corporate Counsel Association and the Leadership Council on Legal Diversity, and UK organisations such as PRIME, have all helped firms to work on the structural challenges.

Bar associations, regulatory bodies and law schools and universities are focused on the need for greater diversity in the profession, and the pressure and demand for firms to play their part continue to grow. Improving diversity and access to the profession needs to be a common goal for all firms. Discussing the topic internally, supporting external initiatives and building a truly inclusive culture within the firm – for example, by reviewing policies, being clear on expectations and recognising biases – are all steps that can easily be taken to achieve these goals.

4. Attracting talent

Approaches to attracting talent currently take many forms. Entry routes into firms are diversifying, while firms are more accepting of different career paths and are focusing on different markets in order to attract the best talent. The employer proposition and the firm's ability to explain, portray and deliver on its promises are thus becoming ever more important.

Firms are facing increased competition for the best talent at entry level and beyond. Lawyers are increasingly prioritising skills and capability development over loyalty or longevity. Increased client sophistication in procurement of legal expertise is changing the nature of work and resourcing at many firms. These and other factors have put significant pressure on the traditional law firm model, demanding greater productivity and utilisation to maintain or improve profit levels.

The changes within the market and the need to attract talent in a variety of ways have created new entry routes to the legal profession, thereby modifying the career model in many firms. The once linear route from university or law school to partnership now has many additional pathways.

4.1 Trainee

This was the sole entry point to most large global firms, offering the prospect of partnership in return for hard work, commitment, dedication and legal excellence. However, for many of the reasons noted above, this is no longer the case. The Law Society's trend reports show that the number of training contracts registered in the United Kingdom between August 1 2009 and July 31 2010 fell by a record 16.1%. After a slight increase the following year, the 12 months up to July 31 2012 saw a

10.5% decrease. This pattern was repeated in the United States, with firms hiring far smaller summer classes.

Although there has been an upswing in recent years, the lower recruitment levels have helped to open up alternative routes into firms via paralegal positions and other legal executive roles, and off-track associate positions.

4.2 Paralegal

While the drive to reduce costs has seen a reduction in training contracts in the United Kingdom, opportunities for paralegals in firms have increased significantly. Paralegal positions have doubled in the last 10 years, whether in more traditional roles within firms or in new centres outside expensive hubs.

Firms are now using this resource option in more diverse ways, whether through career paralegal roles, opportunities with the potential for progression to a training contract or shorter-term paralegal positions.

4.3 Lateral associate

The market for lateral associates is expanding, affording them greater post-qualification opportunities and mobility.

4.4 Staff associate

The staff associate role can take a number of forms: it may represent an off-partnership-track position, provide individual flexibility or be temporary in nature. Easier access to high-quality talent on a short-term basis, coupled with the challenges of meeting client demands and cost constraints, has contributed to eliminating any stigma associated with this resource pool.

4.5 Lateral partner

Once almost nonexistent in certain markets, today movement of partners between firms is increasingly the norm. The most recent economic downturn has quickened the pace as the meaning of 'partnership' evolves – it is no longer a 'ticket for life'. The *American Lawyer* reports that in every year since 2000, over 2,000 partners joined or left Am Law 200 firms.[1] In the 12-month period ending on September 30 2012, the figure stood at 2,691, representing a 9.7% increase on the previous year.

4.6 Implications

It is important to consider all of these different routes into firms, as a targeted approach is essential to attract the best talent. Who are you looking to attract? What approaches are most likely to succeed with this target group? What offerings will be the most attractive for the target audience? Lateral partner recruitment differs greatly from entry-level recruitment, yet many firms that grasp this difference continue to employ ill-suited tactics.

---

1   *American Lawyer*, March 1 2013.

5. Talent development

To compete in a people-oriented business, it is essential for a firm to develop its talent. A talent development offering initially helps to attract staff and also ensures that the needs of highly sought-after clients – which may have been equally hard to attract – can be met.

Global firms with US roots have typically been slower to offer wider business development for lawyers. However, February 2011 saw a clear indication that times were changing, when Milbank publicly announced a multi-year training programme for all associates, in conjunction with Harvard Law School. Covering topics such as management skills, client relations, personal development and business, the programme recognised the need for lawyers to have a rounded skillset and represented a significant cost investment – both direct and indirect – to address this.

Other approaches to developing individuals do not centre on formal training, although this is often one element. Indeed, while no other firm has followed Milbank's approach in forging a similar partnership, many have excellent professional development programmes in place. Equally, numerous strong, people-oriented organisations offer limited classroom-based training, but are highly successful and profitable because they can develop individuals in other, often more productive, ways.

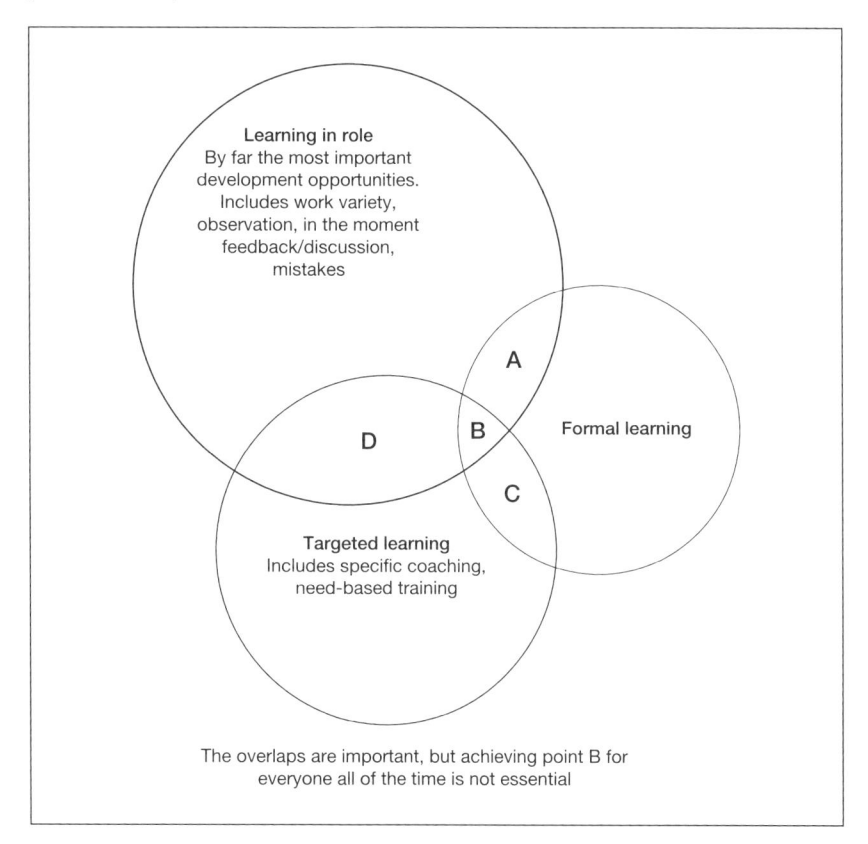

Learning in role
By far the most important development opportunities. Includes work variety, observation, in the moment feedback/discussion, mistakes

Formal learning

Targeted learning
Includes specific coaching, need-based training

The overlaps are important, but achieving point B for everyone all of the time is not essential

The model on the previous page shows the weighted importance of the three areas of learning and development. While the intersections of these areas are where the most beneficial development happens, the challenge is not to reach point B, but rather to ensure that what is in place intersects to some degree. As you consider any formal or targeted training, ensure that it is timely and there is opportunity to practise new skills through in-role experience.

5.1 Work allocation

Development occurs in a multitude of ways. One of the most effective is proactive work allocation that takes into account the development needs of a particular lawyer. This approach is often the most powerful and timely way to develop talent within a firm. In order to allow for active development over a period of time, elements of a transaction, matter or case must be allocated in a considered manner. A number of common situations that frequently arise in large global firms – in part due to the nature of the work – must be avoided for this development approach to be effective.

(a) *The easy route*

Today's firms face time and volume pressures driven by client needs and demands in a faster work environment. It is thus often easier for the partner managing a transaction to delegate elements to an associate whom he knows can handle the piece of work and deliver a quality product, with limited review. Delegating the drafting of a sale-purchase agreement to an associate who has done this before will be easier than explaining the process to, and reviewing the work of, a less-experienced junior associate.

Consider how you are allocating work within the team.

(b) *Financial metrics*

Financial metrics within a firm can inadvertently drive unintended behaviours. Allocating work to an associate for whom the task is new often results in more time recorded than would be the case with someone who has the benefit of previous research and experience. This often results in the recording of a time write-off that can impact on the partner's financial metrics.

Consider whether metrics may be impeding talent development.

(c) *Lack of visibility of development needs*

In larger firms with multiple partners, the understanding of individual development needs arising from performance review discussions and other interactions is inevitably diluted. Such firms may rely on formally implemented 'practice adviser' or 'career development' partner relationships, compared to the one-partner firm mentor/mentee relationship with an associate. Formal relationships may not be as productive, resulting in the loss of some of the positive development aspects of proactive work allocation.

Consider whether you have clarity about the development needs of associates in the firm.

(d)   Changing nature of work
Significant changes in the work undertaken in global firms today create challenges for work allocation. These include the following:
- Commoditisation of work – client pressure and improvements in knowledge management systems and template management have commoditised work once considered to suit junior lawyers. Clients often will not pay for time to be spent on template creation or drafting.
- Offshoring or outsourcing of low-value work – a growing trend is for commoditised or lower-value work to be completed in lower-cost locations, either set up by firms themselves (eg, Allen & Overy and Herbert Smith in Northern Ireland, Orrick in West Virginia) or outsourced. Legal process outsourcing is projected to grow at a staggering 26% compound annual growth rate through 2014, compared to 2.2% in the period between 2007 and 2012.[2]
- Focus on higher-value, challenging transactions and cases – clients are now more likely to split their legal spend across panel law firms, based upon the level of technical expertise needed, type of work and cost. Large firms may see more specialised, higher-value work.
- Fewer smaller matters – many of the above factors have created a trend towards fewer smaller matters, where associates have historically been able to take the lead and build experience.

Consider opportunities to enable individuals to run elements of a project on their own.

On-the-job, work-based development requires one other critical element: feedback. Within the fast-paced, technology-enhanced workplace of today, finding time to provide constructive feedback and discuss performance discussions is often seen as a barrier. However, providing valuable, developmental feedback is not about finding a free hour to sit down for a discussion; rather, it is about developing a routine to provide this frequently.

'Type A' individuals need feedback, recognition and encouragement. Time spent going over feedback in a straightforward fashion can be invaluable. Elements to consider include the following:
- When – be specific about the situation, context and time.
- What – describe what was done or not done.
- Result – articulate the impact, positive or negative.
- Next time – identify what should be repeated or changed.

The need for feedback today is becoming ever greater as 'Generation Y' develops and grows in the workplace. This is covered elsewhere in this book.

Consider whether feedback is being delivered in the above manner.

5.2   Rotations
Movement of talent can take a number of forms and, even within a single location,

---

2   Report on the State of the Legal Market, Georgetown Law, 2013.

can be a powerful way to develop an individual's skillset early on. This model has been adopted for some time in the training contract for trainees joining large firms in the United Kingdom. In the United States, the approach is more mixed: some firms adopt a rotation system for their first-year associates, in part as an attraction tool for individuals leaving law school who have not yet decided upon, or had enough exposure to, different practice areas.

While it is easier to move trainees and junior associates between practices in a firm, creating flexibility to maximise mobility at other levels can enhance development. This is not to suggest that a white-collar litigator should transfer to capital markets, but rather that proactive sharing and movement of resources between certain practices, or even within areas in large practices, can benefit the firm, as well as the individual.

The next level of resource movement is on an international scale. With changes in the nature of work as noted above, working across borders is commonplace. There is significant benefit in having talented lawyers with an in-depth understanding of other jurisdictions, appreciating local challenges and having connections and relationships in place.

Such experience can be built in a number of ways, as outlined below:
- In the past, global or international firms typically set up two or three-year secondments overseas offices. However, in 'the new normal', the financial impacts of such an approach have come under close scrutiny, particularly as the total cost for a secondee is normally around three times his annual salary.
- Transfers from one office to another – on the basis of local employment terms – are increasing as a result of growing trends, such as dual careers, acceptance of greater mobility and the desire to gain experience in the face of fewer secondment opportunities.
- Client secondments provide excellent opportunities for individuals to grow their networks, improve their understanding of clients and develop their skills. Adopting a flexible approach – for example, by considering part-time secondments, shorter placement periods or different approaches to cost management – can help to lower the costs associated with such opportunities.
- Opportunities can also arise for secondments to other firms, on a limited basis. Careful arrangements are needed in such circumstances, and normally an individual should leave his home firm for the period of the secondment.

5.3   **Formal training**

Formal business and legal skills training has an important place in the development of talent in a global firm. The framework below provides an example of the type of business skill offering for associates in a large firm.

There are many ways to deliver elements of the training set out above; it is not always necessary to use external trainers to run programmes in-house. Firms can consider offering business skill training through the following mechanisms.

Trainee	Lawyer	Associate	Senior associate	
Training contract skill development	Business skills training – may include: • Presentation skills • Effective networking	Business skills training – may include: • Financial training • Delegation skills	Business skills training – may include: • Leading negotiations • People management	
Department & firmwide legal skills training	Department & firmwide legal skills training	Department & firmwide legal skills training	Department & firmwide legal skills training	

Mid-career development review — *Partnership process*

Progression through career structure

(a) **Partners/senior associate**
It can be extremely productive when a respected partner or senior associate discusses tools and techniques on various topics – for example, giving presentations or negotiating – and shares specific relevant experiences. This approach has the benefit of being tailored for the firm and audience. It is important that the person delivering the session can share key messages clearly and provide examples, and is recognised for his ability in the area under discussion. There is often a misconception that such sessions need a significant amount of time (eg, a half or full day); in fact, they may be short, with additional follow-ups, if required.

(b) **Panel discussions**
Many of the topics that fall under business skills training do not have one right approach or answer. Consider business development as an example: this can vary across clients, practices and sectors, albeit with some common techniques underpinning different approaches. A panel discussion with a number of senior lawyers provides the opportunity to share and discuss multiple approaches and debate a variety of experiences. A well-moderated session, along with participation from those attending, can yield meaningful results. This approach works well for new and existing partners. An adaptation of this theme is inviting clients to talk about their experience from the other side; they are often prepared to share a breadth of valuable information.

(c) **e-learning**
The quality and accessibility of e-learning options have greatly increased in recent years. E-learning is cost effective and provides a resource that can be reviewed again – for example, ahead of an important presentation. Global firms have implemented e-learning to varying degrees: the spectrum ranges from partnerships with external providers to training on specific topics developed in-house.

(d)   ***Bar associations***
I   This is an excellent resource that can often be forgotten. Proactively using it, and reminding individuals in the firm about what is available and its value, can add to the overall development offering.

(e)   ***Experiential opportunities***
I   Formal training opportunities, in whatever format, are a small part of any integrated learning and development offering. Indeed, it is thought that individuals gain the majority of their development through experiential, on-the-job learning – hence the earlier discussion about proactive work allocation. As part of business skill development, it is important to encourage lawyers to maximise opportunities that can be all too easily passed by, such as the following.

(f)   ***Network opportunities***
I   Client, industry, sector, alumni and bar association events are a selection of opportunities that can arise in any given year. Unless the skills that are desired, discussed and read about are actively used and tested, they will not be developed.

(g)   ***Presentations***
I   Internal opportunities are excellent low-risk scenarios for individuals to build confidence, practise skills and receive feedback. Bar association opportunities, joint continuing legal education presentations and industry groups can all provide stepping stones before making presentations to clients, at seminars or at larger gatherings.

6.   **Talent retention**
Keeping high-quality talent in a firm is more challenging today, for a multitude of reasons. Career development now takes a variety of forms; it is accepted that these may include moving to another employer – for example, another law firm or client – or changing roles for a period of time, in order to build skillsets and capabilities while gaining exposure to a broader variety of work. Expectations of individuals have also changed, so it is important to place an active focus on the careers of associates. Similarly, the availability of career options and willingness of individuals to change careers are far greater. With the industry facing questions about the future of the law firm model and firms grappling with different approaches and roles, the conveyor belt of advancement is slower and more unpredictable.

Analysis of employee opinions has greatly helped efforts focused on retention. At a minimum, exit surveys provide helpful guidance; today's approach is more robust and analytical in many firms than the short confidential discussion of the past, which used to be the only source of feedback. While such discussions still have value, the ability to capture views from departing individuals against specific criteria that can be analysed and measured over time is extremely valuable to direct and guide retention programmes and further internal discussion.

A number of notable changes have been implemented in recent years, with the intent of addressing the challenges in retention.

6.1 **Development partner role**

In recognition of feedback expressed in recent years by departing lawyers, greater attention is now paid to ensuring that all associates in a firm have a partner who is responsible for their development. While the design of this role varies, it is broadly intended to capture a partner's responsibilities for managing feedback, supporting development opportunities through work allocation, providing formal training, ensuring high utilisation levels and ensuring that career goals and progression are actively managed. An annual review and formal follow-up during the course of the year also sit within the role scope.

The role does not place sole responsibility for career development in the hands of the appointed partner – there is a continued expectation of proactivity from the individual – but it does ensure that there is a dedicated point of contact for these important elements.

6.2 **Career structures**

The movement among large firms to define different level of associate roles has, in large part, been driven by a need to stem attrition rates in the productive mid-levels. Surveys revealed that this attrition was primarily rooted in a feeling that partnership was still a long way off – if achievable at all – and that there was no goal or recognition of progress beyond the 'badge' of being one more year beyond law school or qualification. Prior to becoming associates, high-achieving individuals in the legal industry have specific, achievable goals which fall within shorter time horizons – for example, a three-year degree, one-year Legal Practice Course and two-year traineeship. Upon reaching full associate status, suddenly the time horizon expands to a minimum of eight years – today, typically over 10 years – to potential partnership.

The introduction of associate levels has affected many firms in a number of ways:

- It has created a career path with shorter time horizons, which supports the sense of achievement and progression that is important for high-performing individuals in law firms.
- It enables firms to review the development of associates in a formal manner at certain gateways – for example, between associate and managing associate roles. Often a formal review and/or attendance at a development workshop (typically an offsite event aimed at benchmarking certain skills and providing feedback to the associate) is required ahead of advancement.
- Progression is now more likely to be based on the individual's development, rather than on the amount of time that has elapsed since graduating from law school or university, as has been the norm historically.
- Expectations concerning the skills required at differing levels within a firm are now clearer. These are often articulated through role descriptions and competency models that describe the skills and behaviours at each level,
- Clients can be confident that firms are taking development of their lawyers seriously and not merely charging higher rates for lawyers who have witnessed the passage of another year.

6.3 Alternative roles

A greater number of alternative roles exist in firms today to help retain talent. These include the following:

- Counsel/director roles – these are typically for specialised, subject-matter experts where a business case for partnership is not feasible or an individual does not wish to pursue promotion.
- Off-track lawyer roles – these may involve a different contribution expectation, but demand the same level of quality. Professional support lawyers may also fall under this category.
- Management roles – these offer opportunities for talented individuals to step into alternative management roles within a firm, in recognition of the need for professional leadership and management of all aspects of that firm's operation (eg, leading a knowledge management function, taking responsibility for practice management or managing large projects for a period of time).

6.4 Flexibility

In order to retain the best talent, and as part of diversity efforts, firms have recognised the importance of providing greater working flexibility. Although challenging due to client demands and the nature of the work, this is possible to achieve on both sides.

Policies and procedures around flexible working (eg, reduced hours, part-time, compressed schedules) have been scrutinised and revisited in recent years, and a change in mindset is reflected in the drive to remove negative connotations from existing terminology (eg, 'balanced hours' instead of 'reduced hours', 'flexible working' instead of 'part-time'). While this has helped to signal a change in attitude, clients are often ahead of law firms in this area and are expecting to see greater commitment to making changes.

Flexibility is also improving the ability of firms themselves to ramp up resource needs for particular pieces of work, without carrying an ongoing cost. Parts of a matter or transaction may be better handled by a flexible, 'on tap' workforce that is trained and led by a team of lawyers from the firm. This flexible resourcing approach is being developed through improved alumni programmes that enable firms to maintain contact with former employees and so-called 'on/off ramp' policies that allow those wishing to leave a firm for lifestyle reasons to remain in contact, have access to training and have their bar dues paid for by the firm.

In the wider professional services environment, many of the large accountancy firms have spearheaded programmes and initiatives around flexibility. For example, in 2013 PwC introduced 'plan2flex', which is designed to reward leaders and staff who create and deliver against flexibility plans during the busiest times of the year.

6.5 Performance management

Today's large international or global law firm is a different place from that which existed 10 years ago. The economic landscape has changed, resulting in greater pressure on firms to address inefficiencies and maintain standing. Clients are more sophisticated in how they go about procuring legal services, whether through the use of request for proposals, procurement teams, e-billing, panels or a stronger focus on rates and who is conducting the work.

In the post-Lehman landscape, the large number of forced partner departures from firms was seen by many as a watershed. The safe haven of partnership ceased to exist, affecting the mindset of many within firms, such as the recently promoted partner, the mid-career service partner or the highly productive senior partner. Partner performance management – often discussed, but never truly implemented in the way that is commonplace in the corporate world – arrived in law firms and is here to stay. This development is generally a positive one and supports the retention of talent in a number of ways:

- Firms have improved their ability to support and guide partners, in order to avoid any damaging or irrevocable effects of underperformance.
- There is greater clarity regarding the division of partnership talent (eg, between revenue producers, service partners, the next generation and transitioning partners).
- It has created a mechanism for managing transitions – whether into different internal roles, through retirement or to clients – which enables firms to create the required space for upcoming partner talent.
- It fosters stronger, more robust partnerships that are better able to adapt to the 'new normal'.

Clarity regarding talent is important at all levels within any firm. Active performance management needs to cover the full spectrum, from high-performing individuals to those who require active exit management from the business. All too often, both ends can be neglected – for different reasons – until it is too late.

For rising stars – whether junior associates, those closing in on potential partnership or partners themselves – discussions need to be held on a regular basis to identify what support, opportunities and further development are needed to maximise potential and ensure retention. Firms that have truly embraced this concept will be undertaking some or all of the following:

- using the performance review process to support the identification and management of talent;
- proactively agreeing actions for identified talent, covering:
  - experience that the individual should gain in a defined time period;
  - introduction to clients or business development opportunities;
  - assignment of a mentor; and
  - training and development opportunities; and
- scheduling regular discussion and follow-up, with summaries recorded.

Even with the changes currently underway, the law firm model is still founded on the premise that talent will leave; not everyone is going to, or indeed can, make partner. Importantly, this provides an excellent opportunity to generate new clients, through those former employees who had a positive experience with their firm and were appropriately handled during their transition to an in-house role. It is essential to provide transition approaches or programmes at more senior levels, in order to

maximise this potential opportunity. While recognising that transitions may occur for a variety of reasons, the key elements remain the same and include the following:
- early identification of a successor for client work;
- development of plans to seamlessly handle these client relationships and any ongoing work;
- provision of personalised support to the individual transitioning out of the firm;
- clarity on both sides about the parameters and what is on offer; and
- supporting frequent dialogue throughout the process.

Years of positive feelings about a firm can be undone in exceptionally short periods of time when these basic steps are not followed. The lawyer who becomes a new potential client is unlikely to feel inclined to engage the firm that just ostracised him for the last six months, damaged his confidence or did not provide even basic help. Those remaining at the firm also watch transitions keenly.

7. Conclusion

In summary, there is a great deal of change with regard to how large firms manage and develop talent. It is critical that firms respond to the needs of today and anticipate the themes of tomorrow. This chapter's discussion of programmes, initiatives and tools at global firms has highlighted a number of areas for consideration by anyone focusing on talent within a law firm:
- What are the market and client demands and direction?
- How does internal talent need to adapt and develop to address these needs?
- What needs to be implemented to support different approaches to attraction, development, retention or performance management of staff?

This chapter has aimed to share insights and spark ideas around what can be undertaken or considered in any firm. Talent needs attention. Your limited time can be most meaningfully utilised by addressing the questions posed in this chapter and implementing appropriate strategies.

Women lawyers and how to improve gender balance

Rachel Brushfield
EnergiseLegal

1. Introduction

This chapter focuses on women lawyers and how to improve gender balance in the legal profession. It explores the barriers to gender balance and the conditions that law firms need to put in place to enable change.

Gender equality needs to be an integral part of a firm's strategy, with consistent commitment to progressing women that covers the whole firm.

The downturn has hindered the progression of gender balance in law firms, making it a 'nice to have' rather than 'must have' policy. Reasons such as lack of time, money and dedicated diversity and inclusion (D&I) roles are often given for lack of progress.

On the other hand, a recent and genuine concern about the lack of women in law firm partnerships has emerged, and some leading firms are now taking this issue seriously. Interesting changes are thus likely in the coming years.

Recruitment, retention, development and promotion of female partners in law firms are key strategic drivers for future success. Diversity now matters to the corporations that law firms serve. In-house counsel look at a law firm's commitment to diversity when selecting a law firm. Clients are seeking deeper insights and creative solutions – diverse thinking can achieve these. A law firm's partnership needs to reflect the target audience of its clients. Clients want diverse people on their pitch panels and firms that reflect their culture.

Influencing gender balance for sustained change in law firms requires cultural change, flexible working policies and changes beyond the direct influence of the gender balance issue.

Recent research by McKinsey into female talent in law firms and professional services shows that women are as ambitious as men to achieve partnership and see work as the number one priority; the stumbling block is their willingness to do what it takes to achieve this – that is, sacrificing work-life balance, being political and so on.

2. The business imperative of law firm gender balance

Diversity in a law firm is a business imperative and helps to create a competitive advantage. Gender balance is ideal, but what law firms and their clients want is the best talent mix for the firm to achieve its goals and provide an exemplary service.

Research by McKinsey[1] shows that women exhibit five leadership behaviours

---

1 *"Women matter: Gender diversity, a corporate performance driver"*, McKinsey & Company, 2007.

('people development', 'expectation and rewards','role model', 'inspiration' and 'participative decision making') more than men; these behaviours are factors which correlate with superior corporate performance and the number of women in senior management positions. The gap increases significantly once a certain critical mass is attained – that is, when at least three out of 10 board members are women.

Mary Gallagher, the diversity and talent manager at Addleshaw Goddard, says: "A more diverse firm is a stronger business and reflects what our clients want. At Addleshaw Goddard, we are working hard, through a combination of formal programmes and informal support, to inspire women to reach the top and to give them the skills and experience they need to operate at the highest level."

Gender balance provides many benefits to the firm:
- It facilitates improved decision making and different perspectives on a problem;
- It leads to increased productivity and fulfilment, with lawyers playing to their strengths;
- It promotes a more harmonious culture – time is spent on pulling together and being proactive, rather than on politics and factions;
- It strengthens the employer's brand, attracting the best talent to the firm and giving a local and global competitive advantage; and
- It reflects the client target audience – the firm represents the marketplace, from the partnership to the employees.

2.1 Competencies and qualities for career success as a lawyer

Gender balance in the legal profession needs to be looked at within the context of the factors that create career success for lawyers. These are:
- commercial awareness;
- clear specialism in type of law and market;
- strong written and verbal skills;
- adaptability;
- good people skills;
- visibility (eg, via writing articles or doing speeches);
- client generation;
- professionalism;
- self-awareness
- diplomacy and courage in tackling difficult issues;
- political savvy, with an understanding of and ability to work within a power structure;
- understanding the firm's authority structure and operating rules;
- networking for good referral sources;
- making tough decisions for the good of the firm;
- fitting the firm culture;
- influencing and aligning with the most influential members of the firm;
- not being too emotional at work;
- choosing battles;
- keeping private life private; and
- treating others with respect.

From the point of view of the decision makers – primarily senior male partners – career success factors for women are:
- developing legal skills by working on challenging cases and receiving feedback and mentoring;
- satisfying clients' needs in a cost-effective way;
- being willing and able to develop networks and bring in business; and
- having one or more dedicated mentors.

2.2 Current gender balance in law firms

Gender balance in law firms needs to be examined against the backdrop of society as a whole. Men hold nearly 85% of corporate board and executive committee seats in the United States. They account for 90% of the world's billionaires, control most of the world's governments and continue to out-earn women with similar skills and education.[2]

Women make up 46% of the workforce,[3] but represent only 33% of all managers[4] and 9.6% of managers in FTSE250 companies.[5] In the United Kingdom, female partners remain a minority in top law firms, with 23.5% of all partners and 9.4% of all equity partners across the largest 100 UK law firms (by revenue) being female. Sixty six percent of trainees are women, so the drop in numbers is significant.[6]

In a survey of the 50 best law firms for women in the United States:
- 10% of chairpersons were women;
- 12% had female managing partners;
- 19% of equity partners were women;
- 28% of non-equity partners were women; and
- 41% of of-counsel were women.[7]

Across the best 50 law firms for women, certain key factors contribute to the successful promotion of female talent:
- One hundred percent have reduced hour policies;
- Forty four percent have written full-time flex policies;
- Seventy eight percent offer full-time telecommuting;
- Ninety four percent allow reduced-hour lawyers to be eligible for equity partnership; and
- Seventy eight percent provide back-up childcare at a facility.[8]

2.3 Barriers to gender balance

A survey by the World Economic Forum found that the most cited barriers to women's rise to leadership were "general norms and practices" and a "masculine/patriarchal corporate culture".[9]

---

2 Research by McKinsey quoted in "The silent sex" by Alison Beard, *Harvard Business Review*, March 2013.
3 Labour market statistics, November 2012, Office for National Statistics.
4 Annual survey of hours and earnings 2012, Office for National Statistics.
5 Professional Boards Forum, Boardwatch.
6 *The Lawyer* magazine, 2012.
7 NAFE and Flex-Time lawyers, *Executive summary Best law firms for women*, 2011.
8 Catalyst research, Jeanine and Nancy Carter, *Impressions of men and women as leaders*, 2008.
9 "The Corporate Gender Gap Report", World Economic Forum, 2010.

A survey by McKinsey showed that the "double burden" of work and domestic responsibilities was one of the biggest barriers to increased diversity in senior management,[10] with the "anytime anywhere" model of management an additional obstacle.

The existing barriers that hinder gender balance in law firms are multi-faceted and include:
- the law firm model;
- the fee-earning primary focus, which plays to the natural competitive predisposition of men more than women;
- the long-hours culture; and
- the lack of control that lawyers have over their hours, which does not fit with having a family and enjoying a healthy work-life balance.

Gender expert Tom Schuller developed 'The Paula Principle',[11] which states that most women work below their level of competence – that is, they are underpaid and underpromoted. Five factors were cited: discrimination, cost of childcare, lack of confidence, lack of connections in high places, and women actively choosing not to go for promotion in favour of less stress and more family time or better work-life balance.

The benefits that gender balance brings need to be communicated to gain the buy-in of key stakeholders. Gender balance needs to be looked at in the context of an overall integrated talent management strategy, which this book explores elsewhere.

Few firms look at talent management in an integrated way. This is surprising when talent is the only true source of a law firm's competitive advantage. Discussing issues and options around gender balance with employees is important to secure buy-in for any changes in policy and to overcome resistance.

Law firms tend to look within the legal profession or to other professional services firms and rarely look outside. The London Olympics are a useful reference point to gain learnings about the management of gender balance and D&I in the spotlight of the world's media. What can law firms learn from the London Olympics and how they made D&I a success before a global audience?[12]

D&I success at the Olympics was created by:
- thorough understanding of D&I in the context of the organisation's purpose and objectives;
- strong and thoughtful leadership;
- effective delivery with limited resources, people and money;
- observance of strict deadlines as a catalyst for embedding change;
- a compelling vision supported by simple, clear messaging, which ensured that the audience engaged with and committed to it;
- D&I in combination, not isolation;

---

10   "Women Matter", McKinsey, 2010.
11   "The Paula Principle", Tom Schuller, www.paulaprinciple.com/.
12   "Game on! How to keep diversity progress on track", Chartered Institute of Personnel Development, *A guide for employers*, November 2012.

- research, to gain an understanding of how things look through different people's eyes; and
- belief in individualism and the avoidance of stereotypes.

2.4 Hours, not output

Fee-earning capability has been the number one criterion for achieving partnership. Non-fee-earning contributions to the firm and its clients are more important now than in the past: clients are working with fewer law firms, so close client relationships are vital for a firm's success. After a period of unprecedented growth, firms have experienced a challenging time through the downturn. Employees are in need of motivation and energising, especially at associate level, where they are 'caught in the middle' – expensive to use for fee-conscious partners on client projects and less likely to achieve promotion to partner, due to fewer partner places.

Lawyers are measured on fee-earning hours generated, not on output. Historically, law firms have charged by the hour, but rankings based on chargeable hours – with targets such as 1,200 to 1,500 hours per annum – put women with children at a disadvantage, as they tend to do the lion's share of household management and childcare.

Client pressure for fixed fees is changing the commercial landscape, and efficiency and output are becoming more important. This shift may help to address gender balance – for example, working mothers who work part time in order to spend more time with their families are acknowledged to be efficient and productive during their shorter work hours, because they have to be.

2.5 Gender differences

While in the past law firms have been transactional and short term in their thinking, the focus is now shifting towards sustaining longer-term relationships and cross-selling between practice groups.

Research shows that women are different from men on a number of measures. These differences affect gender balance in law firms. The law firm model can be stressful, with tight deadlines, increased competition and pressure from the billable hour model, and are political environments where self-promotion is vital to be visible. Lawyers can be critical, rather than skilled at giving acknowledgement, and women may avoid rejection by not putting themselves forward for promotion, thus affecting gender balance.

Research into gender differences shows that, compared to men, women:
- feel uncomfortable promoting themselves and more comfortable looking after others;
- are more modest;
- are more open to feedback; and
- are more conscientious and perfectionist.

A survey of managers showed that women have lower levels of confidence and lower expectations than men. Twenty three percent of women compared with 35% of men fully expected or hoped to take a management or leadership role when they started work. Younger women report higher expectations than older women.[13]

Women are less likely to apply for a job unless they meet all of the requirements, whereas men will apply if they meet most of the requirements. Equally qualified women are less likely to apply for promotions than men.[14]

Providing training about gender differences increases awareness and aids the communication, motivation, deployment and engagement of talent. As D&I expert Dr Ian Dodds notes: "Lawyering is transactional in nature – task focused – and research shows that men tend to be more transactional and women relational and transformational. The smart firm will use these gender differences to their competitive advantage."[15]

Women are affected by gender stereotypes and expected to have communal qualities – to be givers and sharers and to pursue the common good.

Research shows that success and likeability are positively correlated for men and negatively correlated for women. As women get more successful, they are liked less. Businesses and firms want to promote people who are both competent and liked.

Gender stereotyping can inform expectations of how men and women 'should' behave. For example, it may be acceptable for a man to be assertive and direct, but if a woman communicates in this way, she is seen to be aggressive. All these attitudes affect gender balance.

These gender differences provide useful assets for law firms to leverage for the benefit of clients, business development and the firm itself, especially in a more competitive marketplace:

- building relationships;
- empathy to deal with challenging situations;
- humility, when dealing with successful rainmakers 'ruffling feathers';
- candour and patience;
- collaboration to maximise cross-referral;
- practicality;
- desire to help others, focusing on client needs and customer relationship management (CRM);
- awareness of and sensitivity about feelings, for pay and promotion discussions;
- relationship maintenance – useful in CRM;
- bridge-building to ensure that conflicts that might inhibit productive working are resolved;
- multi-tasking;
- 'soft' selling when promoting the firm to female decision makers at clients; and
- connecting networks, internally and externally, and asking clients for introductions to increase repeat business.

---

13   "Ambition and gender at work", Institute of Leadership and management, 2011.
14   "A business case for women", *McKinsey Quarterly*, McKinsey, 2008.
15   "Transforming leaders – women and the vision thing", Herminia Ibarra and Otilia Obodaru, *Harvard Business Review*, January 2009.

3. Culture

The culture of a law firm has a big impact on gender balance. Male-dominated partnerships affect the culture and are self-perpetuating. Therefore, it is wise to take a proactive approach to accelerate culture change – for example, by having targets to increase the number of female partners.

The acceptance of difference, the absence of presenteism and the acknowledgement of talent can help women to thrive. Creating a policy of open expression, where inappropriate comments are addressed to educate and focus attention on unconscious bias, also helps to accelerate change.

Men can worry about what to talk to women about and, being risk averse, lawyers especially have a fear of causing offence, not being politically correct or mishandling issues. This can prevent them from having career or performance management conversations with female associates at an early point, which could make all the difference to their development and career success.

Diversity initiatives will promote gender balance; inclusive excellence will embed it. A culture that appreciates the uniqueness of all colleagues will attract and keep the best legal talent. Individual differences are business assets. Firms that support individuals to fully utilise their skills and experience will gain collective synergy.

Ensuring that more women reach partnership level may further influence culture.

3.1 Leadership support and buy-in

Strong inclusive leadership of law firms and practice groups is a prerequisite to enable gender balance, while leadership pledges and diversity boards help to illustrate its importance.

The managing partner and senior partner of a firm must be seen to 'walk the talk' in how they speak and act, and must be positive inclusive role models. Partners need to be seen to be active and open about D&I and the need for change. Safe and confidential forums should be provided to allow people to express their views and concerns, free of judgement or fear. This helps to encourage positive mindsets and curiosity about D&I, as well as affording opportunities for staff members to acknowledge their own insights regarding unfair behaviours, attitudes or practices. Inclusive behaviours need to be rewarded (positive reinforcement). Leaders must be equipped to notice passive or active resistance to change and to speak up.

Confronting gender imbalance can be sensitive, so subtle methods of engagement – for example, using video, stories, enactments using actors and personal accounts that evoke emotions – are powerful in their impact.

Collectively, individual practice groups and departments need to support gender balance so that deep systemic change occurs. This is a change in mindset, as well as a change in numbers.

'What gets measured gets done', so making leaders and practice group heads responsible and accountable for improving gender balance is essential. Including measures in annual performance appraisals and bonus allocations ensures that the topic gets attention – this is the language of success.

Giving women positions of responsibility to promote their influence and

visibility – for example, as committee heads – also creates positive role models.
Partners can be engaged in gender balance by:
- understanding their concerns and beliefs about D&I;
- relating gender balance to them in a personal way (eg, an ambitious daughter overlooked for partnership);
- linking what is needed with their own goals; and
- sharing examples of how gender balance has been successful and beneficial elsewhere in the firm and outside.

3.2 Linear career paths

Many women choose to move in-house, as this gives them more flexibility with less pressure. Leaving the profession altogether is another option that is becoming increasingly popular, with many women lawyers choosing to become self-employed, so that they have control over their hours.

Non-fee-earning or less pressured roles, such as that of professional support lawyer, offer women more flexibility to combine work and a family, but as they are not fee-earning, they do not carry the same status or perceptions of success as partnership.

3.3 Flexible working

Certain types of law (eg, commercial and corporate law, where deal deadlines are tight) are demanding, and flexible work can be difficult to accommodate.

Charging by the hour and '24/7 availability' to service clients have created an environment of long hours that is not conducive to working mothers or those seeking a healthy work-life balance.

Working from home is still not seen as 'the norm', except by a few firms. Presenteism prevails, magnified by fear of job loss in challenging and uncertain economic times. In some law firms, lawyers who go part time get 60% of the pay for 80% of the hours, which can be demotivating. Part-time working is often not seen to be compatible with management responsibility. Assuming that lawyers who work part time are less dedicated to their work than those who work full time is a form of unconscious bias.

Research by Joseph Vandello, Vanessa Hettinger, Jennifer Bosson and Jasmine Siddiqi found that when both male and female colleagues sought flexible schedules, people tended to evaluate them more negatively and recommend them for smaller salary raises than when they worked a regular schedule.

In research by The Law Society, 52% of women lawyers felt that to get ahead at their firms, they were expected to work long hours and to take work home in the evenings or at weekends.

One in two believed that negative career consequences were associated with work-family/life policies, and that lawyers who made use of such policies were viewed as 'less serious' about their careers.

Associates and senior associates in particular recorded the greatest degree of interference between their work and family or personal lives.

Women who worked from home reported:

- higher levels of job satisfaction;
- higher levels of organisational support and commitment; and
- a lower propensity to quit their organisations.

Dissatisfaction is statistically significant where women:
- work full time;
- work in City law firms or law firms serving City clients;
- work to a billable-hour model;
- perceive that they have little control over scheduling their working hours; and
- experience higher working pressure.[16]

The availability of flexible working has a big influence on whether mothers return to their employer after maternity.[17]

One survey found that 52% of employers who had not recruited quality part-time employees had an unofficial preference against part-time work, and 9% had an official company policy against it.[18]

Perception is reality, and when companies and firms feel under pressure, a common misconception is that working mothers will be less reliable as they will need to take time off to look after ill children or because of school responsibilities.

Opting out of the profession altogether, becoming self-employed, taking a position as a contract or locum lawyer or joining a more flexible, lower-pressure high-street practice are the alternatives for many, causing a drain of female talent and inhibiting gender balance in big law firms.

The willingness of law firms to change their attitudes to part-time work and commitments will have a significant impact for women. Career breaks, sabbaticals, four-day weeks and longer periods of unpaid leave over school holidays will help, as well as saving firms money in quieter times, such as August.

3.4 Unconscious bias

Bias is normal – it is human nature to like people who are like ourselves and choose to spend more time with them. Helping people to recognise that they have bias helps them to develop inclusive behaviours that become second nature over time.

Bias was originally thought to be conscious – that is, the person is aware of it. It is now acknowledged to occur at an unconscious or 'hidden' level. The topic of bias needs to be introduced sensitively – getting people to notice, admit, understand and accept bias is not always a comfortable process. Lawyers can be very aware of how they come across with their peers, so it is important to create the right environment for team discussion and reflection about bias.

---

16 "An examination of women solicitors' careers, work life balance and use of flexible work arrangements", Professor Janet Walsh, Department of Management, Kings College, University of London, United Kingdom, 2009.
17 "Women's choices in the labour market", Metcalf & Rolfe, National Institute of Economic and Social Research, 2010.
18 "Building a sustainable quality part time recruitment market", Stewart *et al*, Joseph Rowntree Foundation, 2012.

Making both men and women aware of bias is an inclusive approach, which is vital to ensure that the conditions in a law firm are fair and to help gender balance prosper.

In some cases when discussing the D&I agenda, men have felt that they are being accused of doing something 'wrong', that bias is their fault – when actually it is normal. This is an important distinction to share in order for unconscious bias training to be received positively and to enable cultural change.

Unconscious bias training promotes gender balance because it helps to create awareness of the attitudes, beliefs and behaviours that arise as a result – for example, preferring to make eye contact with male colleagues in a meeting or avoiding having a female mentee in case colleagues think that this may lead to an affair, which might damage reputation. Analysing and understanding each bias helps to facilitate change; often such bias comes from parents or teachers. Combining bias-awareness training with performance management increases the likelihood of embedded change. Unconscious bias training also needs to include family responsibilities discrimination.

Specific types of unconscious bias exist – for example, the 'maternal wall bias' regarding what mothers should do and be. This leads to comments such as, "Don't you feel bad leaving the children at home?" or "I couldn't focus on my work if I had a sick child at home."[19] Research by Shelley Correll, Stephen Bernard and In Paik shows that women with children are 79% less likely to be hired, half as likely to be promoted, paid an average $11,000 less in salary and held to higher performance and punctuality standards than childless women.

Providing unconscious bias and gender differences training to those responsible for recruitment, selection and promotion is essential to tackle bias systemically.

Examining the issue of unconscious bias involves reflection, compassion, respect, communication, empathy and awareness. As is the case with employee engagement surveys, taking no action is not an option.

3.5 **Readiness for partnership versus motherhood**

The number of women at partner level is significantly lower than the number of female trainees. The clash between women's desire to have children and the need to gain sufficient experience to be ready for partnership is a major causal factor.

Promotion criteria in the legal profession are shifting away from time served in favour of performance and potential. This change is likely to help to correct the gender imbalance in the profession, especially if talented females can achieve partnership before having children and are thus in a better negotiating position when they return.

Historically, one of the factors affecting gender imbalance at partner level has been the direct clash between the desire of women to have children and the readiness of lawyers at seven to eight years' post-qualification experience (PQE), with enough knowledge and reputation to become a partner. Many women lawyers have chosen not to have children, seeing that they cannot 'have it all'. Talent

---

19   Joan C Williams and Amy JC Cuddy, *Harvard Business Review*, March 2013.

management programmes that focus on talent, not PQE, will help to increase the number of female partners.

The common unspoken attitude to women by male partners needs to be overcome: "If I am looking at a woman in her late 20s, maybe early 30s, I know she is probably going to leave and have children so I don't think that I will promote her."

Law firms are cost conscious and maternity leave incurs costs which directly impact on the equity that partners receive. With clients pressing firms for better value in the current market, this issue is likely to be magnified.

4. Conditions to enable gender balance

Any changes to enable gender balance must be shown to provide added value for the firm and to align with its vision, mission and objectives. D&I, including gender balance, needs to be positioned as a business focus – not just a HR issue – in order to gain respect, support and buy-in. Collaborative working and discussion of issues across practice groups, non-fee earning departments and D&I champions and ambassadors will help to promote change.

Conditions that support the success of women to partnership levels are:
- a spouse or life partner with a flexible schedule or a trusted childcare provider;
- inspirational female role models in more senior positions; and
- a team atmosphere with flexible schedules.

Gender balance can be improved by:
- creating consistent key messages for internal and external communications;
- linking changes to the firm's values and making expected behaviours explicit;
- highlighting the business case for gender balance;
- linking D&I objectives with firm and practice-group objectives;
- putting D&I on the agenda of every project so that it is the norm rather than an 'add-on';
- weaving D&I into projects so that it is part of the fabric and standard practice of the firm; and
- demonstrating the value and return on investment (ROI) that a focus on gender balance brings, including positive press coverage, awards, client wins and positive client satisfaction surveys.

5. Creating a foundation for improving gender balance

Benchmarking and data are important to track and measure success and help to maximise ROI.

Identification of a firm's unique issues is the best starting point to ensure that resources are prioritised appropriately. Feedback from research with talented female associates about the actions that will encourage their retention and success will help to shape firm policies, programmes and networks.

Conducting confidential research through an external provider to elicit honest views about gender and D&I issues can reveal insights, ideas and objections to be overcome, so that a bespoke plan can be created.

Assessing a firm's programmes and policies against those of other law firms and industries enables benchmarking and supports the development of a roadmap, with milestones for change. Such data is useful to overcome resistance and inertia, and helps to justify the investment of time and resources in promoting change.

A D&I audit to assess the diversity, history and culture of the firm can involve interviews, focus groups, questionnaires and policy and complaint reviews, as well as consultation with employees who have complained of bias, in order to make them ambassadors for change.

Conditions to overcome unconscious bias can be created by taking the following measures:
- introducing the topic of bias in a positive way that applies to everyone;
- making addressing unconscious bias a priority for the firm;
- conducting anonymous surveys with current and former employees using an external confidential provider;
- providing unconscious-bias training specific to the issues of the firm;
- creating positive projects for women and men to show their uniqueness and difference in a positive light;
- conducting an organisational D&I audit to examine what employees believe, think and observe regarding possible bias;
- rewarding employees who address bias;
- creating awareness of positive initiatives instigated by employees internally or externally;
- providing a confidential and anonymous helpline for people to share experiences of bias in confidence; and
- auditing candidates who are selected for interview to identify any bias in the recruitment process.

5.1 Targets and quotas

Utilising targets to improve gender balance can be a double-edged sword. On the one hand, they provide a measurable goal to prioritise change; on the other, they can send out messages of unfair selection and development.

A higher proportion of female partners shifts the balance of power, culture and influence at the crucial decision-making level, creating a tipping point for change. Women want to be selected on merit; to select because of gender could delegitimise their hard work, as well as being illegal under employment law.

A law firm's practice groups are naturally competitive, so publishing D&I data and tracking change for each group can be a healthy and unthreatening way to change gender balance, once this is supported by policies and governance. The Law Society in the United Kingdom, for example, is promoting voluntary diversity targets, rather than quotas. Lucy Scott-Moncrieff, president of The Law Society, states: "It's clear that meritocracy isn't working. In many firms, women are still an oddity in boardrooms. Men hold up to 73% of partner-level positions in the UK. Not only are women losing out on career opportunities, firms are losing out on talent. Targets can help change this. Unlike quotas, which rather blindly commit firms to allocating senior positions, targets can help change the corporate culture that is often at fault, not just structures. It's time for firms to 'man up' and invest in women."

Some law firms are introducing targets for the percentage of female partners – for example, Eversheds has a target of 25% by 2016, while Hogan Lovells has set a 10-year target, aiming for 25% by 2017.

5.2 Law firm policies

The lack of transparency in some procedures and practices – for example, how lawyers are selected for promotion – is increasingly coming under the spotlight. Allocation of work is based on relationships – this can be unfair, as it fosters the careers of some lawyers while hindering the careers of others. Informal mentoring has a big impact on career success and powerful senior figures – typically, senior white men – tend to foster the careers of younger white men because of unconscious bias. Networking outside the firm can be a challenge for working mothers, due to childcare issues.[20]

Bias needs to be examined in all policies and processes, including recruitment, appraisals and selection for partnership.

Michael Coles, head of HR for DLA Piper, says: "Creating a gender-balanced workplace, where women and men advance side by side, will I believe require deep-seated changes across both the structure and management of commercial law firms. Becoming a law firm that truly attracts, and more importantly actually retains women will therefore require fundamental changes to the systems that impact women's client and leadership opportunities and their compensation. Those systems must therefore be based upon transparent processes, fair and objective criteria and consistent application. Making these changes should be a strategic priority for any firm that hopes to retain and advance talented women within their workforce."

Law firms need to ensure that:
- gender-neutral selection processes are based on merit;
- assignments are given based on merit, not gender;
- benefits and rewards are gender neutral; and
- robust development and feedback processes exist, with clear milestones and explicit and transparent criteria about what needs to be done to make partner.

5.3 Governance

Governance around D&I and gender balance is more important and effective than women's programmes, networks and unconscious bias training.

Including D&I as one of the firm's values lends it gravitas and weight, while involving the senior partner and managing partner in the D&I committee sends out messages about its importance and ensures that a senior and respected partner will champion it. Lawyers and support staff across all international offices should have access to the D&I committee at both executive and management levels, while D&I data should be consistently measured across practice groups.

---

20 "Diversity in the legal profession in England and Wales: A qualitative study of barriers and individual choices", funded by the Legal Services Board, University of Westminster.

5.4 Rewards and compensation

D&I, like any strategic imperative, needs to be aligned with compensation and have meaningful financial incentives to ensure that partners achieve diversity goals.

The pay gap between men and women is about 20%; according to the Chartered Management Institute, this gap is narrowing, but will take nearly 100 years to close.

5.5 Positive female role models

Role models play an important part in encouraging women in the legal profession. A shortage of senior women lawyers to mentor and inspire the next generation is a consequence of the profession's stage of development.

Female partners at the top of the profession are pioneers and some have adopted 'male behaviours' to get there, which is offputting to some of the next female generation on the way through.

Sourcing successful women from associated professions, such as accountancy, for mentoring programmes in the legal profession helps to accelerate change.

Encouraging successful female partners to share their own personal life and career journeys can be a useful way to inspire, motivate and support younger female legal talent.

5.6 Initiatives to support gender balance

Research shows that organisational change is more effective at supporting gender balance than programmes, women's networks and mentoring. Sponsorship is a key factor in career success and selection for partnership or increased visibility in the firm.

The Glass Ceiling Commission,[21] set up in 1991, has outlined the key characteristics of programmes that remove the glass ceiling. They should:

- have the support of the leader;
- form part of the strategic plan;
- be specific to the firm;
- be inclusive;
- address preconceptions and stereotypes;
- emphasise and require accountability at all levels;
- track progress; and
- adopt a comprehensive, not piecemeal, approach.

Law firms need to take a long-term view and begin grooming women at the beginning of their careers.

Mindset and attitude are also important success factors, and programmes and networks for women can help these to be created and sustained.

The following success factors were shared by female lawyers who had made it to partnership:

- believing in being successful;
- having clear goals;

---

21 National Glass Ceiling Commission, http://nationalglassceilingcommission.org/?page_id=28.

- being willing to make sacrifices;
- taking time to develop skills and learn;
- making time to network;
- being active in the community and bar associations;
- staying optimistic;
- developing resilience;
- having self-belief and confidence;
- showing commitment to a career;
- showing commitment to finding solutions to balance work and personal life;
- taking responsibility for their career; and
- identifying and overcoming fears.

Individual coaching helps women to express their fears and build their confidence in a safe, supportive and confidential space.

Many law firms provide programmes specifically to support the advancement of women, including mentoring, sponsorship and support networks. External industry bodies also exist – for example, the Law Society's Women's Division.

Some women are nervous about being seen to need support and worried about being perceived as weak, but programmes for women do play a useful role in improving the likelihood of gender balance occurring and supporting women in a profession where they are currently outnumbered.

A comprehensive programme with group and individual support specifically for senior female associates supports their professional development, confidence, competence and engagement with the firm, which in turn affects retention and promotion. The cost of programmes in terms of time and money is minor compared with the cost of female talent drain and associated reputational costs.

5.7 Sponsorship

Sponsorship is when a more senior member of staff champions a less experienced colleague – for example, by discussing cases and big clients with them and promoting their qualities to other partners.

The majority of high-performing women do not have a sponsor or, if they do, this relationship fails to work effectively. Research by a New York-based taskforce for talent innovation[22] showed that sponsorship conferred a statistical benefit of up to 30%, with more stretch assignments, promotions and pay rises.

The strong merit-based tradition of the legal profession can make introducing formal sponsorship programmes difficult. These should be designed carefully and tailored to each firm's culture.

5.8 Mentoring

Formal mentoring programmes create a structure to provide consistency of mentoring to counter any unconscious bias and give a fair chance to all. They also improve the quality of mentoring.

---

22   Center for talent innovation – sponsorship, www.worklifepolicy.org/index.php/pageID/22.

Forming mentoring circles is a time-effective approach, with mentees benefiting from shared experiences and a diverse group, and enhanced commitment from mentors. These also can create future networks to facilitate cross-referral.

5.9 **Women's networks**

A cross-firm external network can provide stronger support and avoid the confidentiality issues that arise in an internal firm network, as well as avoiding the exclusion of men or cynicism. Ernst & Young, for example, is proactive in its stance towards gender balance, with an active women's network.

Women's networks need to have a clear purpose and focus to be effective – for example:
- learn more about employees and clients;
- increase the number of women at partnership level;
- raise awareness of the challenges that women face; and
- help supervising partners to understand and manage and motivate women better.

Networks for women can also provide insights to help drive business development for the firm and improve talent attraction and retention, both of which can engage male decision makers in investing time and money in them. It is important to adopt an inclusive approach to women's networks, inviting men as 'friends' and ensuring that they get the same benefits as women. Coles comments: "The DLA Piper Women's Network provides women with a platform where they can network together and with clients externally; find mentoring support to achieve their personal objectives; help to develop the careers of their contemporaries or more junior employees and socialise and attend targeted events."

Factors that make a successful network are:
- clarity of purpose and structure;
- a strong business case which seeks benefits for the firm as well as its members;
- good leadership, clearly defined roles, visible champions and passion;
- courage and a willingness to tackle difficult issues and speak the truth; and
- a collaborative, outward-looking and inclusive approach.

5.10 **Profile and communication of D&I initiatives**

D&I – including gender balance – needs to be communicated, internally and externally. Rotating high-performing lawyers into diversity roles helps to raise the profile of D&I, while recruiting a full-time diversity and inclusion expert demonstrates the firm's commitment to it.

The communication strategy needs to be integrated and should include:
- communication of the diversity committee's purpose and activities to all employees;
- annual publication of diversity goals and achievements in the press and on the firm's website;
- hosting of joint D&I events with clients;
- dissemination of the firm's strategic diversity statement and plan via email or

- the firm's intranet;
- quarterly meetings to discuss progress, successes and concerns;
- inclusion of D&I on firm retreats with partners;
- inclusion of D&I on all committee agendas; and
- accessibility of information on D&I and unconscious bias, available to all on the intranet.

5.11 Technology as an enabler

Technological advances are creating exponential change in the world of work as well as across the legal profession. Cloud technology, information portals (eg, to access previous cases) and knowledge sharing facilitate new ways of working. Tablets, 24-hour access and social media all support working in different and more flexible ways that give people more choice regarding when and how they work. The world of work is gradually shifting and modernising – all of which helps to support working mothers especially to stay in the profession, contribute and succeed, without compromising work-life balance.

6. Conclusion

Progressing D&I and improving gender balance are ongoing processes, and the number of female partners in law firms is representative of business and society as a whole. Change will not happen overnight; but just as law firms need to think long term as well as short term, so small steps forward to support gender balance will lead to bigger changes in future and will attract both sought-after clients and the cream of talent.

The market for law firms is increasingly global and can be developed only through exposure to widely diverse people, cultures, ideas and viewpoints. Firms that put gender balance and genuine diversity and inclusion at the heart of their DNA will reap the rewards, building a healthy employer brand and attracting the best talent and clients for sustainable business success globally. Ultimately, it is likely to be client pressure that creates the impetus for change and a healthier gender balance in law firm partnerships.

Effective teamwork and collaboration

Heidi K Gardner
Harvard Business School

1. Introduction

The greatest asset in any knowledge-based organisation, such as a professional service firm (PSF), is the expertise of its professionals. In recent decades, most top-tier PSFs have focused on expertise specialisation, creating narrowly defined practice areas and rewarding professionals for developing reputations in ever more precise niches. The collective expertise in such firms has thus become distributed across people, places and practice groups.

Increasingly, however, the growing complexity and integrative nature of client issues demand that professionals collaborate with others throughout the firm (and often around the world) who have the complementary specialist expertise necessary to develop and serve clients. Further, the continuing globalisation of business means that the clients of PSFs are demanding seamless, multinational service. Counsel must frequently collaborate across geographic and cultural boundaries with far-off partners to ensure that work is aligned with the client's global strategy and accounts for country-specific issues. For example, a patent dispute in China might require lawyers in the United Kingdom to collaborate with litigators in Shanghai who not only are highly qualified in subject-matter competence, but also have a deep understanding of the language, culture and political ramifications of identifying, maintaining and protecting trademarks and overall brand strategy in the region.

Many PSFs have therefore concluded that to gain or even maintain competitive advantage, accumulating star talent is no longer enough. Rather, in order to maximise the value and output of such individuals, their diverse and distributed knowledge must be integrated. By bringing together professionals with different bases of expertise, a collaborative approach to serving clients has the potential to develop more innovative outcomes that are customised to the specific needs of the client, thereby increasing satisfaction and repeat business. Moreover, as individuals in a firm bring together their distinct expertise and knowledge to form innovative solutions, they may create entirely new types of service that can attract new clients.

Some of the very drivers that are forcing firms towards a more collaborative client-service approach, however, are the same factors that make collaboration increasingly difficult. Collaboration involves knowledge and expertise sharing, introducing colleagues to one's own clients, and working across structural and interpersonal barriers to pitch work and serve clients. Such collaboration requires trust – both a deep respect for a colleague's competence ("I trust you not to make a blunder") and a belief in his integrity ("I trust you won't undermine my relationship with my client"). My research shows that when people face high performance pressure – the sort of high-stakes client situation where it is most vital to access and use the firm's best experts – collaboration becomes harder because professionals tend to become risk averse and may attempt to exert control by limiting access to their client. Ironically, collaboration suffers just when it should be most beneficial. Section 2 of this chapter explores the challenges of collaboration in today's legal environment.

By developing and leveraging a well-honed collaborative capability, PSFs can work efficiently and effectively across knowledge gaps, enabling them to perform the complex, multidisciplinary work that their clients increasingly demand. My research demonstrates how collaboration benefits not only the firm, but also the individual lawyers who work jointly with other partners to serve and develop clients. Section 3 of this chapter focuses on the outcomes of collaboration.

If the benefits of collaboration make it worthwhile to invest in overcoming the challenges, the question becomes, "How do we achieve greater collaboration?" My research has investigated not only best practices of firms with a long-standing tradition of collaboration, but also other firms' transitions from highly individualistic to more collaborative working. Section 4 of this chapter provides specific steps that law firms, their formal leaders and individual lawyers can take to lay foundations for enhanced collaboration.

2. Challenges to collaboration

2.1 'Collaboration' defined

Collaboration occurs when a group of knowledge workers integrate their individual expertise in order to deliver high-quality outcomes on complex issues, typically extending over time and across discrete projects as they identify new approaches and initiate further engagements. In addition to offering up their expertise, these professionals must help, advise, stimulate and counterbalance each other. In this way, 'collaboration' is different from mere 'assembly' (where experts simply contribute 'their piece' and someone pulls inputs together) or purely sequential, interdependent work (where a lawyer builds on others' prior work and hands his work over to the next partner). Although it may not involve face-to-face working, collaboration does require repeated or ongoing interactions, to allow the generative recombination of different people's information, perspectives and expertise. The outcome of collaboration is more than simply the sum of participating partners' unique knowledge.

Collaboration is often confused with cross-selling, but they are different. Pure cross-selling occurs when partner A introduces partner B to his own client, so that B can provide additional services. Although A may provide some level of oversight to ensure that his client is satisfied with B's work, he is unlikely to get deeply involved in the content. In contrast, collaboration involves specialists working substantively together to deliver a project, rather than experts working separately in their disciplinary silos.

Lawyers who spend much of their lives delivering client work through matter or

deal teams might wonder what the fuss about collaboration is all about. This section explores four major challenges to effective collaboration in PSFs:
- establishing trust;
- managing dynamic collaborative arrangements;
- navigating the star-based system typical to many PSFs; and
- dealing with performance pressure.

2.2 Establishing trust

We have all heard horror stories about a decades-long client relationship jeopardised by one mistake. The risks of involving a new partner with one's own client are real, and taking the leap of faith to involve others requires two forms of trust: relational and competence trust. 'Relational trust' is the willingness to make oneself vulnerable to another person, such as the partner with whom one begins a new collaboration. It arises from the emotional bonds that connect co-workers and develops through shared experiences, reciprocal disclosure and demonstrations that individuals will not take advantage of each other. This trust gives professionals confidence that they can introduce colleagues into their most valued client relationships without concern that the collaborator will introduce friction, 'steal' their client or undermine the client relationship in some way.

'Competence-based trust' is the belief that another individual is competent, reliable, professional, well prepared and dedicated to his work. When professionals develop mutual competence trust, they are more likely to rely on and use each other's knowledge. The closer someone else's expertise is to one's own, the more easily and accurately competence can be judged and trust established. When lawyers from different practices work together, however, they may initially have to bridge dissimilar 'thought worlds' – for example, new jargon, differing assumptions or unfamiliar approaches – that make it harder to trust each other's competence.

Changes in the legal sector – including firms' rapid growth and internationalisation, along with heightened individual mobility – make it more challenging than ever for lawyers to develop mutual trust, even within the same firm. For example, when firms grow through lateral hiring or mergers, it becomes difficult for partners to know, let alone trust, their colleagues. To the extent that new entrants come from firms with significantly different norms and cultures, trust may be even harder to establish. Although a lawyer will be applauded for bringing his book of business to a new firm, his new colleagues may think twice about introducing him to their key clients when they consider his deftness at transporting critical relationships. Research also shows that the more tightly intertwined a group of lawyers were in their legacy firm or practice – as measured by the amount of business they referred to one another – the less integrated they are likely to become in a merged firm.[1]

Internationalisation also raises cross-cultural issues that pose challenges to collaboration and building trust. For example, legal training differs significantly across jurisdictions and lawyers develop different competencies based on their exposure to

---

[1] Briscoe, F, and W Tsai "Overcoming Relational Inertia How Organizational Members Respond to Acquisition Events in a Law Firm", *Administrative Science Quarterly* 56.3 (2011): 408-440.

client work of varying sophistication. If a partner is unable to predict the capabilities of lawyers in another country, he will likely hesitate to bring them into his client work. Although partner-level capabilities may even out considerably as careers progress, other divisions based on different cultural norms can remain. Consider, for instance, the assumptions that a hard-charging New York lawyer might make about his Dubai-based colleague's perceived delay in responding to a possible client opportunity; and on the flipside, the Dubai lawyer's difficulties in trusting his impatient colleague who fails to appreciate the importance of building relationships before trying to sell additional work. Without deliberate interventions to foster relationships, integrate newcomers and build confidence in others' competence, partners may feel insufficient trust in their colleagues to engage in collaboration. Worse, failed attempts at collaboration may kill the desire to work together in the future.

2.3 Managing dynamic collaborative arrangements
Collaboration begins with finding the right expert who has both complementary knowledge and a willingness to engage in joint working – and both aspects become harder to find in firms that expand rapidly. As one partner in an international firm recounted: "I used to know enough about my partners' work that it would take me only one or perhaps two phone calls to locate even the most esoteric expertise I needed. Now [after a series of mergers], the firm has a lot more experts available, but finding them is exponentially trickier. Plus, people no longer feel the same personal accountability to each other that makes them interrupt their own agenda to help on another partner's client. I feel like I need to negotiate or incentivise, whereas before people would just do the right thing for each other."

It becomes even more difficult once the relevant parties have committed to working together. Traditional teams formed to tackle a specific matter or deal typically have clear goals, a defined leader and a relatively clear hierarchy to facilitate smooth working. In contrast, collaboration increasingly happens among peers who are experts in their own domains and have their own sources of power and prestige. Even when the partner who 'owns' the client is nominally 'in charge' of the engagement, collaborators need to mutually establish task allocation and decision-making norms. Moreover, these working arrangements must be continually renegotiated, as partners who lead one engagement must defer to their former followers on the next. Reordering the status hierarchy may be simple in principle, but it is often a difficult, politically charged act. Lastly, integrating highly specialised expertise is cognitively complex and can generate competition and conflict when lawyers have even slightly misaligned objectives.

2.4 Star-based talent management and culture
As we know, the legal profession is filled with 'stars' – the lawyers who have cultivated a distinguished reputation for their extraordinary legal wisdom and client-handling prowess. Many firms, though certainly not all, have evolved to cater to these stars through their various structures and systems. The problem is that the individual hero is often at odds with a collaborative approach.

Lawyers tend to consider themselves a breed apart and some research does back up the idea that, in general, they have a set of personality traits that differ from the mainstream population.[2] For example, lawyers tend to be introverted and are sceptical and self-protecting, rather than trusting. On average, they show a stronger predisposition towards autonomy, rather than teamwork. Indeed, there is a degree of self-selection in the profession: people with these characteristics are attracted to it, and the characteristics are then reinforced through formal legal education and socialisation into law firms where such personalities dominate.

These characteristics suggest that collaboration may not come naturally to the average lawyer. Research shows that for people who have strong autonomy preferences, group work can be constraining and frustrating, and may undermine their satisfaction with their work. They may avoid working collaboratively and concentrate on aspects of the task that allow them to work alone, free of the obligations and constraints that come from working with others. Because they avoid collaboration, they tend not to build the kinds of skills and knowledge that enable smooth cross-practice working and thus continue to perceive the costs of collaboration as high.

Importantly, however, research also shows that individual preferences are malleable: as people gain experience of interdependence, they grow more accepting of it and even come to prefer it to solo working.[3] In part, these preferences shift as people learn how to collaborate: it becomes less time consuming or daunting and they begin to understand the benefits outlined below, such as the ability to do more sophisticated client work.

The diffuse power structures typical of PSFs make collaboration difficult to foster and even harder to demand. Professionals' so-called 'star power' stems largely from their relationships with clients, which are vital to the firm. In general, clients tend to prefer working with specific individuals year after year, rather than holding strict allegiance to the PSF itself, and partners hold a much stronger bargaining position relative to their firm than is found in more centralised hierarchical models typical of corporations. Directive decision making runs counter to the prevailing culture, so it is prohibitively difficult to mandate or push actions down the hierarchy.

Promotion systems that foster individualism and perhaps rivalry can also interfere with attempts to promote collaborative practices. Many law firms use an 'up-or-out' model, a 'tournament system' in which associates either meet certain production targets and move up or are encouraged to move out.[4] Pitting professionals against each other for promotion makes it hard for them to see the immediate value in sharing knowledge and expertise; once these competitive values become ingrained as an associate, it is unsurprising that the winners find it counterintuitive to collaborate once they become partners.

Lastly, the compensation system in some firms is perceived as a barrier to collaboration. Too often, a firm espouses the desire for partners to collaborate, but

---

2   Richard, L and L Rohrer, "A Breed Apart?", *The American Lawyer* (2011): 43-46.
3   Wageman, R and F M Gordon, "As the twig is bent: How group values shape emergent task interdependence in groups", *Organization Science* 16.6 (2005): 687-700.
4   For an in-depth examination of these effects, see M Galanter and T Palay, *Tournament of Lawyers: The Transformation of the Big Law Firm* (Chicago: University of Chicago Press, 1991).

then carries on remunerating people for individual results. Even the most altruistic partner is unlikely to sacrifice potential financial rewards indefinitely.

2.5 Performance pressure

In today's hyper-competitive marketplace, professional firms and their leaders face unprecedented pressure to deliver superior results. All lawyers would like to believe that they use the challenges of a high-stakes client situation to shine, showing off their own and the firm's best talents. Paradoxically, however, my research shows that the pressure to perform exceedingly well drives people towards lower-risk options, with sub-optimal outcomes.[5]

"We were seriously feeling the heat ... it was a make-or-break project for us. We threw our best and brightest against the problem, but the more we rallied our team, the worse it got. I still don't know what went wrong," moaned one high-ranking partner in a 'Big Four' accounting firm that participated in my research. This – unfortunately widespread – effect shows how performance pressure can be a double-edged sword: although it motivates people to ramp up their efforts, they may also inadvertently react in ways that are ultimately counterproductive.

Performance pressure occurs when someone must deliver exceptionally high-quality performance. Because their projects are so important, those facing performance pressure generally have the time and resources needed to complete the work; the trouble is that they stop using these resources effectively. High stakes breed anxiety among team members, their clients and their bosses. Consequently, performance pressure leads people to become risk averse.

Rather than becoming more innovative and pursuing best solutions for their client, teams under pressure start thinking of their matter as something that cannot be allowed to fail. This failure-prevention mindset leads them to opt for solutions that can be easily justified and to use proven approaches that are focused on narrowly defined performance objectives. By definition, these outputs are less innovative because novel solutions seem risky. In addition, individuals facing performance pressure seek control, which lowers their desire to collaborate – it feels safer to complete the work oneself. Together, these insidious effects of performance pressure can greatly undermine the collaborative process.

3. Benefits of collaboration

At this point, it would be unsurprising if the reader asked, "If collaboration is so difficult, why bother?" Indeed, this is the response I repeatedly hear in my interactions with some lawyers. In contrast, other lawyers contend that their success completely depends on collaborating.

I have initiated an extensive research programme to investigate these differing effects, examining the outcomes of collaboration on both law firms and individual lawyers who engage in collaborative client work.[6] The findings presented here are

---

5 For more on the causes, consequences and handling of performance pressure, see Gardner, H K, "Coming Through When It Matters Most: How Great Teams Do Their Best Work Under Pressure", *Harvard Business Review* 90, No 4 (April 2012).
6 To request updates on this ongoing research, please email the author: hgardner@hbs.edu.

based primarily on empirical analysis of data from two law firms, chosen for their contrasts along key dimensions including size, breadth of global reach and growth process (mergers and acquisition versus mostly organic). Both are multi-practice, 'big law' firms, with partners in each exhibiting a wide range of collaborative behaviours – from those who work rarely with other partners to those who work almost exclusively in collaboration with others. Both firms have shared many years of archival data with me, on condition of anonymity. I have conducted further extensive studies of multiple additional professional service firms across a range of sectors and have tested the extent to which findings from the initial set of law firms can be generalised to other law firms and beyond.

In general, the research revealed that collaboration – while certainly not without its costs, risks or challenges – provides significant benefit for the firms and lawyers that participate. This section outlines how these benefits arise and some of the conditions under which collaboration becomes more beneficial for the different constituents. Although the results may corroborate what highly collaborative partners already believe, the evidence presented here provides the first empirical confirmation of the benefits of collaboration in professional firms.

Figure 1: Effects of cross-practice collaboration on revenues

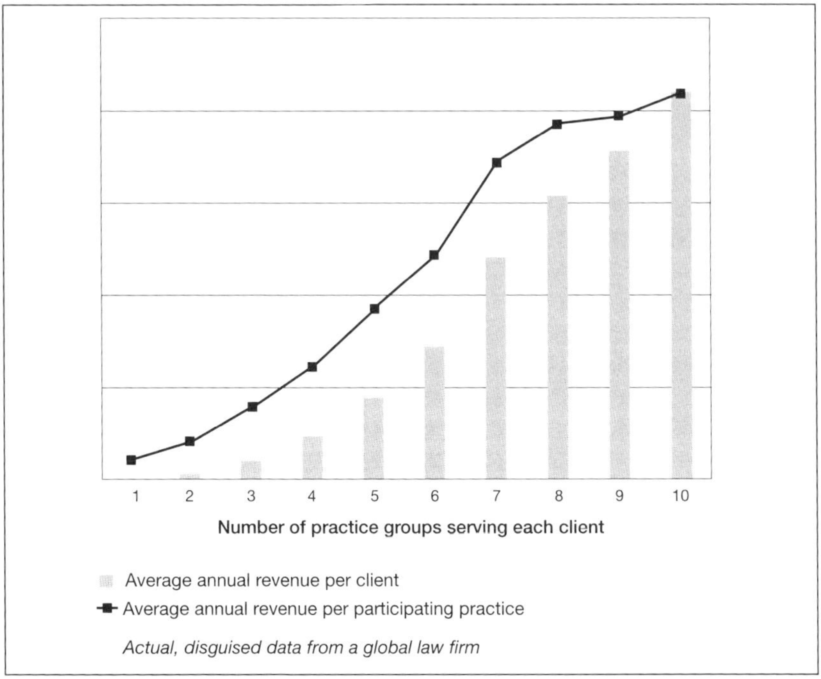

Number of practice groups serving each client

Average annual revenue per client
Average annual revenue per participating practice
Actual, disguised data from a global law firm

3.1 Firm-wide benefits

Figure 1 illustrates the effects of cross-practice collaboration on one firm's client revenues. Each bar on the chart represents a set of clients, defined by the number of practice groups (eg, real estate, employment) that serve each client in the set. The height of the bar represents the average annual revenue that the firm gets from each client. The line shows how the average revenue per practice depends on the total number of practices that are involved in serving that client. What is clear from this pattern is that multi-practice client service brings in significantly more revenue than can be explained by mere cross-selling. The jump from, say, five to six practices involved with a client is greater than just one-fifth; this increase implies not only that additional work is being carried out within an individual practice, but also that each additional practice changes the nature of the work itself. There are two possible reasons for this increase: higher-value work and increased retention of clients and professionals.

(a) *Higher-value work*

An obvious benefit of getting more practices – and therefore more partners – involved with a particular client is greater availability of intelligence (sleuthing, as well as brainpower): with more touch points, partners should be able to better understand client issues, be proactive in spotting opportunities and ultimately deliver greater value. Collaborating with lawyers from another practice also improves one's perspective of issues such that even highly experienced partners can see their clients' problems through a new lens. As one partner explained, "Although I was generally aware of what my colleagues in the employment practice did, it never occurred to me how much value they could add to my own clients until I had the chance to engage on a joint matter [that a third practice pulled them both onto]. After that, I began to see opportunities where their expertise could make a significant impact, and that's how I started a really productive cross-practice collaboration."

Because cross-practice collaboration can result in higher-value and more sophisticated work that is less likely to become commoditised, it commands higher prices. Moreover, a collaborative approach to client service has the potential to develop innovative outcomes that are customised to the specific needs of the client, increasing satisfaction and repeat business. As input from multiple experts allows a firm to take on more challenging and complex work for clients, partners can create a virtuous cycle of generating more sophisticated, bespoke and rewarding work from their clients.

(b) *Increased retention of clients and professionals*

Collaboration institutionalises client relationships. In general, when there are more lawyers serving a client, the risk of any single individual absconding with the client if he leaves the firm decreases. Yet even when multiple professionals serve a client, it is no guarantee that they cannot leave *en masse* and take the client relationship to their next firm. This phenomenon of leaving with an intact team is known as a 'lift-out'. Lift-outs occur when a firm hires a high-functioning group of colleagues, who are often successful in taking many of their clients with them to the new firm.[7] Lift-

---

7 Groysberg, B and R Abrahams. "Lift outs: how to acquire a high-functioning team", *Harvard Business Review* 84.12 (2006): 133-140.

outs, however, are generally constrained to individuals working within a single unit. This reasoning suggests that there is stronger retention of clients who are served by a team of cross-practice professionals, as opposed to those served by either sole partners or groups of partners from within the same organisational unit.

Additionally, collaboration may reduce professional turnover. The more that a professional works in teams, the more he comes to identify with the firm and the less he sees himself as 'lone wolf' or 'franchisee' (terms that professionals in highly individualistic firms used to describe themselves in interviews). Stronger organisational identification means that professionals are more likely not only to stay at their firm, but also to engage in pro-social, firm-building activities such as mentoring junior lawyers. These activities, in turn, enhance the desirable retention of high-performing associates.

3.2 **Benefits for individuals**

Even if collaboration benefits the firm, however, it will be nearly impossible to implement if lawyers are not convinced of the benefit to them personally. Analysing nearly a decade's worth of timesheet records and a host of other archival data has allowed me to begin answering the "What's in it for me?" question. The findings are organised below according to whether the focal lawyer is on the receiving side of work (ie, being asked to collaborate on a project for another partner's client) or the originating side (and must therefore decide whether to involve others or do the work alone). While most partners will, of course, do some of each, my research suggests that the way in which each sort of collaboration benefits a lawyer may be different; therefore, they are analysed and discussed separately.

(a) Collaborating on projects for others' clients –'receiving work'

My results show that collaborating with a wider group of partners on their projects boosts a lawyer's amount of billed revenues in the subsequent year, even when other factors that we would expect to affect individual billings – for example, one's office, practice group, organisational tenure and present-year revenues – remain constant. Detailed discussions and interviews with hundreds of practising lawyers show that these effects stem primarily from the trust that develops through collaboration. Trust in colleagues is the key ingredient that enables knowledge sharing and collaboration. When partners work together, they form bonds of trust that allow them to work more effectively to produce high-quality outcomes. Collaboration gives them the opportunity to observe and understand each other's capabilities and specific areas of expertise. This first-hand experience of each other's work increases competence trust, which is essential for facilitating collaboration.

Cross-practice collaboration (ie, participating in work originated by partners in a different practice) is especially valuable. Usually, professionals are likely to know the reputation of those who work in their own speciality area or practice group, but may be unfamiliar with an outsider's areas of expertise or quality of work. Collaborating with them can be the most reliable way to learn about each other's reputation. This reasoning explains why cross-practice collaboration is more beneficial than within-practice collaboration.

Statistics further demonstrate that the main benefits of collaboration stem from the focal lawyer's ability to attract more work in subsequent years – not only from those with whom he has worked directly (either on their or others' projects), but also from partners in the firm with whom he has had no prior working relationship. In general, reputations spread either through first-hand experience or through third-party information. My data suggests that both avenues are viable channels in law firms.

The benefits of collaboration in securing additional work from both prior collaborators and unfamiliar partners are especially visible for lateral hires during their first three years. Once lateral hires join a new firm, they must establish their own reputation in terms of both character (relational trustworthiness) and ability (competence trustworthiness). This is the case even in firms that carefully vet lateral candidates and where existing partners have a say in hiring decisions. My findings suggest that working on others' matters is a valuable way for a recent lateral hire to develop his reputation and thereby attract increasing amounts of work.

(b) *Collaboration and rainmakers – 'sending work'*

Collaboration can also enhance one's ability to originate work. My research shows that for work that a partner originates, the more of this he shares with others, the greater his book of business grows in subsequent years (again, controlling for other factors that are likely to affect individual billings, such as one's office, practice group, organisational tenure and present-year origination level). Specifically, subsequent-year revenues from a rainmaker's existing clients increase the more he involves partners from his own, and other, practices. Additionally, inviting own-practice and other-practice partners to collaborate is a strong predictor of revenue growth from new clients (ie, those which the firm has not served for at least a decade, if ever), although cross-practice collaboration is a significantly stronger predictor of new client revenues.

The ways that collaboration affects rainmaking are likely to be different, depending on whom one collaborates with. For example, sending work to other partners in the same practice can be considered a substitution effect: as the expertise of partners within the same practice is arguably fungible, involving them simply frees up the rainmaker's time either to deepen existing client relationships or to seek out new clients.

In contrast, involving partners from other practices has multiple consequences. First, it allows a partner to learn how to do complex, multi-disciplinary client work and develop an external reputation for this sophisticated sort of client service. Additionally, collaborating across practices allows partners to develop a cadre of trusted professionals who can help deliver sophisticated, high-quality and high-value work. Knowing that he can rely on a trusted team gives a partner the confidence to pitch additional multi-disciplinary work to new or existing clients.

4. How to achieve greater collaboration

This chapter has addressed the challenges of collaborating in today's PSFs, including establishing trust, navigating the star-based system typical to many firms and handling the interpersonal challenges of working within dynamic collaborative arrangements, especially when facing performance pressure. The following section suggests ways that law firms, their leaders and individual lawyers can address these challenges and lay the foundation for enhanced collaboration.

4.1 Building trust through talent management processes

Professional development leads to competence-based trust by creating transparency about the expertise and capabilities of lawyers at any given level.[8] Ideally, formal professional development should be based on principles of active learning – in the form of case studies, simulations and role playing – and involve significant interaction with partners, rather than being conducted solely by external providers. Giving partners a chance to engage with associates and each other allows them to learn what others know and establish competence trust.

Informal professional development in the form of on-the-job learning remains the most important way for junior lawyers to develop their capabilities and demonstrate their trustworthiness. A partner who invests time in coaching and giving real-time feedback will not only enhance the technical skills of the recipient, but also foster the junior lawyer's ability and willingness to provide further feedback to those with whom he works.

A comprehensive development plan for associates should also include assessments that measure their performance against competency benchmarks. Transparency about abilities at any given tenure or level is especially crucial as firms expand globally. Given the heterogeneous nature of legal training across jurisdictions, it is up to each firm to develop a robust internal system to allow lawyers to understand what they can reasonably be expected to know and how they can demonstrate their increasing capabilities.

Performance against these assessments should be linked to a merit-based promotion system. In firms that implement an alternative, non-partnership track (eg, counsel), it is especially important to set and communicate standards and a progression path commensurate with these professionals' increasing abilities. This sort of talent management system gives professionals within the firm reliable indicators of what can be expected from lawyers at any given level and thus fosters competence trust.

International secondments – temporary transfers to another office within the same firm – are another important way to build interpersonal familiarity and relational trust, standardise skills across jurisdictions and increase lawyers' awareness of, and competence in, others' trust. For example, one global firm saw cross-jurisdiction referrals increase threefold in participating offices in the first year following the implementation of a secondment programme for associates.

4.2 Modifying the star-based system

(a) Shifting desire for autonomy towards preference for collaboration

Strong preferences for autonomy act as a deterrent to joint work, but overcoming this

---

8   For more information on professional development in 'big law', see Gardner, H K and P Andrews, "Professional Development at DLA Piper – Building the Strength of Global Legal Talent", Harvard Business School Case 413-001 (2012) and the related instructor's note.

obstacle can lead to the benefits associated with collaboration. As previously mentioned above, lawyers generally have personality traits, such as scepticism and low sociability, that make collaboration seem less appealing, if not outright distasteful. Research demonstrates, however, that individual preferences for strict autonomy begin to fade as people gain experience with interdependent work. As they collaborate more, lawyers can learn communication and interpersonal skills that enable smooth interchanges of work with other partners, which poses different challenges than merely delegating work to junior lawyers. In addition, with increased collaboration, they build knowledge that is essential for cross-disciplinary work, such as familiarity with the technical jargon used in other lawyers' practices.

In my own research, I frequently hear that lawyers need to take a 'leap of faith' in starting collaborative working – for example, introducing another partner to their client. After some initial growing pains, collaboration often starts to build momentum as lawyers learn how to collaborate efficiently and effectively, and begin reaping rewards in terms of client satisfaction and the 'fun' or 'thrill' of doing increasingly sophisticated work. One implication for individual lawyers is that they must overcome their negative perceptions of joint working in order to get involved and invest in learning to collaborate effectively; finding a trusted partner who is experienced in collaborative working will likely jump-start the learning process.

One implication for firms is that they need to create structured opportunities for people to become familiar with partners from other practice areas, so that they develop an appreciation for what those lawyers might bring to their own clients. Some firms, for example, devote part of their annual partners' retreat to a series of 20-minute 'road show' presentations, where partners highlight the work that they do and explicitly focus on potential growth opportunities for lawyers in other practices. In short, although many lawyers' initial preferences might predispose them towards solo working, the evidence shows that 'seeing is believing'. Once familiar with collaboration and its benefits – through their own experience and perhaps aided by the firm's efforts – lawyers will generally come to a better appreciation of collaborating.

(b) *Compensation*

So far, my research has explored collaboration in a range of professional service firms where compensation systems span from highly individualistic 'eat what you kill' approaches to those with more balanced weighting for origination and execution credits to modified lockstep systems. Each has its challenges and it is beyond the scope of this chapter to explore them in detail. But a few principles are essential to keep in mind. The first two are based on the concept that people care not only about how much people are rewarded in comparison to each other, but also about the way in which compensation decisions are made (ie, distributive and procedural justice, respectively).[9]

---

9   For a discussion of the intersection between collaboration and compensation in professional service firms, see Gardner, H K and K Herman, "Marshall & Gordon: Designing an Effective Compensation System (A)", Harvard Business School Case 411-038 (2011) and the related Instructor's Note.

First, people's behaviour is strongly affected by their beliefs about distribution of rewards. Ultimately, collaboration depends most of all on trust. If firms espouse the value of team-based client service and collaboration, partners expect to be rewarded for demonstrating this behaviour. When people perceive that their firm's compensation system unjustly rewards lawyers who hoard work, for example, collaboration suffers. By contrast, in a lockstep system where pay is based on seniority rather than performance, they may not be motivated to undertake the complexities and risks of collaboration unless they are convinced that others are also making equal efforts at collaborating. Lockstep systems tend to work best either in smaller firms where personal relationships provide such assurances or in firms where sophisticated systems coupled with a strong culture provide transparency about collaboration efforts and thus maintain a sense of fairness.[10]

Second, the way that a firm implements any given compensation system will affect people's perceptions of fairness, in turn shaping their willingness to collaborate. Professionals must understand what actions are rewarded and how they are measured; communication is especially critical when a firm changes any aspects of its compensation system. Professionals must also believe that their firm has reliable ways to capture the performance metrics on which compensation is based.[11] They must also have faith in those who make the compensation decisions. The decision makers must be seen as competent and unbiased, with enough information to make accurate decisions, no vested interests in outcomes and as little susceptibility to internal politics as possible.

Third, it is crucial to remember that compensation takes on exaggerated importance in people's minds when it is their main way of figuring out how much the firm values them. In contrast, the best firms provide abundant psycho-social rewards, such as recognition for excellent client work or firm-building initiatives, formal and informal feedback (even for partners), opportunities to represent the firm or practice at prestigious external events, high-integrity colleagues, increasingly challenging and interesting client work and a brand name that people are proud to identify with. In these firms, compensation still matters, but people pay far less attention to it than in places where 'the number' is their only signal of their worth.

Lastly, a well-designed compensation system can help to foster joint working only when it is paired with other collaboration-enhancing approaches (eg, hiring lateral partners with a demonstrated track record of successfully working across practices) and a broader reward system that emphasises interdependence, rather than competition. No 'silver bullet' compensation scheme determines collaboration; rather, a holistic approach that aligns compensation, culture, other talent management practices and leadership is necessary.

---

10 Allen & Overy is one firm that attempts to foster global collaboration through transparency and related means. See Gardner, H K, M Chen and D Lau, "Leading Global Collaboration: Allen & Overy Opens in Vietnam," Harvard Business School Case 414-018 (2013) and the related Instructor's Note.
11 For an in-depth examination of one firm's system of measuring and communicating performance metrics, see Gardner, H K and A Lobb, "Collaborating for Growth: Duane Morris in a Turbulent Legal Sector", Harvard Business School Case 413-110 (2013) and the related Instructor's Note.

5. Micro-dynamics of collaboration: effectiveness under pressure

One of the best ways to facilitate and increase collaboration is to make it a positive experience. In order for people to understand that the benefits of collaboration outweigh the costs, the process has to be both productive and relatively frictionless. When people have an opportunity to contribute, they have to believe that their individual expertise and knowledge are valued and used by the team. Working jointly is never as simple as working alone, but the perceived costs of collaborating can be reduced if people take steps to improve coordination efficiencies and reduce interpersonal conflicts.

As discussed in section 2 of this chapter, performance pressure can undermine the collaborative experience because team processes often become dysfunctional when people are 'under the gun' to deliver exceptional outcomes. When stakes are highest, teams often become risk averse, defer unnecessarily to status or authority (rather than actual expertise) and value shared knowledge more than unique expertise. If teams are able to spot the onset of performance pressure, however, they can take steps to mitigate these adverse effects and even turn the situation into one where they are highly motivated to shine in the face of their challenge. Below are several approaches that can help to ensure that collaboration enhances, rather than undermines, productivity.

First, every team needs a kick-off meeting. Even if a group has been working together extensively, taking the time to have an explicit conversation about who is best able to contribute in which ways to the group's goal can help to mitigate unhelpful conflict and ensure that each member's expertise is fully leveraged. Unfortunately, my research shows that when team members are highly familiar with one another, they are most likely to skip this step, but are also more likely to jump to conclusions about who has what sort of expertise. They often rely on outdated information and fail to see how each person can optimally participate. An effective kick-off discussion – sometimes needing as little investment as 15 minutes – unearths and acknowledges relevant expertise, and opens up possibilities for a more creative or customised solution that delights clients, rather than merely satisfies them. These kick-offs may also highlight knowledge gaps, so that team leaders understand where additional resources may be required.

Once the team has the right resources and understands each person's potential contribution, the key is making sure that they use this knowledge optimally. Under performance pressure, teams often default to relying on knowledge that feels safe – that is, knowledge that is easily justified or commonly held – rather than on unique expertise built through individuals' idiosyncratic experiences. Too often, stressed teams will also prematurely shut down debate, because contributions that challenge their emerging consensus feel like unnerving distractions. The best leaders will periodically interrupt the team's natural progression to ask whether each person has contributed at least as much as was initially expected, and then redirect the team if anyone's answer is 'no'. Actively listening to inputs, inviting less senior members' opinions and acting as role models to encourage openness to dissent or challenge are all ways that team leaders can create an environment of psychological safety in which the team welcomes innovative ideas.

The partner leading the collaborative effort is responsible for ensuring not only that each expert contributes his unique knowledge, but also that such knowledge gets incorporated into the output. Effective partners often deputise a senior associate to help monitor the team's knowledge flows; the partner can intervene when necessary to highlight any important knowledge that was inadvertently left out. This approach avoids wasting valuable expertise and encourages team members to pay greater attention to more novel inputs. When team members listen to and integrate their collaboration partners' unique knowledge, it leads to more sophisticated outcomes that provide greater value to the client and to a more productive, meaningful experience that motivates people to engage in future collaboration.

6. Conclusion

Collaboration is increasingly essential in today's law firms. The complex, international and integrative nature of legal work requires professionals to combine their specialised expertise in order to successfully serve the most attractive clients. Partners who collaborate realise the benefit of generating more sophisticated, innovative and lucrative work. While collaboration undoubtedly entails risks and coordination costs, these challenges can be mitigated by implementing appropriate measures. Lawyers who develop their own collaboration capabilities and network are likely to reap both intellectual and financial benefits.

Creating effective relationships

Sarah Martin
Coombs Martin

1. **Introduction**

   A successful lawyer, today more than ever, needs to be talented at developing strong professional relationships. Whatever kind of lawyer you are and whatever position you hold in a firm, forging good sustainable relationships with clients and colleagues is fundamental to driving the success of your practice and your career.

   Like other professionals, lawyers are trained to use their intelligence to become technical experts and to deliver a technical service. As many know to their benefit, developing and succeeding with clients and leading or managing others require a different kind intelligence: the intelligence to understand and manage emotions, which lies at the core of good relationships.

   Many senior lawyers throughout the world have spent their careers honing this intelligence through years of experience. In the rapidly changing landscape of legal practice, it is also one of the most important skills that they can develop and manage in younger lawyers within their firms.

   In most parts of the world, legal professional training and development are still largely focused on the law and technical legal requirements, particularly at entry level. In the United Kingdom, legal professional training as a whole is under review, and there is a strong and welcome lobby for inclusion of a broader skillset. Good lawyers can no longer afford to rest on their technical laurels.

   While formal professional training maintains its narrow focus, it is all the more important for law firm leaders to recognise the value of:
   - using their own emotional intelligence to develop and manage the talent in their firms; and
   - helping to develop the emotional intelligence of their colleagues.

2. **Emotional intelligence**

   In essence, 'emotional intelligence' refers to our abilities to recognise and understand emotions in ourselves and others, and to use this awareness to make better decisions and manage our behaviour and relationships. In other words, it is about developing a good sense of how your actions are perceived and experienced by others and how you respond to their behaviour.

   Recent developments in neuroscience have shown that in many situations our brains are wired to give emotions precedence. The limbic system where emotions are processed is the root from which our brain developed. Messages entering our brains via our senses come through the limbic system. Emotional areas are interwoven into the neural circuits connected to the rational neocortex, so the brain's first reaction to an event – particularly in high-stress situations – is going to be emotional.

Overview of the five components of emotional intelligence, D Goleman[1]

	Definitions	**Hallmarks**
Self-awareness	Can recognise and understand one's moods, emotions and drives, as well as the effects of these on others.	Self-confident. Realistic self-assessment. Self-deprecating sense of humour.
Self-regulation	Can control or redirect impulses and moods. Think before acting.	Trustworthiness. Integrity. Comfort with ambiguity. Openness to change.
Motivation	Passion for work goes beyond money or status. Goals pursued with energy and passion.	Strong drive to achieve. Optimism even in failure. Commitment to organisation.
Empathy	Can understand the emotional make-up of other people. Treat people according to their emotional reactions.	Expertise in building and retaining talent. Cross-cultural sensitivity Customer service.
Relationship management/ social skills	Managing relationships and building networks. Can find common ground and build rapport.	Effective in leading change. Persuasive. Builds and leads teams.

Although we all have emotional set points, it is possible to learn how to manage the reactions and thoughts that follow so that they do not become hijacked by emotional responses.

3. **The importance of emotional intelligence**

Recent studies suggest that there is a higher correlation between emotional intelligence and success than between intelligence quotient (IQ) and success. It seems that people who develop their emotional intelligence tend to be the highest performers and earners.[2]

The good news for talent management is that unlike IQ, which changes little from childhood, emotional intelligence can be learned over time and at any age. It takes time, effort and practice, but the investment can reap huge rewards for the individual and those who interact with him, including colleagues and clients.

Why is developing emotional intelligence particularly important for managing legal talent now?

3.1 The economic context

As the economic squeeze gets tighter, clients of law firms are becoming more demanding and competition for legal jobs is tougher. More than ever, lawyers in many jurisdictions are suffering from exhaustion, broken relationships and depression, and are turning to alcohol and drugs. Despite the financial rewards, the costs to health and happiness can be high. As a result, many talented lawyers are leaving the profession. Developing emotional intelligence is a foundation for the understanding and support required to manage and counter the effects of these demanding conditions. It also helps to build resilience.

3.2 The changing nature of the lawyer's role

Studies on motivation[3] reveal that an individual's intrinsic motivation levels are significantly increased if he understands and buys in to the purpose of what he is doing and has a reasonable degree of autonomy in his work. Lawyers, in particular, tend to like autonomy and having a sense of the 'big picture'.

Yet an overall sense of purpose and a fair degree of autonomy are increasingly rare experiences in legal practice, as it has become more specialised and commoditised in many jurisdictions. Individuals can end up having limited knowledge of the big picture and little scope to make decisions. In this environment, frustrations and tensions can build to a point where they boil over or simmer and create resentment and disengagement. Senior lawyers can bring their emotional intelligence to this problem, explaining the overall purpose of the work to their more junior colleagues, so that they have an appreciation of how they are contributing. They can also try to give junior lawyers more opportunities to participate in client interactions and face-to-face meetings.

As many observers of legal markets have commented,[4] the legal profession is subject to unprecedented change from globalisation, the global economic downturn, rapid development of information technology and the liberalisation of law firm structures. Change on such scale creates greater complexity, uncertainty, ambiguity and anxiety. The shift to short-term performance and higher monetary rewards risks making relationships within firms more transactional and losing the 'give and take' of strong long-term bonds. If this continues, firms may become reluctant to invest in

---

1   Daniel Goleman (1996) *Emotional Intelligence,* (1998) *Working with Emotional Intelligence,* Bloomsbury.
2   Daniel Goleman (1996) *Emotional Intelligence,* (1998) *Working with Emotional Intelligence;* Bloomsbury, T Bradberry and J Greaves (2012) *Leadership 2.0,* Talentsmart.
3   Ryan, R M & Deci, E L (2000) "Self Determination Theory and the Facilitation of Intrinsic Motivation, Self Development and Well-Being", *American Psychologist* Vol55 no1, Jan 2000, Greaves.
4   R Susskind (2013) *Tomorrow's Lawyers,* Oxford University Press.

and develop people over the longer term, and there will be more uncertainty for individuals over their legal careers. Firms may also find that they do not have the buy-in for implementing necessary changes. In these circumstances, it is all the more important to build mutual support and reduce uncertainties within the firm as much as possible.

3.3 Limitations of current legal training

Legal training is presently narrow – some would say that it is even worse than this. One observer[5] contends: "Lawyers are trained to be aggressive, judgemental, intellectual, analytical and emotionally detached. This produces predictable emotional consequences for the legal practitioner: he or she will become depressed, anxious and angry a lot of the time." This may be an extreme view, but it has some truth in it.

3.4 The legal 'character'

Like any group of professionals, lawyers have differing personalities and traits. While not wishing to make generalisations about the character of lawyers, some similarities are worth exploring to appreciate the impact of developing emotional intelligence.

(a) Being challenging

As highly intelligent people, lawyers have an inbuilt talent for challenging, questioning and making clever points. Some may also feel the need to prove that they are right. Although this gives the immediate satisfaction of winning the argument, it can also destroy respect and trust, eroding the quality of the relationship. Legal talent management can help individuals to appreciate the impact of this approach on their clients, colleagues and leaders, and to understand how undermining trust with any of these groups will ultimately be counterproductive.

(b) Quest for feedback

Like many high achievers, lawyers often need the approbation of their clients and colleagues to maintain their self-esteem. In such a demanding environment, they need to know how they are performing and to feel supported by their leaders, knowing that if something goes well it will be recognised, and in circumstances where they need support, they will be sure to get it. They need specific, timely and actionable feedback from people they respect. Good emotional antennae are needed to find the fine balance between promoting confidence and giving the necessary support, so that individuals develop and do not crumble under pressure.

(c) Need for challenge

Lawyers, like other professionals, have a strong appetite for challenging work.[6] One of my clients has spent his professional life working on international transactions and travelling constantly. In his spare time, he runs marathons and has climbed to

---

5   Martin Seligman (2003) *Authentic Happiness*, Nicholas Brearley Publishing.
6   Thomas J Delong, John J Gabarro, Robert J Lees (2007) *When Professionals Need to Lead*, Harvard Business School Press.

Everest base camp. He has a constant need for new challenges in and out of work. If you are challenge-driven, developing your emotional intelligence is particularly helpful for appreciating the impact that you have on others when you focus solely on achieving the task in hand. Developing self-awareness can also help you to work out how to stay motivated.

(d) *Fairness*

Lawyers, unsurprisingly, have a strong sense of the power of fairness. In any important firm decision, they will want to have their say. Significant emotional intelligence is required to create 'decision justice': taking time and care to explain things well, to listen and understand the different points of view and to communicate why the decision does or does not reflect the input. This emotionally intelligent approach allows you to build the long-term trust and mutual support required for future decisions.

(e) *Tendency to search for the negative*

One of the reasons that lawyers are in the high-risk category for demoralisation, according to a leading psychologist, is that many have a natural tendency to look for the negatives. The legal mind that looks for problems and imagines the worst in order to protect against it is a wonderful talent as far as the client is concerned. As one major client said: "It's terrific working with Jim, because he does all my worrying for me." Emotional intelligence can help to prevent that mindset becoming pervasive in all aspects of life as explained in the work on motivation and learned flexible optimism.[7]

4. Developing emotional intelligence: the five components

4.1 Self-awareness

The starting point for understanding the impact that we have is to develop a good level of self-awareness. It takes time, honesty and courage – inevitably, we discover things that are unsettling – yet the benefits can be long term and widespread. First, we should focus on improving our own performance and interactions. Then, having experimented on ourselves, we can use this knowledge to enhance our skills of managing, developing and leading others.

Over several years, I have been asked by firms and individual lawyers to help them with different aspects of their professional relationships. The following case studies are drawn from this work and illustrate the development of different components of emotional intelligence. Names and other facts have been changed.

(a) *Case study*

"Anyone can become angry – that is easy. But to be angry with the right person, to the right degree, at the right time, for the right purpose, and in the right way – that is not easy." Aristotle, The Nicomachean Ethics

---

7   Martin Seligman (1990) *Learned Optimism*, Pocket Books.

Caroline was a partner in a major firm. The quality of her relationships with her team had plummeted. She had worked in M&A for years and was successful, but she was burnt out by the highs and lows, did not enjoy going to work and felt under-appreciated and angry.

The benefits of increasing her self-awareness are set out as a starting point using the Johari window model below.

Johari window

Solicit feedback ⟶

Self

Self-disclosure

	Known	Unknown
Known (Others)	Public self The arena: I see the pluses and minuses about myself and so do others.	Hidden to self My blind spots: I don't see these pluses and minuses about myself, but others do.
Unknown (Others)	Private self The façade: I see these things about myself, but keep them hidden.	Sub-conscious self The unknown: buried to both myself and others.

Adapted from Luft, J (1970) Group Processes: An Introduction to Group Dynamics, Palo Alto, CA: National Press Books

The aim was to increase the size of the upper-left-hand box, called 'the arena', by seeking feedback and being as transparent as possible. In this way, we are operating with fewer blind spots and without wasting energy hiding behind a façade, making us more effective in building our relationships over the long term.

I collected anonymous 360-degree feedback from some of Caroline's colleagues. There were strong themes. They sang her praises for conscientiousness, loyalty, authenticity and passion, but also mentioned volatility, mood swings and a propensity to wear her heart on her sleeve.

As part of the exercise Caroline shared her feedback from two psychometrics: MBTI and FIRO-B.

Of the many psychometric instruments designed to help increase self-awareness, MBTI is the most popular for raising awareness of overall personality, with over 2 million users each year. Based on the work of Jung and developed by Myers and Briggs, it looks at four dimensions of how people manage their energy, take in information, make decisions and explore or seek closure. It has its critics, but it works very well to show and develop appreciation of differences in personal preferences and approach. One of its major strengths is that it is non-judgemental and so easier to share results in order to appreciate differences.

FIRO-B was developed by Schutz from research on interpersonal relations and conflict, to help submarine crews work together for long periods. It identifies how you tend to behave towards others and how you want them to behave towards you. It provides information about three fundamental dimensions of interpersonal needs – inclusion, control and affection – and the extent to which we differ in how much we want and how much we signal we want. It is particularly good for raising self-awareness when working with teams.

Caroline's MBTI feedback showed that she had a 'feeling preference' in taking decisions. Her FIRO-B showed that she wanted and expressed a high level of affection.

After discussing the combined feedback, Caroline appreciated that she had a blind spot about the overt intensity of her emotions. She began to see what a destabilising effect her behaviour was having on her colleagues by creating volatility, uncertainty and emotional exhaustion. This made them more anxious, guarded and unlikely to appreciate her positive behaviour. It seriously affected her gravitas. With this in mind, she became strongly motivated to work on a plan to channel her emotions for the benefit of herself and her team, enabling them to flourish in a more predictable environment.

(b) *Improving self-awareness*

As obvious as it may sound, simply asking people to think about self-awareness is a good starting place. They can note strong reactions and triggers, try to work out what is happening and why and look for patterns. Recognising feelings as they happen can reduce the chance of them reappearing uninvited.

As we have seen, objective constructive feedback is powerful. It is usually difficult to get, particularly for those higher up in the firm. Asking a trusted colleague for open and honest feedback can work. In practice, anonymous 360-degree feedback from several colleagues is more helpful and will include a mix of positive and negative comments.

I always encourage lawyers to concentrate on the positive feedback first, but this is not always straightforward. We are all programmed to seek out the negative or problematic and work on it. Lawyers excel at this through a natural disposition enhanced by years of training and practice. So seeing the positive comments first, resisting the urge to flip the page and taking the time to digest them is an essential part of setting the context for the areas that need work.

Psychometric instruments are widely used and helpful if they are employed with a purpose and the feedback is fully discussed. Other useful tests are the highly regarded personality instrument NEO, which includes a dimension on neuroticism, and the Hogan Development Survey, which highlights aspects of your personality that can derail your progress and leadership capabilities.

The critical thing to remember on developing self-awareness is that it is far from a linear process and many mistakes give useful information about what to do differently. It is difficult to start noticing things of which we were previously unaware and which we do not particularly like.

4.2 Self-regulation

Self-regulation is more than managing emotional outbursts. It involves regulating our responses and tendencies over time into desired reactions and behaviour. To achieve this, the individual has to put his immediate needs on hold and think of the impact on others and of longer-term, more important goals. It is also about achieving balance and reducing volatility and over the long term it builds resilience.

(a) *Case study*

Nicola was a lawyer with an international firm. A highly intelligent woman in her mid-forties who rose rapidly through the firm, she was known for her ability to win business with her quick solutions-based approach. Nicola also had a reputation for intimidating others intellectually.

The senior partner was concerned that this attitude was limiting both a very talented lawyer and the rest of her colleagues, who were afraid to venture their views. It was my role to help Nicola to improve her relationships with her colleagues and develop her team.

I began by seeking feedback with an anonymous 360-degree process. Hearing different viewpoints was essential to gain Nicola's attention, to help her understand how others experienced her and to recognise blind spots. She found some of the feedback difficult to accept. Her peers at times experienced her as scary, dismissive, often interrupting, not listening and dogmatic, with a strong need to be right. She recognised the comments from her partners and knew that she had to improve if she were to advance in the firm. She saw how her need to demonstrate her intellectual capacity was destroying trust with her colleagues. This realisation was critical for developing the motivation to change, the humility to recognise that her current ways were counter-productive and the determination to practise on the job in the coming months.

Nicola developed a practical plan focused on areas for change, and created a safe practice zone with feedback from a trusted colleague. She started with the perceived lack of listening and managing her need to be right. She practised trying to wait until the other person had finished his point, avoiding interruptions and listening carefully to gain a deeper understanding. She started with one colleague and explained to him what she was doing and why. She then asked others to remind her if she interrupted. She knew that giving full attention and listening would show respect and build trust, her underlying goal.

She focused on how to recognise, acknowledge and use the valuable contributions of others. She put aside her embarrassment about praising people for their ideas and was genuine and specific in recognising their value. She resisted the temptation to try to 'trump' them. If she had things to add, she found positive ways to do so. Her aim now was not to show them she was smart (which they knew), but to encourage the smartest bits of them and build their trust. She saw that focusing on flaws in the ideas of others can invoke self-doubt, is intimidating and destroys trust.

I asked her to make notes about how this felt, what she noticed, heard and learned and the impact she saw on others, emphasising the importance of recognising her emotions about these changes.

After six months, we took additional feedback from her peers. They reported that Nicola was no longer belittling people with her intellect, but listening more carefully and interrupting less. She had learned to value their contributions and no longer felt a need to outplay them. She became more relaxed, continued to build trust and was seen as a much more effective and successful partner in the business.

What is happening here and why does it take so long? Recent developments in neuroscience have helped us to understand this a little better. The neocortex, which learns technical skills and cognitive abilities, gains knowledge quickly. The development of emotional intelligence involves the emotional centres of the brain as well as the neocortex. These seem to need to unlearn old habits and learn new ones through repetition and practice over time, in order to develop new neural pathways that become ingrained habits. During this time, numerous relapses into the original default behaviour are likely to occur, until the new one takes over as the default option.

(b) *Improving self-regulation*
Through self-awareness, we start to identify what we are trying to manage. In practice, it is best to choose one or two things to focus on at a time. The aim is to recognise trigger signs and then practise remaining objectives, taking control of our inner voice and modelling the behaviour we would like to see in our colleagues. Sharing goals with a trusted colleague, as Nicola did, helps to hold us to account and improves our chances of success.

Increased self-awareness also helps us to assess our energy levels and take time to recharge physically and emotionally, exercising self-regulation to avoid falling prey to the prevalent burn-out. It can help to shake off anxiety and irritability and to build resilience.

Self-regulation applies to positive as well as negative emotions. Being overexuberant and overenthusiastic can overwhelm colleagues, while overconfidence and excessive optimism can impair sound decision making.

4.3 Motivation
We hear so much about how lawyers are suffering from disillusionment, fatigue and lack of motivation.

Having a passion for what you do and are trying to achieve is an important part of the emotional skillset for any partner in a law firm in order to win clients and do a good job for them. Equally, it inspires younger lawyers and helps them in turn to develop their own passion for their work.

Part of developing emotional intelligence is to become aware of your own strengths and those of colleagues. Law firms make sound investments when they take the time to discover the particular strengths and passions of their individual

Creating effective relationships

lawyers. This is not just about technical expertise, but natural talents as diverse as networking, courage and creativity. A whole body of research demonstrates the increased motivation, energy and performance levels that occur when people are playing to their strengths. Looking at individual roles and, where possible, reshaping these to facilitate tapping these strengths will lead to greater satisfaction and lessen the unhappy and disillusioned exodus of young talent.

4.4 **Empathy**

Empathy is at the centre of social awareness – it is the ability to pick up what is happening for another person and put yourself in his shoes. It is the capacity to understand what he is feeling, even if you do not feel it yourself, and to resist the tendency to project your own emotions onto others. It involves developing highly attuned antennae to gather critical information.

(a) *Case study*

George was, in the words of his senior partner, "a fantastic lawyer". The main challenge for George was how to manage himself and his people. He headed up a significant department in the firm and I worked with him to develop his management and leadership of the group.

We started with self-awareness. George already knew that he needed to manage his time better, have more structure in his department, delegate more effectively, relinquish some control and run a more organised office. These were some of the goals he set for the coaching. He had tried to achieve some of these before, but to no avail. People thought that he had lost his motivation, but in reality he was frustrated.

It was here that I saw the full power of 360-degree feedback to invoke natural empathy. His colleagues' comments fell into clear themes: praise for the creation of a successful department, his innovative legal and client-facing skills, passion and high standards. As he anticipated, the challenges arose in management of himself and the department: taking on too much work, perfectionism, lack of willingness to delegate, cancelling meetings at the last minute, a fire-fighting approach and a lack of respect for procedures. The chaos made it difficult for others to become involved.

George's motivation to change was rooted in his empathy and deep respect for his team. His reaction to the honest and open comments that they had made was, "I see that some people suffer more than I had realised; it needs sorting out."

This set him on the road to practical solutions, including recruiting an excellent personal assistant, ruthless tidying of his office, setting up regular meetings and asking others to take him to task if he tried to cancel them, delegating routine and administrative tasks and developing techniques for delegation of more complex matters. George was able to free up more time to spend on his award-winning legal work and start mentoring junior lawyers to explore creative solutions that met clients' changing needs. His team had less ambiguity to manage and felt more respected.

(b) *Developing empathy*

Learning to appreciate the differences of others requires listening and observation to tune into how they may be seeing things. Research shows[8] that in appreciation of a message, words account for only about 7%, tone of voice accounts for about 38% and body language accounts for about 55%. So, while lawyers are experts of the written word, they must also develop keen powers of listening and observation – the foundation skills for empathy. Experience and intuition then help to build the ability to recognise the different emotions that everyone brings to the workplace.

'Careful listening' inevitably means to stop talking, anticipating, interrupting. It requires practice, as seen in section 4.2(a). Practising empathy also involves developing objective observation, trying to see others' emotions while staying neutral and picking up on different moods and energy levels. The more time invested in getting to know clients or colleagues, the easier it becomes to appreciate how they see things and to adjust your responses and behaviour accordingly. MBTI is an excellent psychometric for appreciating how people see, approach and respond to things differently.

4.5 Relationship management

Clients often state that they consider technical expertise as a basic requirement and that they select their lawyers on the basis of personal qualities and relationships. As one private equity client puts it, "You may as well choose someone you get on with, as you have got to spend a lot of time with them."

Lawyers who are willing to invest time listening carefully and understanding their clients' challenges, standing in their clients' shoes and owning their legal issues with passion have a much better chance of winning and retaining business. This means making time for face-to-face meetings regardless of location, maintaining regular contact and alerting clients to interesting trends and developments. It involves building a deep knowledge of clients and developing a personal consistency over time.

(a) Developing relationship management with clients

Talent management has an important role to play in encouraging a change of mindset from the transactional, chargeable-hour, short-term approach, to one of long-term relationships. This involves a renewed focus on developing empathy with clients, understanding the environment that they operate in internally and externally, thinking about the drivers of their profitability and growth, listening to what is concerning them, thinking about their organisational structures and decision making. This is the world of the in-house lawyer, with a talent set that should be of fundamental interest to the independent lawyer who wants to create enduring client relationships. At the heart of this talent lie the fundamentals of emotional intelligence: self-awareness, listening skills, awareness of others, motivation and empathy.

These skills are best learned from an experienced lawyer and law firms can enhance their talent by treating this as an essential element of on-the-job training. There are stories of young lawyers who have not yet met a client, despite being in their second or third year of work. They need to see and hear first hand what it takes

---

8   Mehrabian, Albert (1971) *Silent Messages* (1st ed).

to understand and engage in a client's issues and develop a passion to take on their work. Likewise, they should be able to understand how experienced lawyers develop and maintain networks and how to put their energies into forging their own.

(b)   *Developing relationship management with colleagues*
Engaging our awareness to manage interactions successfully and build positive long-term relationships applies equally outside and inside the firm. Investing time to find common ground and build rapport will help to sustain relationships through trickier times.

Whether we are working with individuals or leading teams, most relationships are built on reciprocity and collaboration. Empathy includes understanding what is important to others and what you have that they may value. Thanks, recognition, praise and challenging work are all often underestimated in this context. Lawyers place a high value on genuine praise from someone whom they respect. Celebrating successes even in tough times reinforces the effect.

Listening skills are central to effective relationships – concentrating on hearing everything that is being communicated before responding, noticing silences and looking for the important non-verbal signals. Listening with full attention and genuine interest in what the other person is saying demonstrates respect. It will help you to identify your colleagues' strengths and harness them to increase motivation.

As we have seen, feedback is vital and has most impact when it is concise, clear and given as soon as possible. Constructive and balanced feedback meets a strong desire in lawyers to develop. It is most effective when it is as factual as possible and the intention is to benefit the learning of the recipient, rather than to be critical or demonstrate superior knowledge. Using a style of "It would be even better if…" can make it more readily accepted.

Relationship management inevitably includes handling difficult conversations. Many lawyers shy away from these, and conflicts at work tend to fester. Tackling tough conversations is a separate topic, but if an interaction is going to be tough, it is best to start with self-awareness and a good understanding of the other person's position.

Finally, it is important for leaders to model – as consistently as possible – the skills and behaviour that they wish to see in others. Remembering that only about 7% of communication is through words, it is best to have face-to-face interaction whenever possible.

Cultural intelligence – an indispensable talent

Peter Alfandary
PRA CrossCultural

1. **Introduction**

Austrian-American psychologist Paul Watzlawick once stated: "What is true is not what I say but what the other person understands."

Language is full of nuances, mistranslations and 'false friends'. Even between native English speakers, confusion can reign. 'Quite good' to an American means very good. To the British, it implies that something is just OK. When Americans table an idea, they postpone discussing it. The British, on the other hand, put it on the immediate agenda.

Words such as 'benefits' (*advantages* as opposed to *profits*), 'director' (*board member* as opposed to *manager*), 'agenda' (*list of meeting points* as opposed to *diary*) and 'realise' (*become aware of* as opposed to *achieve*) may mean different things to native and non-native English speakers.

We must avoid the overuse of colloquialisms. In one recent 20-minute presentation to an audience of European lawyers, an eminent speaker used the following words : 'recoil', 'gutted', 'cram in', 'crib sheet', 'chipper', 'soak up', 'clinch', 'bandwidth', 'air time', 'straight from the off' and 'bee's knees'. For some listeners, each of these words acted as a distraction and each distraction detracted from the overall message. Their use was at best culturally insensitive, at worst damaging to the speaker's credibility.

Idiomatic expressions, used extensively by British and Americans, confuse and are counterproductive. We should avoid throwing 'curve balls' to non-native English speakers or asking them to 'step up to the plate', and we should all stop 'beating around the bush' if we are going to 'hit the ground running' as culturally intelligent lawyers.

As our profession becomes increasingly international, it is crucial that lawyers understand the nuances and differences of the new markets and jurisdictions in which they are required to operate.

The legal profession worldwide is experiencing dramatic structural change. With increasing market saturation, many firms are beginning to look beyond their own backyards. Whether opening new offices or strengthening international strategic alliances, leading firms are increasingly casting their gaze internationally – both for clients and for market presence. The big boys are getting bigger and clients – who have always been king – are now exerting their regal powers with unprecedented vigour.

As the legal market becomes increasingly homogenous and difficult to navigate, cultural intelligence (CQ) is becoming more and more important.[1] Defined by two leading researchers and academics, Ang and Earley, as "an individual's capacity to function effectively across cultures", CQ is now a crucial skill for any lawyer seeking to work in an international context.

Fundamentally, legal services are still made up of two key elements: the 'What' and the 'How'.

The What is our technical ability as lawyers – no matter what the discipline or practice area in which we operate. Excelling in the What is not only a *sine qua non*, but is now treated by clients as a starting point. Legal excellence has become no more than a base expectation – we are increasingly being judged on how we deliver our services, not just on the services themselves.

As the legal market becomes more and more saturated, as law schools churn out wave after wave of legal talent, a lawyer's competitive edge is no longer about simply his or her ability to litigate, but rather his or her abilities to build, nurture, manage and deepen client relationships. We are fast approaching a stage where the only real differentiator that most firms now have is the quality of their service delivery; historically, this is a skill that some lawyers have been sorely lacking.

As markets open, firms merge and the legal profession becomes increasingly international, CQ has become an integral part of any good lawyer's portfolio.

2. Cultural intelligence and culture

IQ as a measure of intelligence has been with us for over a century.

Some of the very first IQ tests were devised as early as 1905 by two Frenchmen, Binet and Simon. Over the years, IQ testing has had many critics, but it continues to be used in some sectors as a measurement tool.

In the 1990s, the business world partly shifted its focus to emotional intelligence (EQ) – in essence, an individual's ability to combine thinking with emotions so as to understand and empathise with others. Following the work of Daniel Goleman, EQ continues to be seen as an important tool for successful leadership.

CQ focuses not on our intellect or emotions, but rather on our ability to work effectively and efficiently across cultural and national boundaries.

CQ is now a recognised management tool and skill. The subject is vast and the research voluminous. Cultural differences in business have now been studied, analysed, categorised and explained in depth by prominent researchers and academics, in addition to Earley and Ang, including leading thinkers such as Trompenaars, Hampden Turner, Hofstedde, Hill, Livermore, Rosinski and Hall.

3. What exactly is culture?

In essence, culture is the 'Who', the 'What', the 'Why' and the 'How' we behave

---

[1] For further information on cultural intelligence (and used as sources for this chapter) please see *Coaching across Culture*, Rosinski; *Wired for Culture*, Pagel; *Bridging the Culture Gap*, Carte and Fox; *The Mindful International Manager*, Comfort and Franklin; *Beyond Culture*, Hall; *Riding the Waves of Culture*, Trompenaars and Hampden-Turner; *Culture and Organizations*, Hofstede; *The Cutural Difference*, Livermore; *When Culures Collide*, Lewis; *Cultural Intelligence*, Earley and Mosakowski; *Cross Cultural Awareness*, Victor; *Introduction to Comparative Legal Cultures*, Papadopoulos; *Cultural Intelligence*, Van Dyne, Ang and Livermore; *Figuring Foreigners Out*, Storti; *Thinking, Fast and Slow*, Kahneman.

when viewed collectively by others with whom we interact, as well as by ourselves as part of the group to which we consider that we belong. It is, as Hofstede has said, "the collective programming of the mind which distinguishes the members of one group from another". Furthermore, and as Pagel states, we are all "wired for culture".

Culture is like an iceberg. When we first land in another country, the cultural differences hit us at their most simplistic level and without any noticeable effort on our part. We immediately notice differences in language, dress, smells, signs, climate and food – these represent the visible part of the iceberg.

The invisible part of the iceberg, the mass below the waterline, is much bigger and more significant than its tip.

Dwelling just below the surface are marked distinctions in how we communicate, deal with conflict, manage our time and approach problems. There are deep-rooted differences in perceptions of professionalism, etiquette, right and wrong, and acceptable behaviour.

Lawyers who want to succeed in international markets must constantly ask themselves important questions: "What makes individuals in this particular culture different from those with whom I normally interact? What style of communication do they prefer? How do they make decisions, manage their time, analyse problems and deal with conflict?" The answers are less obvious than you might think.

The culturally intelligent businessperson and lawyer must spend time addressing these questions and must strive to become an expert at functioning effectively across cultures. In so doing, he or she can deepen professional relationships with both colleagues and clients.

4. **The 21st century paradox**

It is both simplistic and true to say that we live in an increasingly globalised and increasingly small world.

It is equally banal to observe that we live in a world where communication has changed beyond all recognition and expectations. Ours is a world of email, social media and smartphones, where instant reactions, initial views and quick answers are expected of each and every one of us. We live in a world where quality 'thinking time' is in ever-shorter supply.

We also live in a world where English has become the *lingua franca* of the business community and where it is difficult to compete without knowledge of English. Despite the near ubiquity of a common language, communication has not, in fact, become any easier. The globalisation of the English language has given rise to a paradox: we may all speak English, but that does not mean that we are all speaking the same language.

Take, for example, a group of German, Japanese, British, Brazilian, American and French businesspeople, sitting around a table negotiating. They may all be speaking English, but that does not guarantee that they really understand each other.

Worst of all, a common understanding may be assumed: the participants in our meeting may have fallen into a 'trap of similarity', that dangerous place where we assume understanding, but where in reality we end up with miscommunication, misunderstanding and inaccurate presumptions.

Intercultural miscommunication is a key obstacle to effective cross-border business, a problem that is only exacerbated by the increasing speed of our communications, where we have seconds to react, where replies are expected immediately and where we are afforded precious little time to think.

Competing Across Borders, a recent survey of global executives published by *The Economist* Intelligence Unit, concluded that "misunderstandings rooted in cultural differences present the greatest obstacle to productive cross-border collaboration", while at the same time recognising that "effective cross-border communication and collaboration are becoming critical to the financial success of companies with international aspirations".

The legal profession is not immune to this. If our clients are worrying about cultural intelligence, so too should we. We are not above falling into the trap of similarity. There are no exceptions to the rule – even for lawyers.

5. Lawyers are like everyone else

Every client and every lawyer walks into a conference room (or gets on to a conference call) carrying a suitcase containing his or her unique cultural baggage.

Or to put it in other terms, we all walk in with our iPods containing our unique and very specific choices of music. Culturally, we assume that because we all own iPods, we all have the same music on them. The reality, obviously, is that some lawyers have jazz and opera on their iPods, while others listen only to hip hop and metal.

Similarly, a Mac and a PC may be used to perform the same tasks, but they are built, designed and programmed entirely differently. In this case, the trap of similarity is the assumption that because the Mac and PC are both computers, they can talk to and understand each other immediately and intuitively. The truth is that communication is possible, but only with additional software.

Some lawyers and some clients are Macs, whereas some are PCs.

CQ is the software that all lawyers now need if they are going to excel at the How.

The good news is that, perhaps unlike IQ, CQ can be taught and is therefore integral to 21st century talent management.

6. The culturally intelligent lawyer

In order to succeed, lawyers need to develop an increased understanding of the 'Why' involved in cultural differences, along with a greater degree of personal self-awareness and a willingness to adapt behaviour and develop strategies appropriate to a variety of cross-cultural encounters.

Effective talent management in both law firms and in-house legal departments will need to encompass what the leading researchers have identified as four fundamental factors:
- Motivation – for lawyers, this refers to the partner, associate or general counsel's drive and energy to adapt cross-culturally and deal with increasingly apparent challenges with clients from different cultures or with lawyers in different jurisdictions
- Cognition – the lawyer's level of understanding about culture and how it shapes both the business and legal environment in which others operate.

This factor includes an understanding of one's own culture and how it is perceived by others.
- Metacognition – the lawyer's ability to strategise when working with clients and colleagues in other cultures. Despite current market pressures, this means finding the time to observe, prepare and plan for dealing with differences in the way that legal concepts are explained or advice is delivered.
- Behaviour – the lawyer's ability to change his or her behaviour, use of language and verbal and non-verbal actions when interacting with others.

Advice to an Asian client cannot necessarily be given in the same way as to a US client. A German chief executive or French general counsel may need to be dealt with differently from a Brazilian chief executive or British general counsel. Also, the client's reaction to the same advice may differ depending on his or her culture of origin.

How often we have we heard the complaint (in both international law firms and in-house legal departments) that the Paris/London/Moscow/New York/Mumbai/Frankfurt/Sao Paulo office just do not seem to understand what we really are saying, what we really want and what the client needs…?

CQ is about suspending judgement. It is about working smarter, particularly with the continual stress we are under as lawyers. It is in times of stress that we need to be most wary, as we all tend to revert to stereotype: the British become more British, the French more French, the Japanese more Japanese, Americans more American.

It is also about understanding not just the differences between legal systems, but also how different cultures view crucial issues such as time, deadlines, risk, formality, directness, uncertainty or even the very purpose of meetings.

6.1 Points of cultural difference

(a) *Time management*
In some cultures, such as Germany, the United Kingdom and the United States, time is thought of as highly linear. Diaries are respected religiously, meeting times are rigorously adhered to and interruptions are disliked. People concentrate on one activity or relationship at a time and deadlines are observed. These monochronic cultures are diametrically opposed to their polychronic equivalents.

In South America, most of Southern Europe, Africa and parts of Asia, time can be viewed differently and may be seen as more of a guideline than a rule. People may well multitask and can focus simultaneously on multiple relationships. If new circumstances arise, timetables and deadlines may well change, without incident.

Italians or Brazilians do not believe that there is much of a problem if a meeting or conference call starts 15 minutes late. By this time, the American or German will have interpreted the delay as either disrespect or lack of seriousness or professionalism.

(b) *Meetings*
Closely linked to concepts of time are the ways that meetings tend to be conducted in different cultures. In France, for example, meetings have been described by one senior executive (perhaps unfairly) as "intellectual orgies". Although clearly

hyperbolic, in less time-orientated cultures, meetings may well start and finish later than planned and, in extreme cases, may seem like nothing more than ill-disciplined shouting contests or intellectual boxing matches.

Monochronic cultures will tend to have much more structured meetings, where a strict agenda is followed and pre-approved topics are discussed. The purpose of these meetings is to conclude with an action plan that either reflects the decisions taken at the meeting or agreements regarding next steps.

Americans, British and Germans, for instance, will often be surprised at how tolerant their Latin counterparts are of participants who go 'off point', who digress, talk on their phones or talk among themselves while others are speaking.

(c) *Communication styles*

In 'low-context' cultures such as the United States and the Netherlands, communication will tend to be very direct and unambiguous. Indeed, it may be so direct that it is sometimes misinterpreted as rudeness. In other 'high-context' cultures, such as Japan or the United Kingdom, the unsaid may well be as important as the said. The Dutch or American listener will need to learn the skills and acquire the patience to successfully decode the message.

The British, in particular, need to learn that they are often nigh incomprehensible to the rest of the world. Their indirectness and use of metaphor are not only hard for foreigners to understand, but also often interpreted as hypocrisy. The British use of understatement, humour and self-deprecation is a source of much confusion and misunderstanding. This is hardly surprising when being "a little bit disappointed" means "very angry", when "I am not certain that I completely agree" means "I do not agree" and when the remark, "That is a courageous proposal" means that the suggestion is ridiculous.

(d) *Decision making*

The culturally intelligent lawyer must understand that, for example, the French or German client may require a great deal of analysis (and time) before making a decision. In cultures that are risk averse and certainty orientated, the value of taking time is highly important. In its most simplistic form, a comparison between a 'typical' French and US executive would tend to indicate that while the American would spend, say, 20% of his time on reaching a decision and 80% on its actual implementation, the reverse may well be true of the French counterpart.

This would tend to explain the often-heard criticism in some European circles about Americans 'knee jerking' into decisions without having sufficiently analysed the consequences. Conversely, Americans often complain of the European condition of 'paralysis by analysis'. With further examination, however, it becomes clear that these different approaches may well stem from deeper issues: an analytical, possibly Cartesian education system, as opposed to a faster, holistic, even heuristic approach.

Equally, the contrasting way that failure is (or is not) stigmatised in certain cultures may have a direct effect on decision making. The 'can do' attitude and the less judgemental attitude to past failure so prevalent in the United States should help in understanding the American approach to decision making.

(e)   Attitudes towards rules and relationships

The degree to which relationships take precedence over rules presents yet another interesting cultural variation for the international lawyer.

In so-called 'universalist' cultures, such as the United States and much of northern Europe, rules tend to be inflexible, regardless of particular circumstances or relationships that foreigners may consider relevant to the issue at hand. By contrast, in 'particularist' cultures, such as the Middle East and many southern countries, far greater weight is given to duties and obligations that may arise either from individual relationships of from the specific circumstances prevalent at the time.

One of the founding fathers of cultural intelligence, Trompenaars, illustrated this dilemma with the following example: "You are a passenger in a car driven by a very close friend. He hits a pedestrian. You know he was driving at 45 km per hour in an area where the maximum speed allowed is 35. His lawyer says that if you testify that he was only driving at 35 km per hour, it will save him from serious consequences. What right does your friend have to expect you to protect him by testifying that he was driving at the lower speed?"

Even among lawyers – in all of whom, one would assume, the rule of law is to some extent ingrained – a clear cultural split exists. There is a culturally split difference of opinion between those for whom what is right will always be right and to be fair is to treat everyone alike, and those who lean towards the belief that what is true and fair in one situation might be wrong in another.

(f)   Other researched and recognisable cultural variations

Extensive literature exists to help our understanding of cultural differences, which include a multitude of other categorisations. A non-exhaustive list appears below, all of which is relevant to the culturally aware lawyer. Many factors will be familiar and all are important to think about when dealing with different cultures (whether internally or with clients):

- formality versus informality in relationships;
- short-term versus long-term planning in strategy formulation;
- hierarchy versus equality in management;
- analytical versus systemic thinking (ie, dissecting a problem into smaller elements as opposed to adopting a more holistic approach);
- assertiveness versus modesty;
- individualist versus collectivist team behaviour;
- preference for stability versus change;
- harmony versus confrontation;
- deductive reasoning (concept and theory based) versus inductive problem-solving (case and experience based);
- bias towards analysis versus pragmatism;
- discussion-based (with an emphasis on a verbally direct but emotionally restrained approach) versus engagement-based (where the emphasis will be more confrontational and emotionally expressive) negotiations;
- reserved and calm mannerisms versus displays of emotion; and
- preferences for risk versus certainty.

The culturally intelligent lawyer understands and works with all these differences. He or she sees them played out daily, by clients and colleagues across jurisdictions.

The culturally intelligent lawyer has a sound basic understanding of the differences between common law (reflexive) and civil law (legicentric) legal systems.

The culturally intelligent lawyer appreciates the importance of being a 'cultural guide' and will be able to identify and explain foreign concepts in detail and without being asked. The culturally intelligent lawyer will explain the concept of discovery to the client who has never litigated in a common law business environment, and will be aware that common law principles of full disclosure may seem as absurd to the client as playing a game of poker with the cards face-up.

The culturally intelligent lawyer is as alive to jurisdictional differences in matters of compliance, corporate governance and contractual principles as to concepts such as good faith, materiality, reasonableness, best efforts and evidentiary truth.

The culturally intelligent lawyer knows that hierarchy and negotiation styles vary greatly across cultures, as do the structure and purpose of meetings. Some cultures respect age and seniority; some favour silence in negotiations; some will be uncomfortable with displays of anger or emotion; and in some the ultimate decider may not even be present at a critical meeting.

Finally, the cultural intelligent lawyer will be acutely conscious of the comparative importance of relationship building from culture to culture. In the role of a business developer, he or she will accordingly vary the 'investment time' spent on winning new work from both existing and prospective clients.

It is indeed a very rich, complex and varied world we live in, and it is one in which the culturally intelligent lawyer must focus on the part of the iceberg that is below the waterline.

7. Stereotypes and culture

In our efforts to become more culturally aware, it is imperative to discuss stereotypes. None of us is without prejudice and cultural stereotypes permeate our thinking much more than we might care to admit.

In the same way that we are all wired for culture, we are also wired subconsciously towards bias, generalisations and stereotyping. We have already observed that in stressful environments, nationalities and cultures tend to revert to stereotypical behaviour, but stereotypes and generalisations can be both dangerous and useful.

They are dangerous because they are oversimplistic and, when misused, they can lead to lazy thinking or bigotry. They are useful because – where tempered with the knowledge that they are generalisations and must be thought of as such – they can provide us with essential shortcuts to better understand and interpret the group behaviour of others.

Indeed, an understanding of stereotypes – even if these are untrue, misleading and baseless – is important, in that they can help us better understand the way that others view us. They help us understand preconceptions that people might have of us – preconceptions that, even if based on stereotypical and inaccurate understandings of our respective cultures, still inform the way we are viewed and the ways we will be treated.

Self-awareness is a crucial part of cultural intelligence.

It often comes as a surprise to the British to hear that others often perceive them as hypocritical. That perception is primarily the result of the British predisposition to use a coded language that is understated, emphasises indirectness and relies on humour and self-deprecation.

The important lesson for the British to learn is that what they perceive as a normal, polite way of conversing can be viewed as a far more insidious, negative and potentially obstructive form of communication.

Understanding how others perceive us, especially when that perception is incorrect, is a fundamental part of effective communication.

8. What can go wrong without CQ

Language skills are now a *sine qua non* for lawyers.

Like technical ability, they are only the starting point in our increasingly competitive market. Commoditisation of legal services has become an unstoppable force in our homogeneous world. Differentiation, while still achievable, is ever more elusive.

Without CQ, the 21st century lawyer cannot excel. Without CQ, expectations between in-house legal departments within the same group but in different countries, or between the different country offices of international law firms, may fail to be met.

Without CQ, local legislation or local procedures may not be properly understood, time and deadlines may be mismanaged, styles of legal advice between lawyers or with clients may become confusing, advice may be misinterpreted or misunderstood, legal concepts will become lost in translation and nuances will be missed or misconstrued.

Stress levels between offices and between lawyer and client, already at record levels, will rise still further and compound misunderstanding. Time will be wasted, legal costs will increase and clients will be dissatisfied.

If we accept that the How is a critical part of the service equation, then we can no longer risk having our lack of CQ jeopardise client service or lead to mistakes.

9. Practical dos and don'ts for the 21st century lawyer

In his book *Thinking, Fast and Slow*, Daniel Kahneman makes the crucial distinction between unconscious thinking, which we do approximately 90% of the time and is often based on heuristics, and 'effortful thinking', which is slower, more deliberate, more considered and inherently more reliable and accurate.

CQ is about suspending judgement. It is about taking a step back. It demands effort, often patience and an element of conscious rewiring.

No list of dos and don'ts can be exhaustive, but suggestions for our profession should at least include the following:

- Do seek clarity by asking questions about the local and legal culture in which you are operating.

- Do think of the questions that the client has not even thought about asking and deal with all jurisdictional surprises in advance.
- Do consider what is the 'question behind the question' and what has prompted the person to ask it in the first place.
- Do take account of others' preconceptions about you.
- Do highlight deadlines, major points, key questions and major risks in your emails, then phone the recipient to ensure that these are clearly understood.
- Do invest time in appreciating colleagues' different ways of 'lawyering'.
- Do ask colleagues about the client's level of cultural awareness and his or her cultural expectations.
- Do listen actively and intelligently and spend more time listening than speaking – most lawyers wrongly believe that the Almighty gave them two mouths and only one ear, whereas a quick look in the mirror will reveal that the reverse is true.
- Don't assume similarity.
- Don't assume understanding – in fact, don't assume at all.
- Don't speak too fast.
- Don't write long paragraphs in emails, each containing a multitude of key points.
- Don't use jargon, idiomatic expressions or colloquialisms.
- Don't make the mistake of believing that adapting your style or behaviour involves a loss of your own cultural identity – it simply means working smarter.
- Don't wait to be asked – a good lawyer offers information and explains the journey that the client is embarking upon.

A final word for the native English-speaking reader: the greatest burden is on you.

Now that English has become the *lingua franca* of the legal and the business world, native English-speakers have it easy. Never forget, however, that its pre-eminence brings with it obligations and responsibilities.

We need to speak more slowly; we need to be clearer; we need to signpost our conversations and summarise key points – we must ensure that we communicate with precision, clarity and empathy for others.

10. Conclusion

CQ is to be embraced.

The good news is that, perhaps unlike IQ, CQ can be taught. It is already on the curricula of some major international law firms and is taught in a number of leading business schools. It is not, however, just a skill to be embraced by major firms or global in-house legal departments. It affects every lawyer working in an international environment.

CQ is an integral part of excellence in terms of client service.

It is therefore not an optional talent or a soft skill. It is a critical hard skill that we all need to hone.

Lawyers from every jurisdiction need to become cultural guides if they are to become better lawyers.

There is a saying that "tourists take their culture away with them on their travels; voyagers leave theirs at home".

The 21st century lawyer needs to be a voyager, not just a tourist.

The final piece of good news is that to help guide them on their voyage, every lawyer possesses an internal GPS, a cultural satellite navigation system.

Our clients are switching on their GPSs. We should all be doing the same.

The author extends thanks to Adam Alfandary for his editorial contributions.

The future of legal talent management: adopting an innovative mindset for future challenges

Shelley Dunstone
Legal Circles

1. **Introduction**

   What challenges will law firms need to address in managing their legal talent over the next five to 10 years? How will firms need to change and adapt?

   There is no single answer. Employment conditions vary from country to country. In some places talent may be freely available and easily replaced, whereas in others there is a shortage. Law firms vary in their challenges and aspirations – there are large firms, small firms and solos, offering an array of different services. Some have sophisticated approaches to talent management and others have little experience with it.

   To begin, two challenges must be acknowledged:
   - We are writing for a global audience, because generalisations cannot apply everywhere in the world; and
   - We are writing about the future, because no one can foresee exactly what challenges will present themselves.

2. **Likely future challenges**

   Some insight into future challenges can be gleaned from general employer surveys, as some of the results will apply equally to law firms. An example is the Randstad Salary, Benefits and Workplace Trends Survey 2011-2012.[1] It reports that the top three challenges for employers are:
   - attracting talent for the next growth phase;
   - retaining top performers; and
   - increasing performance and productivity.

   According to this survey, the three main productivity challenges for employers are:
   - developing leadership skills for the next growth phase;
   - filling critical vacancies created by business expansion; and
   - addressing knowledge loss created by increased employee turnover.

---

1   Report of a survey of 530 key decision makers from a range of companies across Australia between November 2011 and February 2012 (conducted by ICMA Group, Belgium).

The most important leadership competencies nominated in the survey are:
- motivating and inspiring others;
- adapting to changing business demands; and
- building trusted relationships.

The Australasian Legal Practice Management Association conducted a survey of law firms, entitled "Hot Issues in Human Resources for the Australasian Legal Industry in 2013".[2] In this survey, the top three issues rated as "highly important" by over 40% of respondents were:
- finding quality staff;
- retaining employees/managing talent; and
- developing organisational leadership capabilities.

Other issues that were rated as "very important" by over 40% of respondents included:
- managing poor performance;
- promoting effective use of social media; and
- managing mental health in the workforce.

Issues that were ranked higher in importance than in the previous year included workforce diversity and equal opportunity issues, and ageing in the legal profession.

Future challenges for the legal profession may include the following.

2.1 Attracting and retaining lawyers

Law firms could encounter skills shortages as a result of hiring fewer law graduates during the financial crisis. Despite challenging economic conditions, high staff turnover could continue. Employees (including the growing numbers of women entering the profession) are increasingly demanding flexible ways of working. Younger workers are more inclined to seek a higher purpose in their work and are attracted to employers that demonstrate corporate social responsibility.

Questions to ask could include the following:
- How can we recruit more lawyers with the right qualities and skills?
- How can we keep our lawyers satisfied in their employment so that they will stay with us?
- What can we do to make legal practice a more meaningful and fulfilling career for our lawyers?

2.2 Training

Young people tend to change jobs more frequently and to seek a more varied career than their predecessors. It might become more difficult to hire lawyers with the right type of experience, and law firms will need to become better at training new graduates. However, legal process outsourcing and disruptive technologies are reducing the amount of beginner work that is available for new law graduates.

---

2   Survey results are available at www.alpma.com.au.

Clients are less willing to pay for junior lawyers to learn at their expense. Yet younger employees increasingly expect and value professional development, including mentoring.

Questions to ask could include the following:
- How can we challenge the conventional wisdom that it takes two years' experience for a new graduate to become productive and profitable?
- What tools can we develop to help junior lawyers to become more productive, more quickly?
- How can we get better at mentoring our lawyers?

2.3 Career development

In some places, reduced barriers to entry are allowing non-lawyer providers to compete in the market for legal services. Commoditisation and 'supermarketisation' of legal services are leading to an expectation of lower prices; but at the same time, lawyers want higher salaries and want to do work that is intellectually challenging.

As more people change careers, age is no longer an indicator of seniority. A new law graduate might have years of valuable business experience to offer. Lawyers in larger firms have shorter shelf lives: for example, an 'out at 55' policy is becoming more common.

Questions to ask could include the following:
- How can we keep our lawyers intellectually stimulated?
- How can we manage our mature-aged graduates more effectively?
- How can we better harness and utilise the wisdom of our most senior lawyers?

2.4 Legal practice development

It is increasingly necessary for all lawyers to bring business into the firm, but not all have the skills to do so. The Internet provides a valuable platform for professionals to promote their services, but there is a distrust of social media and an uneasy tension between personal branding and firm branding.

Questions to ask could include the following:
- How can we help our lawyers to build their skills in practice development?
- How much freedom should we give our lawyers to utilise social media in their professional capacities?
- To what extent should our lawyers be allowed to promote themselves, as opposed to promoting the firm?

2.5 Succession planning

For many lawyers, partnership has become a more remote prospect, because the firm is 'top heavy' or unwilling to dilute the partnership equity pool. Equally, for many younger lawyers, partnership does not hold the allure it once did. However, a new generation of partners will need to be found, to keep the firm going and to ensure that outgoing partners are paid a fair amount for their career-long investment in the firm.

Questions to ask could include the following:
- How can we provide a satisfying and rewarding career path and create a sense of belonging in the firm for those who are not partners?

- How can we encourage younger lawyers to become interested in partnership?
- What skills development can we offer to equip our lawyers to become our 'succession plan'?

3. What is meant by an 'innovative mindset'?

A 'mindset' is a mental attitude that determines how you will interpret and respond to situations. Your mindset is your own unique way of thinking about what is possible.

'Innovation' is doing new things, or doing things in new or better ways.

So an 'innovative mindset' is a mental attitude of being willing to try new things.

It is very easy to say, "We are innovative", but it is hard to do, because humans are creatures of habit. It is much easier to keep doing the same things in the same way than to take the risk of trying something new.

The legal profession is conservative. Lawyers (at least in common law jurisdictions) are required to follow precedent; they must look to the past to find solutions. But they are not the only ones who are prisoners of precedent. All humans can find themselves stuck in precedent at times, because that is how the brain works.

Throughout your life, your brain takes in pieces of information and arranges them in patterns in your memory. As new information comes in, your brain does a search to see how it might fit with other information already stored in your memory. When you look for an idea, your brain goes straight to its store of similar ideas and retrieves them. The shelves of your brain are stocked with examples of things that you have seen, done or heard of before.[3]

In effect, your brain offers you a selection of templates (or 'precedents' in lawyer-language). This explains why many people find it difficult to think laterally and why brainstorming sessions often produce little in the way of truly novel suggestions. The conversation goes something like this: "What should we do?" "Let's brainstorm some alternatives." "Well, what did we do last time?" "What are our competitors doing?" "What is best practice in this area?" "Let's not reinvent the wheel."

It is not easy to visualise a wholly new way of doing things. And when you do, plenty of people will tell you why your idea will not work. It is seen as safer to follow what others have done.

However, those who persevere with their new ideas attract attention and can build competitive advantage.

Here is an example of a lawyer who has achieved this with his law firm.

3.1 Case study: breaking free from precedent

Kain Corporate and Commercial (Kain C+C) is a law firm with a team of 29 staff (including 20 lawyers) based in Adelaide, Australia, offering services in corporate, commercial and M&A law.

This firm is extremely popular among lawyers seeking employment. One reason for this is the substantial amount of charitable work it undertakes.

The firm's founder, John Kain, says: "Compared to the overwhelming majority of

---

3   William Duggan, " How Aha! Really Happens", *Strategy + Business*, Issue 61, Winter 2010

the world's population (and many parts of Australia's population), we occupy a position of rare privilege – materially, socially and in many other respects. With this privilege comes responsibility – to use our good fortune to help those less fortunate."

With this philosophy, he resigned his partnership at an established commercial law firm and set up his own firm based on a unique model, which seeks to achieve two things:

- Do good work to help people in need, in a meaningful and sustainable way; and
- Change the way that people think and behave, to encourage them to use their own good fortune to help others.

The vehicle through which this is achieved is the Kain C+C Charitable Foundation, which has the mandate of "unlocking compassion to change our world".

Since its establishment in 2005, the foundation has raised more than A$500,000 in cash and has performed more than 4,000 hours of volunteer work on foundation projects.

Having a 'higher purpose' at the heart of the legal practice has brought business benefits such as ease of attraction and retention of staff. John says: "The business benefits are a welcome side effect; but that's not why I established this model. I chose to do it because it's the right thing to do." He adds: "It does help to create a unique culture, which is now deeply ingrained. It gives our business a soul. Working here is more than just a job."

Each team member makes a fortnightly donation (which is automatically deducted from gross salary) to the foundation. The business then matches those donations, dollar for dollar. But this is only the start. John states: "It is not a donation-only business. It is only hands-on work that changes the way people think and behave."

Therefore, each team member also commits to spending the equivalent of one day per year performing volunteer work through programmes sponsored by the foundation. Local programmes include providing free legal advice and computer training for homeless people at a pro bono clinic and mentoring disadvantaged young people to help them transition to work. The firm's billing targets are adjusted to reflect time spent on foundation projects.

Internationally, the firm has developed the Uganda Project, to help the plight of children who have been orphaned due to HIV/AIDS, war and disease. A team from the law firm (and from its partner organisations) regularly travels to Uganda to undertake physical work such as building houses and other infrastructure, assisting at a medical clinic, working in an orphanage and donating clothes, books and toys. The visit lasts for two weeks: one week is funded by the firm and the other by the team member. The firm contributes to the travel costs.

In a blog entry published on the firm's website, one of the participants wrote: "It was just like any childcare centre in Australia, with one major disheartening difference – the children we were playing with had no family. I helped feed and play with a young child called Nicole. Soon after, Nicole would not let go of me. The whole time with her I could not stop thinking that my newborn nephew of three weeks would have already received more gifts and affection than she will receive in her lifetime."

The charitable activities also provide leadership development opportunities for the staff. Leading the group travelling to Uganda presents a unique leadership challenge. The work is hard and confrontational. The leader must be able to encourage team members who are out of their comfort zone and may feel upset by what they see. To lead such a group requires maturity and self-assurance.

Better teamwork is another benefit. When someone is away working on a foundation project, someone else must cover his or her work. Staff recognise that they are all part of a single team contributing to good work in the community.

Philanthropy is at the heart of everything the firm does.

John accepts that other law firms also engage in philanthropic or pro bono work and allow their staff to take time away from the office to work for charity. However, he says that his firm's model is different: "We don't simply encourage or allow it; we demand it." Instead of having staff members do bits and pieces of charitable work, "we orchestrate all of our efforts to produce a more effective overall result". When job applicants are interviewed, they are told very clearly what the firm's expectations are. Commitment to the philosophy and the work of the foundation is a prerequisite for joining the firm.

At Kain C+C, the foundation work is given the same priority as client work. It is not something that is done in people's spare time. This in itself is a major mindset shift. In most law firms, client work always comes first.

'Mindset' is a way of thinking about what is possible. Where there is no precedent, the assumption is that if something were a good idea, people would already be doing it. It requires vision to imagine that it would be possible to run a law firm like this.

So how did John conceive of the idea for this innovative way of running a law firm? He says that the idea came from his personal conviction that "if you can, you should". He realised that it would be difficult to develop a new model within an existing business structure. He also recognised that a piecemeal approach does not bring about lasting change.

There was no precedent for such a law firm, so he had to make it up as he went along. He says: "Some of my lawyer friends mocked me, but I am not concerned about what other people think. If you are always looking over your shoulder, you will end up with mainstream thinking." Another key was not to worry about making mistakes, "as long as they are not huge mistakes, and we do not repeat them".

It may sound as if this firm does not place a great emphasis on financial success. On the contrary, John has been methodical in ensuring that the firm is run in a business-like way. He recognised that the foundation could be sustained only if the law firm were financially sound and successful. The firm has a corporate structure and is overseen by an independent board which takes an objective view of its business activities.

The foundation, too, is run as a business, with strict corporate governance. It applies the following seven criteria in deciding which projects will be supported:

- Hands-on support – involve both financial and hands-on support from the firm or its corporate partners.
- Scalability – be replicable by the firm or its corporate partners in other locations or contexts.
- Sustainability – be self-sustainable with a continued, long-term impact beyond the firm's period of support.
- Measurability – generate identifiable outcomes measurable by short and long-term key performance indicators.
- Preventability – address the causes of problems, rather than treating the symptoms.
- Most in need – receive limited government funding or philanthropic support.
- Minimal resources – have low administration costs, solid and proven administration and strong volunteer support.

A major benefit of this approach is the genuine pride of the firm's staff. One lawyer recently related a conversation with a taxi driver about her work. The public perception of lawyers is not always positive. It is not always easy to tell a stranger, "I am a lawyer," because of the reaction that you might receive. This lawyer, however, was extremely proud to say that she was a lawyer and to tell the taxi driver about the good work being done by her firm.

To find out more about the Kain C+C model, visit www.kaincc.com.

4. **Competing for talent**
    Law firms compete against each other for the lawyers that they require. How can an innovative mindset lead to competitive advantage in the market for legal talent?
    Competitive advantage is derived from two things:
    - what you have (ie, your strategic assets); and
    - what you do with these strategic assets to create value.

Your strategic assets are your inherent strengths, which usually include intangible things such as core competencies, firm culture and reputation. Competitive advantage is based on strategic assets and enhancing your strategic assets can build competitive advantage.

It is important to be clear about:
- what sort of law firm you have;
- what sort of talent you want to attract; and
- why your targets will be attracted to your firm.

Law firms wanting to improve their competitive advantage in the market for legal talent should develop the following as strategic assets:
- their ability to adapt to a changing environment; and
- their reputation for being innovative with talent management.

5. The role of the leader in promoting innovative thinking

5.1 The challenge

People in organisations are not always receptive to new ideas. Time and other resources are limited. People do not like to take risks that could be perceived as mistakes. The safe, the easy, the usual way and "what we did last time" all exert a powerful pull.

Conformity is a strong human trait which is driven by the desire to be liked and accepted by others. Humans evolved under harsh and uncertain conditions. There was safety in numbers and even the earliest humans formed tribal or kinship groups for protection. Membership of these groups was a matter of survival. When we are genetically programmed to see expulsion from our social group as a dangerous prospect, 'fitting in' becomes paramount.[4]

Suggesting an untried idea, seeming different or eccentric, challenging the status quo – according to our finely tuned instincts, all of these behaviours have the potential to attract scorn, condemnation and rejection.

Solomon Asch's 'conformity experiments' in the 1950s demonstrated people's reluctance to speak up against majority opinion. In these experiments, subjects were placed into small groups. Only one person in each group was a genuine, unwitting subject; the rest were confederates planted by the organisers. Each group was shown a drawing of a 'standard' line of a certain length, followed by three other lines of varying lengths. The subjects were asked to identify which of the three lines was identical in length to the standard line. The answer was clearly the second line. However, under directions from the organisers, the confederates unanimously selected the incorrect line. The 'real' subject answered last. Over the course of multiple trials, 75% of the subjects agreed with the incorrect judgement of the majority at least once.

In organisations, this phenomenon is manifested in the following sorts of beliefs:

- "It has always been done this way and it seems to work – why should we risk changing it now?"
- "Everyone else seems to accept things the way they are, so who am I to question them?"

Whereas the purpose of innovation is to stand out, many people would prefer to blend in. Most people strive to earn the approval of their peers, so putting forward an unusual, unproven idea can feel risky.

In a study reported in the *Harvard Business Review*,[5] researchers sought to identify the factors that cause employees to bring ideas to their bosses or to withhold them. They interviewed 200 employees of a leading high-technology company – the very place where you would expect to find a flow of creative suggestions. Yet approximately half of the employees indicated that they felt it was not safe to speak

---

4 A good book on this subject is *Executive Instinct: Managing the human animal in the information age* (2000) by Nigel Nicholson (Random House).
5 Deter and Edmondson, "Why Employees are Afraid to Speak", *Harvard Business Review* May 2007 pp23-25

up. In particular, they were reluctant to put forward creative ideas for improving products, processes or performance.

When questioned further about this, there were three types of response:
- Some people said they had experienced a hostile reaction from a manager in response to a previous suggestion.
- Some related stories about people who had spoken out publicly and were suddenly "gone from the company".
- For many of the employees, it just felt risky. They did not know what would happen if they made a suggestion. Some were worried about embarrassing their bosses in public. Some felt that their suggestions would be resented.

These responses demonstrate that you cannot expect people simply to volunteer their suggestions. Leaders need to invite ideas and develop a climate where people feel comfortable to offer their suggestions.

The researchers commented: "We found the innate protective instinct so powerful that it also inhibited speech that clearly would have been intended to help the organisation. In our interviews, the perceived risks of speaking up felt very personal and immediate to employees, whereas the future benefit to the organisation from sharing their ideas was uncertain." They concluded: "Making employees feel safe enough to contribute fully requires deep cultural change that alters how they understand the likely costs (personal and immediate) versus benefits (organisational and future) of speaking up."

5.2 Give priority to innovative thinking

In his book *The Seven Habits of Highly Effective People*,[6] Steven Covey presents a "Time Management Matrix", in which activities are classified as urgent or non-urgent and important or not important. He makes the point that our time is usually taken up with urgent things that clamour for our attention. To get ahead, we need to make time for the things that are non-urgent, but important: "We react to urgent matters. Important matters that are not urgent require more initiative, more proactivity. We must act to seize opportunity, to make things happen. If we don't ... have a clear idea of what is important, of the results we desire in our lives, we are easily diverted into responding to the urgent."[7]

Covey tells a story about a professor who fills a big jar, first with rocks, then with gravel, then with sand and finally with water. At each stage, he asks the students: "Is the jar full?" At the end of the demonstration, he asks the students: "What is the point of this illustration?" One student responds: "No matter how full your schedule is, if you try really hard, you can always fit some more things into it!" The professor says: "No, the point is that if you don't put the big rocks in first, you'll never get them in at all."

Thinking innovatively about your talent management is important, though rarely urgent. If you do not make time for it, it will not get done. It will not shout for attention until some crisis occurs. Treat it as a 'big rock'.

---

6   Stephen R Covey, *The Seven Habits of Highly Effective People* (1989) The Business Library, pp146-162.
7   *Ibid*, p151.

5.3   **Ask the questions that others are not asking**

Questions provide a catalyst for innovative thinking. Competitive advantage goes to those who ask the questions that others are not asking.

A number of questions regarding future challenges in legal talent management were posed at the start of this chapter. While there may not be immediate answers to all of these questions, the important thing is that they are asked. This is the first step towards finding innovative solutions.

(a)   *An innovation story*

If you were out in a boat on the open sea, how would you know where you were? These days, you would use your satellite navigation system. But 300 years ago, there was no way of accurately determining your position. You could work out your latitude by studying the sun – the higher the sun at noon, the closer you were to the Equator. But there was no way of working out your longitude.

In 1714, after a spate of bad shipwrecks, the British government offered a prize of £20,000 to the person who could devise a practical method of determining longitude at sea.

As years, then decades passed with no solution, many people believed that the problem could not be solved. 'Finding the longitude' became a slang term for any crazy activity or impossible task. Cartoons began to appear in the press showing lunatics doing all sorts of odd things.

Astronomers believed that the answer lay in charting the moon and stars, so that is where most of the research was invested. It was also known that longitude corresponded to time: local time changes by one hour for every 15 degrees travelled to the east or west. So if you knew the time at your starting point and the time at your present location, you could work out your longitude by calculating how far you were from your original starting point. The problem was that clocks did not keep time at sea, because they relied on pendulum mechanisms which were disrupted by gravity and the motion of the sea.

The prize was ultimately won by John Harrison. He suggested that clocks could solve the longitude problem and worked on creating one that did not require a pendulum. People thought that he had gone mad. However, he made it a lifelong project and was finally awarded the prize for his H4 pocket watch.

Where are the 'pendulums' in your business – the things you assume cannot be changed? Question those assumptions!

5.4   **Invent problems to solve**

The inventor of a product called 'Honey Spread' was interviewed after he had sold his creation to a local food manufacturer. Honey Spread has the consistency of a gel: it does not form sticky strings like runny honey. This consistency is achieved through the addition of pectin. When asked what had inspired him to add pectin, the inventor replied: "It was just one of many things I tried." When pressed further, he said impatiently: "Look, I'm a product developer. It's my job to find problems and solve them. I was just trying to make honey not sticky."

His leap of imagination was not the idea to add pectin. It was asking the question: "How can I make honey not sticky?" How many people would even think of asking this question? Most people would assume that honey is just sticky; they would not conceptualise this as a problem to be solved.

What questions are your competitors not asking? What problem could you usefully identify and solve?

6. **An innovative mindset for the future**

   As a leader, you will need to work on cultivating an innovative mindset in yourself, your executive team and the culture of your firm.

   How an innovative mindset permeates a law firm

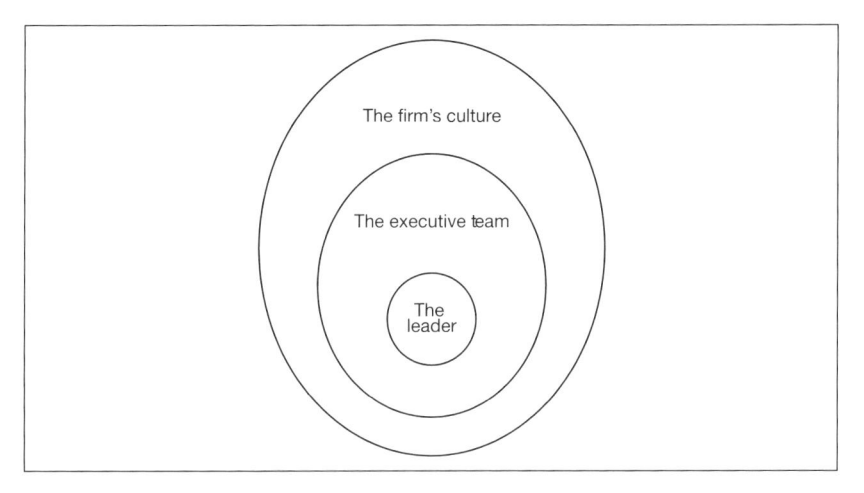

   [Diagram: concentric ovals showing "The firm's culture" containing "The executive team" containing "The leader"]

   6.1 Developing an innovative mindset in yourself

   Innovation is pioneering. When we seek to innovate, we enter new territory where many answers are unknown, with no precedent for what we should do next.

   (a) *Challenge your worldview*

   Your worldview is the way that you see the world. It encompasses the framework of ideas and beliefs through which you interpret the world. Your worldview influences the way that you think and behave.

   You may regard something to be impossible, while someone else considers it to be easily achievable.

   To challenge your own worldview, contrast it with the worldviews of others. The more diverse the group, the more diverse the ideas. Mix with other businesspeople. An advisory board can provide fresh perspectives by including people from a range of different disciplines.

   (b) *Take care of yourself*

   Work on maintaining the spark within you. Do something each day to keep yourself energised, enthusiastic and optimistic.

Delegate work to ensure that you have time to think about the future. Build in some time for recreation and enjoyable interests. Even getting up and going for a walk outside the office can refresh your mind.

Renaissance artist Leonardo Da Vinci knew the value of seeing things in perspective. He said: "Every now and then go away, have a little relaxation, for when you come back to your work your judgment will be surer; since to remain constantly at work will cause you to lose the power of judgment. Go some distance away because the work appears smaller and more of it can be taken in at a glance and a lack of harmony or proportion is more readily seen."

(c) **Stimulate your mind**

Ideas can come from seemingly random sources. Read more books and broaden the range of subjects that you read about. As you read, write down any insights that occur to you. Find some interesting podcasts that you can listen to while you drive, wait or exercise. If you do not own an iPod or other type of MP3 player yet, consider getting one – a wide range of information is available in audio format.

(d) **Allow time for reflection**

Creative breakthroughs arrive unexpectedly, often while you are relaxing or doing something unrelated to your work. You have probably already had the experience of spending a day thrashing out a difficult problem, only to solve it with a fresh idea the following morning. Sleep enables previously unconnected thoughts to come together and produce new insights.

History is full of discoveries which appeared as flashes of insight – but only because the discoverer had been agitating the problem. To produce new insights, the brain needs time to reflect. First, work hard on the problem consciously, then take a break and allow your mind's unconscious processes to do their work.

6.2 **Building an innovative mindset among your executive team**

Your team will look to you for clues as to how to spend their time and energy. If you want them to put effort into innovative thinking, you must make this clear to them.

'Groupthink' is the enemy of innovation. It is a condition in which group members persuade themselves that their collective opinion is valid, without adequate exploration of other possibilities.

(a) **Ask, don't tell**

Ideas come from curiosity. Admitting that you do not know all the answers and encouraging others to do likewise leads everyone to explore new possibilities.

Ask 'naïve' questions, commencing with a signal that your intention in asking such questions is to help the group to explore new possibilities. Make it clear that you do not know the answers and it is not a test, but that the questions are intended to act a catalyst for creative thinking. You might say, for example, "I don't know what the answer to this question might be, but I think it could help us to expand our thinking on this issue...."

Some individuals will use their forceful personalities to push particular points of view, inhibiting the expression of contrary positions. During discussion, ensure that everyone has a chance to be heard and encourage people to keep an open mind instead of adopting entrenched positions.

Encourage a variety of responses. As the twice Nobel Prize-winning scientist Linus Pauling said: "The best way to have a good idea is to have a lot of ideas."

Try some creative thinking techniques in your discussions; many books are available which offer such approaches.[8] Have patience with the process, because new ideas take time to develop.

(b) *Encourage curiosity*

Encourage others in your team to exercise and express their curiosity by proposing their own questions for discussion.

Innovative ideas come from challenging entrenched assumptions. Instead of rewarding the best idea, try rewarding the best question.

(c) *Gather the right people at the right time*

Each one of us is the product of our life so far. We have all had a unique childhood, education, working life and experiences of the world. We all have different personalities and see the world through different eyes. No wonder it can be so hard to understand each other!

Some people naturally see opportunities and find it easy and enjoyable to think laterally. Others are more likely to tell you why the ideas will not work. Both approaches are necessary, but not at the same time. People who take a negative approach could be valuable when it comes to evaluating ideas and managing risk. But when you are trying to generate a range of new ideas, these people may not be the best to have in the room.

To make good decisions, we need the input of both types of person. We need to anticipate the problems and prevent them from occurring. A focus on risk prevention is not helpful at the idea generation stage, but becomes important later on, when potential obstacles must be identified and addressed.

The key is to know which people are oriented towards opportunities and which are more likely to see the obstacles, and to utilise their respective strengths.

In making this assessment, you could rely on your experience of each individual or use one of the personality testing tools that are available.[9]

(d) *Think like a scientist*

Inevitably, you will sometimes encounter resistance to new suggestions. You will not know whether an idea will work until you try it. Set up an experiment or pilot programme; try it in one practice group or with some enthusiastic individuals who are opinion leaders in the firm.

If the results you hoped for are not achieved, do not give up. Change the conditions of the experiment and record what you learn at each stage.

---

8   A classic is Edward de Boon's *Six Thinking Hats* (1985, Penguin Books).
9   For example, the QO2 available from Team Management Systems Pty Ltd measures a person's "Opportunities/Obstacles quotient". Visit www.tms.com.au.

6.3   **Cultivating a culture of innovation in your firm**
If you want the people in your firm to think innovatively, you must lead by example. You may be a strong supporter of innovation, but you must actively demonstrate this. People cannot read your mind – they can only observe you.

(a)   *Set the mood*
Leaders set the tone in an organisation. If a leader is interested only in short-term results, people will think short term. If a leader seems downcast or weary, that feeling will spread throughout the organisation. Moods and emotions are contagious, so make an effort to keep your mood positive

(b)   *Mix people up*
Get everyone involved in generating solutions. Legal practice can be a solitary sport. Within teams, homogeneity of thought can develop which inhibits the creation of new ideas. Encourage opportunities for diverse groups of people in the firm to come together.

(c)   *Be aware of words, actions, reactions*
To build a culture of innovation, everyone in the firm needs to know and believe that thinking creatively is part of their job and that their ideas will be valued.

Leaders can easily stifle innovation without meaning to. The things you say, the things you do and the way that you react to new ideas all communicate your beliefs about the value of innovation.

Ensure that you are modelling the behaviours and attitudes that you wish to see in others.

7.   **Conclusion**
Today's talent management practices were once considered novel ideas. At one time, they did not even exist. Somebody had to be the first to propose these solutions.

Changing circumstances call for new solutions. Your firm's ability to adapt to change with innovative talent management solutions can build competitive advantage. A reputation for innovative talent management can assist you in attracting the talent you want.

The task of instilling an innovative mindset starts with the leader.

About the authors

Peter Alfandary
Founder, PRA CrossCultural
peter@pra-development.com

Peter Alfandary is an English solicitor with over 30 years' experience as an international law firm partner. He trained at Lovells and was one of the founding partners of Warner Cranston, which merged with Reed Smith in 2001.

Mr Alfandary provides cultural intelligence consultancy advice worldwide to law firms and international corporations. He is senior guest lecturer at ESCP Europe, and additionally advises professionals on business development.

Mr Alfandary was educated at the French Lycée in London. He received his LLB from the University of Kent and his LLM from the London School of Economics. He was awarded the Legion of Honour, France's highest decoration, for services to Franco-British business.

Marc Bartel
Partner, Heidrick & Struggles
mbartel@heidrick.com

Marc Bartel is a partner in Heidrick & Struggles' London and Paris offices. He is the managing partner of functional practices EMEA, managing partner of the law firm practice and EMEA leader of the global legal, risk and compliance practice.

Mr Bartel focuses on the legal sector in industry and private practice. He specialises in classic legal in-house positions and partner searches for law firms, national and international clients, covering corporate and regulatory affairs (lobbying), risk, tax, audit and compliance.

Before joining Heidrick & Struggles, Mr Bartel held various senior management positions – from chief operating officer to Asia regional managing partner to deputy chief executive – within leading international law firms, including Lovells, Linklaters and Jeantet. Mr Bartel began his career as a practising attorney in Boston, then Paris. He led the first alliance of European law firms before working as a management consultant at Hildebrandt in the United States.

Rachel Brushfield
Director, EnergiseLegal
rachel@energiselegal.com

Rachel Brushfield is a career, talent, learning and development strategist and coach and the founder of EnergiseLegal and Energise – The Talent Liberation Company. She has over 25 years' experience of helping the legal profession to embrace change, with a career heritage in marketing and brand strategy and communications, including with global communications group WPP. Ms Brushfield is a published author, with books on talent management (February 2012) and professional development (October 2012), and has written extensively for legal magazines including *Managing Partner* on topics such as emotional intelligence, talent drain and female career success. Helping women to 'blow their own trumpet' for career success is a specialism, through both events and articles for The Association of Women Solicitors. Ms Brushfield also creates content for law firm intranets for cost-effective professional development.

About the authors

Clients include Baker & McKenzie, Mayer Brown, Clifford Chance, Jaguar Landrover and Cranfield University. Energise is an official business partner of The Telegraph Media Group.

Jay Connolly
Chief talent officer, Dentons US LLP
jay.connolly@dentons.com

Jay Connolly is the chief talent officer of Dentons with responsibility for human resources, recruiting and training functions, delivering best practices and ensuring consistent standards. He advises the firm's leaders on opportunities to enhance all aspects of talent management, including recruitment, performance management, diversity, training and development, and compensation and benefits programmes for everyone at the firm.

Mr Connolly joined legacy firm SNR Denton in 2011, with a wealth of experience in talent management and human resources leadership and expertise from a variety of industries. Prior to joining SNR Denton, he worked at Clifford Chance LLP in London and then New York as the director of HR for the Americas. Mr Connolly has also worked at the LEGO Company, where he had HR responsibility for the United Kingdom, Italy, Benelux and Nordic regions. He began his career with Unilever and undertook variety of roles across sites in the United Kingdom.

Kevin Doolan
Partner, Eversheds LLP
kevin.doolan@outlook.com

Kevin Doolan is a partner in Eversheds and a member of the firm's management team based in London. Following his law degree, he undertook an MBA at Henley Management College and, in his role as head of client relations, he has been responsible for business development activities for more than 10 years. He also trains extensively from associate to partner level in networking, growing existing clients, winning new clients and designing successful pricing strategies.

In his academic work, Mr Doolan is a faculty member for the Lawyers Management Programme at IE Law School in Madrid, teaches on the ground-breaking US LawWithoutWalls Programme and on the master's in international management at the London School of Economics and Political Science.

With a particular interest in the pricing of professional services, he recently developed the Harvard Law School Case Study on Pricing, and teaches this as a visiting professor on its Executive Education Programme.

Shelley Dunstone
Principal, Legal Circles
shelley.dunstone@legalcircles.com

Shelley Dunstone helps lawyers to build profile and attract clients. She is an Australian lawyer and a former partner of a mid-sized Australian commercial law firm. In addition to her legal qualifications, she holds a degree in management (marketing) and a graduate diploma in applied finance.

For the past 30 years she has immersed herself in the legal profession as practitioner, educator, recruiter, career mentor, author and consultant. She has served as a director of the Australian Legal Practice Management Association (ALPMA) and was the inaugural chair of ALPMA (SA). Ms Dunstone presents at conferences throughout Australia and internationally.

In 2001 she established her firm, Legal Circles, which helps lawyers to have better businesses and more satisfying careers.

Heidi K Gardner
Assistant professor of organisational behaviour, Harvard Business School
hgardner@hbs.edu

Heidi K Gardner researches, teaches and speaks on topics related to leadership, collaboration and teamwork in knowledge-based organisations, particularly professional service firms. Her current research analyses the benefits and costs to firms and individuals of working collaboratively, and investigates how leadership and organisational design support collaboration, innovation, and high-quality client service.

Professor Gardner has published in multiple peer-reviewed journals, the *Harvard Business Review* and numerous edited volumes. She teaches executive programmes at both Harvard Business School and Harvard Kennedy School, focusing on professional service firms, leadership, talent management and teamwork.

Professor Gardner previously worked for McKinsey & Co and was a Fulbright fellow. She earned a BA from the University of Pennsylvania, a master's from the London School of Economics and a master's and PhD from London Business School. She has lived and worked on four continents.

Sarah Hutchinson
Vice president, The University of Law
Sarah.hutchinson@law.ac.uk

Sarah Hutchinson is a qualified solicitor in England and Wales specialising in legal education, with 10 years' experience on the board of the University of Law. She is also the university's account director for its global law firm clients.

Ms Hutchinson is responsible for overseeing all external relationships and new product and market developments at the University of Law.

Ms Hutchinson is the chair of the International Committee of the Law Society of England and Wales. She also chairs the Academic and Professional Development Committee of the International Bar Association.

Tony King
Director, Clifford Chance Academy, Clifford Chance LLP
tony.king@cliffordchance.com

After qualifying as a solicitor and a stint teaching law, Tony King joined one of the firms which created Clifford Chance as a tax lawyer.

Mr King has been involved in professional development at Clifford Chance since 1988. He helped to introduce the global legal-technical and business skills programmes for people at all levels in the firm. He has worked on the firm's competencies and all HR processes which go with them (eg, appraisals, performance management). He has also put in place the firm's structure of development and assessment centres for its lawyers, up to and including candidates for partnership.

Mr King is the chair of the City of London Law Society's Training Committee, the immediate past chair of The Law Society of England & Wales' Education & Training Committee and the immediate past co-chair of the International Bar Association's Academic and Professional Development Committee.

Sarah Martin
Partner, Coombs Martin
sarah@coombsmartin.com

Sarah Martin is a founding partner in Coombs Martin, an executive coaching consultancy in London.

Ms Martin originally trained as a lawyer. She worked in M&A with Allen & Overy and was senior counsel in the chairman's office of BP PLC. She has over 20 years of business, legal and corporate governance practice at board level, combined with advanced training and experience as a business coach.

Ms Martin has been coaching professionals and executives since 2007. Her focus is on leadership in professional services firms. She holds an LLB from Manchester University and an MSc in management as a Sloan fellow at London Business School. She is an accredited business coach and a special adviser to the International Bar Association Law Firm Mentoring programme.

Moray McLaren
Consultant, KermaPartners
Moray.Mclaren@kermapartners.com

Moray McLaren is a consultant at KermaPartners, where he assists law firms on strategy and planning and more effective business development. He has worked with professional service firms – and particularly law firms – since 1997, gaining experience across Africa, Asia, Europe, Latin America and the United States. Mr McLaren is an associate professor at IE Business School (which is ranked by the *Financial Times* as Europe's leading business school), a member of the MBA faculty and its representative within Law Without Walls, a global collaboration among the world's leading law and business schools. He is the founder of IE's Lawyers' Management Programme.

Mr McLaren gained an MBA in law firm management in 2000. He is a trained business coach and a member of the Circle of Experts for the Financial Times Innovative Lawyers Report.

Jonathan Middleburgh
Senior director, Huron Legal
jmiddleburgh@huronconsultinggroup.com

Jonathan Middleburgh is a lawyer, an occupational psychologist and a leadership development expert. He is a first-class graduate in law from Worcester College, Oxford and taught law at the Universities of Chicago, Oxford and Kings College, London before embarking on a career at the Bar.

Mr Middleburgh has a wealth of experience nurturing leadership talent in law firms and legal departments. He designs and facilitates workshops on a range of workplace psychology issues, including coaching, career counselling, individual/personality difference and stress/wellbeing. He has a breadth of experience in pre-partner and partner development programmes, 360-degree feedback, individual assessment and assessment/development centres.

Mr Middleburgh coaches lawyers and executives who work in a wide range of international and domestic law firms, legal departments and Fortune 500 companies.

Rebecca Normand-Hochman
Founder and director, Mentoring Collegium Limited, Institute of Mentoring
rebecca.normand-hochman@instituteofmentoring.org

Rebecca Normand-Hochman is the founder and director of the Institute of Mentoring, which provides insight, research and advice to advance mentoring best practices in the legal profession.

As a Franco-British former lawyer, Ms Normand-Hochman practised international finance law in London and Paris. Her experience as a lawyer with Allen & Overy in Paris laid the foundation for her present work in talent management.

She has carried out extensive research on law firm talent management, and her work draws on best practices and collaboration with leading experts in leadership, change management, coaching and mentoring.

Through her work with the Institute of Mentoring and the involvement of a number of law firm partners, talent management experts, coaches and business school professors, Ms Normand Hochman is currently focusing on the subject of mentoring. She is pursuing research and providing advice to adapt best practices to the specificities and challenges that relate to the practice of law.

Since 2012, she has been leading the main talent management initiatives of the International Bar Association Law Firm Management Committee. These include coordinating this book, *Managing Talent For*

Success, and leading the IBA Law Firm Mentoring Programme. She is an officer and advisory board member of the Law Firm Management Committee.

Simon Pizzey
Director, Huron Legal
spizzey@huronconsultinggroup.com

Simon Pizzey is a certified business coach who works with clients in the legal sector. The focus of his coaching work is on leadership, personal development and performance.

Mr Pizzey is a solicitor who commenced his career specialising in dispute resolution. He then became managing partner of two law firms, providing strategic leadership, managing the businesses and developing partners and staff. As a director of Huron Consulting Group, he now works with law firms on strategy and performance management.

With his unique background and understanding of the culture, environment and dynamics of law firms, Mr Pizzey brings a deep-seated empathetic approach to the coaching relationship and can offer valuable insights.

Mr Pizzey holds an MBA in legal practice from Nottingham Law School and is a graduate of the Meyler Campbell Business Coach programme accredited by the Worldwide Association of Business Coaches and the Solicitors Regulation Authority for England and Wales.

Amber Sharpe
Psychologist
as@ambersharpe.com

Amber Sharpe holds an MSc in cognitive neuroscience; a BSc (Hons) in psychology and anthropology; and an LLB. Her LPC influenced her to focus her research and clinical interests within the crossover between the disciplines of psychology and law.

Her current work is focused on introducing mentoring principles and methods into professional firms and advising young and start-up companies. Her London W1 consultancy also provides clinical advice, where this can facilitate individual client development and growth.

Robert Sharpe
Psychologist
rs@robertsharpe.com

Robert Sharpe is a chartered psychologist with a clinical and mentoring consultancy in London W1. He holds a PhD in psychology and specialises in relationship development, resilience building and mentoring of law firm partners and partner-track associates. He is director of mentoring psychology at the Institute of Mentoring.

Dr Sharpe is an accomplished seminar leader and workshop facilitator who regularly advises senior management of law firms, ranging in size from major internationals to single-office, local firms. He has extensive experience in cross-cultural cooperation in the workplace, having consulted within more than 20 law firm offices in Europe, Asia, Australia and the United States.

The author of three popular applied psychology books, Dr Sharpe also carries out legal reporting, advises on strategy and facilitates the on-boarding of lateral hires. Responsive, available and collegial, he is equally at home advising on high-level strategy or practical specifics. His passions are one-on-one mentoring and development of individual excellence.

Caroline Vanovermeire
Principal, Heidrick & Struggles
cvanovermeire@heidrick.com

Caroline Vanovermeire has expertise in solving leadership challenges and critical business issues facing international organisations, having partnered extensively with global firms across a wide range of industries in Europe, Asia and the United States. She has a strong track record in strategic and operational talent management.

Prior to joining Heidrick & Struggles, Ms

Vanovermeire was the director of consultancy services talent management at Hudson Global Resources, where she led multiple projects including building talent pipelines, strategic resourcing, assessment and development assignments, and retention and succession planning. Previously, she was a senior consultant at TMP/Ernst & Young/De Witte & Morel.

Ms Vanovermeire obtained a master's degree in psychology from the Catholic University of Leuven and a master's degree in human resources management from Antwerp University. She is an accredited coach and is fluent in Dutch and English, with a working knowledge of French.

Sally Woodward
Founding principal, Sherwood PSF Consulting
sally.woodward@sherwoodpsfconsulting.com

Sally Woodward has nearly 30 years' experience as consultant and coach to individuals and groups of senior lawyers and business services professionals on personal development and leading change. She also designs and facilitates partner retreats and workshops, and advises HR specialists on the development and management of top talent. Clients include many top law firms in the United Kingdom, the United States and Europe.

Ms Woodward practised as an IP lawyer and taught at Cambridge University before spending 12 years in a senior business management role at Freshfields, for which she set up its first professional support functions and managed a variety of strategic projects.

Ms Woodward has an MBA from London Business School, is a visiting professor at Instituta Empresa, Madrid, on its global legal management programme; and is an associate member of the faculty of Meyler Campbell, the leading training organisation for business coaches.

Related titles in the same series

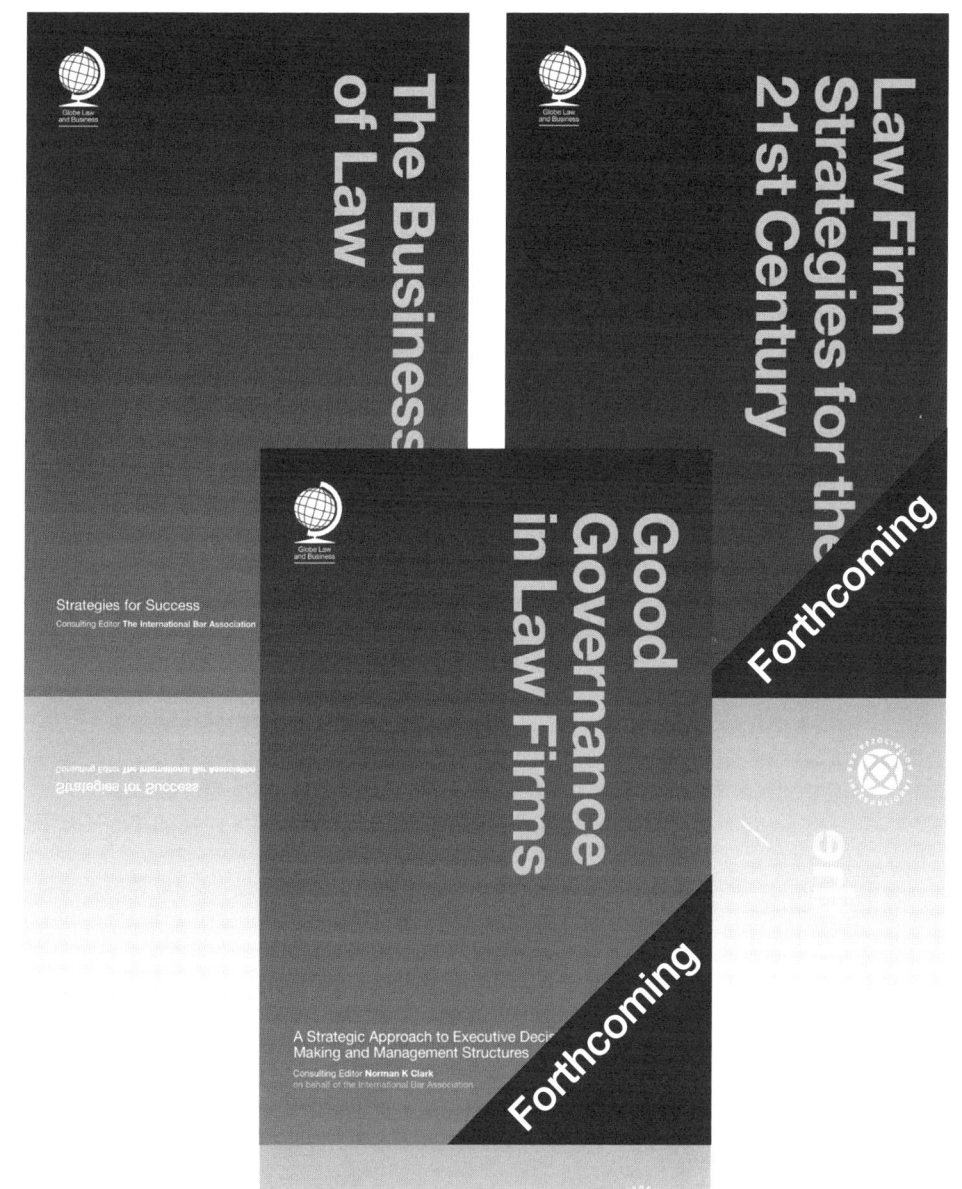

The Business of Law
Strategies for Success
Consulting Editor The International Bar Association

Law Firm Strategies for the 21st Century
Forthcoming

Good Governance in Law Firms
A Strategic Approach to Executive Decision Making and Management Structures
Consulting Editor **Norman K Clark**
on behalf of the International Bar Association
Forthcoming

for further details and a free sample chapter go to
www.globelawandbusiness.com